C000172771

## MOTORWAY SERVICES ARE BORING –

motorways are boring – but they're a necessary and convenient evil when you need to break the journey.

However, we think there's a lot more to good pit stops than strong coffee and the loo. The nation's highways and byways take us through some beautiful countryside. They skim fabulous towns and villages unseen through the crash barrier, and equally wonderful eateries.

Between us, we've hunted out original, quirky and soothing places to stop within easy reach of arterial routes. Places that we – aged thirty-something and seventy-something – think will appeal to like-minded people, whether you're travelling with friends, meeting family or riding solo.

For us, that means good-quality, preferably local food from makers and growers, space for children and pets to let off steam, fascinating attractions and knockout views, no more than 15 minutes' drive from a junction. It's places with conscience that care about the provenance of their ingredients and their impact on the environment. It's eating and resting better and supporting local businesses without adding much to overall journey time. It may even mean transforming your journey.

The notion of 'special' has long been at the heart of Alastair Sawday's guides, but we know that it's highly subjective. We recognise that one person's idea of special is not necessarily another's, so do expect variety.

These venues have been included simply because we like them and we do our best in the text to highlight why. Our opinions and tastes are ours alone and we hope you will share them. Do remember that the information in this book is a snapshot in time and things may have changed since we published it (we hope for the better).

You'll find a 'how to' guide at the back of the book which will guide you through the maps, symbols and information provided.

# *The* SMALL PRINT

Second edition
Copyright © 2018
Printslinger Co. Ltd
Published in November 2018
ISBN-13: 978-1-527225-98-5

Printslinger Co. Ltd,
17 Cornwallis Crescent, Bristol BS8 4PJ, UK

**SERIES EDITOR:**
Alastair Sawday

**EDITOR:**
Laura Collacott

**PAGE LAYOUT & PRINT PRODUCTION:**
Jules Richardson

**SUB-EDITOR:**
Emily Walmsley

**DESIGN:**
Ryan Thomas

**RESEARCHERS:**
Ross Bryant, Claire Holmes, Helena Kaill, Dana Wilson, Kitty Bocking

**MARKETING AND PR:**
Naomi Paget, Big Ideas Consultancy

**ACCOUNTS & ADMINISTRATION:**
Sheila Clifton

**PRINTING:**
Printed in England by Pureprint

**SALES:**
Signature Book Representation (UK) Ltd
+44 (0)845 862 1730
sales@signaturebooksuk.com

**DISTRIBUTION:**
Central Books Ltd
+44 (0)20 8525 8800
orders@centralbooks.com

Photo credits:
Cover © incamerastock/Alamy Stock Photo
p.6 © Iris Thorsteinsdottir iristhors.com
p.10 © Derek Beattie Images/Shutterstock.com
p.54 © Steve Silver Smith/Shutterstock.com
p.96 © DaBrick/Shutterstock.com
p.120 © Richard Bowden/Shutterstock.com
p.154 © Theo Duijkers/Shutterstock.com

p.172 © Aleksey Dushutin/Shutterstock.com
p.188 © Steven Musgrove/Shutterstock.com
p.222 © Paul Nash/Shutterstock.com
p.248 © Konstantin Tronin/Shutterstock.com
p.294 © Paul Cowan/Shutterstock.com
p.342 © Richard O'Donoghue/Shutterstock.com
p.368 © Shaiith/Shutterstock.com

# The
# EXTRA
# M1LE

*Delicious Alternatives to Motorway Services*

# The CONTENTS

# TRAVELLING WELL
## with the Extra Mile

Roads less travelled – they are all around us. Yet we plough on down the motorway, however little we love it, forgetting how delightful it can be to go off piste and see more of this gorgeous country. Worse, we resign ourselves to having to stop at one of those grim service stations.

Let us encourage you to take a break from the strain, to turn your journey into something memorable. It may take an extra 5 or 15 minutes, but they are well spent. Just a few extra miles for delicious food, views across ravishing countryside and places where you can relax. All it takes is a bit of planning, or spontaneity, to get away into the silence of rural Britain.

Those of us born in the 40s and 50s will remember what fun journeys used to be, with stops at pubs and ponds, and picnics in meadows. (Often, I admit, it was to wait for Dad to fix the boiling radiator.) Car journeys were not dreaded as they are now; they were often full of unexpected encounters, startling diversions, spontaneous visits to village inns, conversations with strangers to ask the way. Nowadays we plan ahead to avoid the worst of the traffic and then grit our teeth and head into whatever there is. But there are other ways.

The sheer variety of these places 'off the highway' still amazes me. The 1st edition took me and my wife to a stunning, recently uncovered and restored private garden near Taunton, then to a village café, numerous pubs, a National Trust house and even to a farm. It has been fun, we have discovered parts of Britain we knew nothing of, and our journeys have been enriched.

These wonderful places are part of our campaign to enable people to escape driving convention and experience real food. They are run by remarkable people, many of them driven by a passion for decency and origins when it comes to food and place. You will find no junk food, no grim commercialism, nothing tacky and over-hyped. You will find organic breads and cakes, home-cured meats, sausages from nearby farms, superb coffees and fine vegetarian meals. But that is not all. There are places here to bring a smile to the face and a twinkle to the eye: fun, unusual, original and colourful spaces for you to relax into. We won't get it right every time, so do keep us informed and, even more importantly, please let us know of your own discoveries so we can share them with others.

Do go the extra mile. You will, I acknowledge, add to your carbon footprint a little, but you will also add minutely to the quality of your life. If we help you transform one tedious, long and stressful journey into a pleasure, then we have done our stuff.

One last word: this book, although produced with my support, is not part of the much-loved Sawday's guide and web collection. (The company is now in the hands of its employees.) Those are uniquely honest and brilliant guides to the best places to sleep all over the UK and Europe, and the best UK pubs. This, however, is a new venture, a guide to the best of informal eating near main roads, and a campaign to help transform Britain's food industry. The vast bulk of the work has been done by Laura, and I salute her – as I also salute Jules, Sheila, Ryan, Ross and Naomi.

Go on – forget the ubiquitous branded coffee and flapjacks and the fast food, you already know what they taste like! Follow us and be surprised by something more nourishing.

## Alastair Sawday
☞ GOES THE EXTRA MILE

# The
# EXTRA
# M1LE

*Off the motorway and into the unknown*

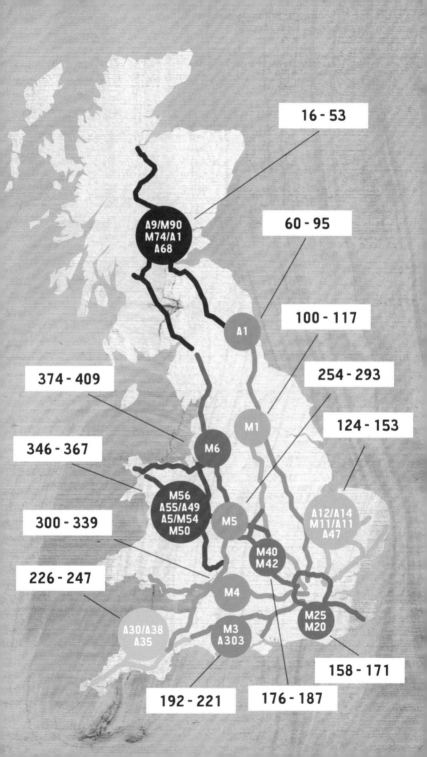

16 - 53

60 - 95

100 - 117

254 - 293

124 - 153

A9/M90
M74/A1
A68

A1

374 - 409

M1

346 - 367

M6

A12/A14
M11/A11
A47

300 - 339

M56
A55/A49
A5/M54
M50

M5

226 - 247

M40
M42

M4

M25
M20

A30/A38
A35

M3
A303

158 - 171

192 - 221

176 - 187

# SCOTLAND
## A68 / M74 / A1

*A Highland fling through the heart of Scotland*

# SCOTLAND

## M90 / A9

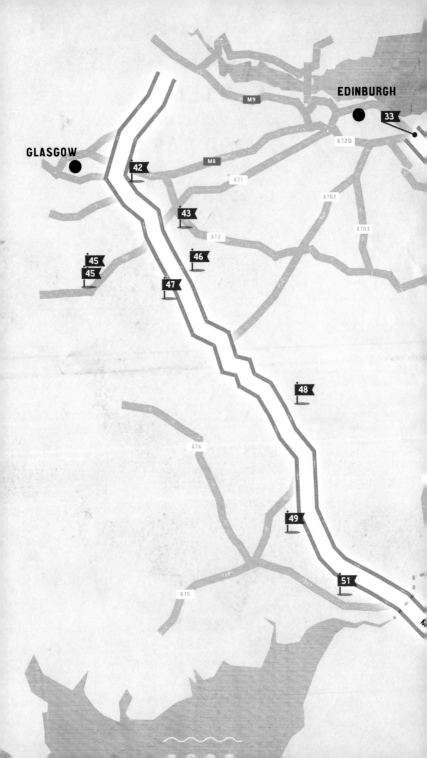

# SCOTLAND

## M74 / A68 / A1

BERWICK-UPON-TWEED

A 697

NORTHUMBERLAND
NATIONAL PARK

A68

A1

SLE

GARDEN CENTRE
# *Speyside* CENTRE

JUNCTION A95: 9 MINUTES

A local landmark, the Speyside Centre is tucked among the boughs of a pine forest at the edge of the Cairngorms. It was nearly devastated by a fire two years ago but, undaunted, the family have shuffled the buildings around to accommodate the garden centre, antiques shop and café while work is completed on a glittering new building (due to open in spring 2019). The plant selection is excellent, the antiques well worth a rummage and the playground ideal for little ones to burn off some energy. There's something for everyone here – even before you've eaten.

Grandad's old workshop has been colonised by the tearoom, famous for its clootie dumplings (a spiced fruit pudding, for the uninitiated), which can also be bought to take away. The lunches are equally good: be sure to have a slice of carrot cake. Grab a table on the terrace (known here as the 'sit ooterie') to watch the red squirrels, butterflies and birds drift around as you eat. Magical.

Opening hours
Mon-Sat 9am-5pm
Sun 10am-4pm

Speyside Centre, Skye of Curr, Dulnain Bridge PH26 3PA
WWW.HEATHERCENTRE.COM   01479 851359

CAFÉ
# *Rothiemurchus* CENTRE

**JUNCTION AVIEMORE; 4 MINUTES**

The rambling Rothiemurchus Estate covers one of the largest remaining areas of ancient Caledonian pine forest, which once enveloped Scotland. Stretching from the River Spey to the Cairngorm Mountains, it's a precious pocket of wildlife and sweeping scenery.

It's been under the stewardship of the Grant family since the 16th century, and they encourage visitors to come and enjoy the landscape. Take a pony trek, fish the loch, try an all-terrain Segway, hire bikes or enjoy an easy stroll to Loch an Eilein, voted the UK's best picnic spot – keep your eyes peeled for red squirrels, osprey and turkey-like capercaillies as you go.

And if it's a picnic you're after, look no further than the fantastic farm shop and Druie Café. It's stuffed with produce from the estate and surrounding area – Highland beef, heather honey, smoked salmon sandwiches, homemade fudge and artisan cheeses – while the bright café does an excellent line in light lunches, fluffy cakes and locally roasted coffee.

**Opening hours**
Mon-Sun 9.30am-5pm

(V) (P) (V) (P) (↻)
(🚶) (📶) (GF)

Rothiemurchus Centre, Rothiemurchus PH22 1QH
**ROTHIEMURCHUS.NET   01479 812345**

CAFÉ · SHOP · GALLERY

# *Laggan* STORES

JUNCTION DALWHINNIE; 10 MINUTES

You're not imagining things if you hear the squawk of a parrot as you walk into Laggan Stores: Kara the African grey is a popular resident and loves to entertain visitors to the shop, café and gallery. You'll get a warm welcome from owners Stuart and Gordon who supply the village with a carefully considered range of Scottish produce and gifts as well as a well-stocked dresser of groceries. Bread is brought in fresh daily, along with croissants, and the excellent coffee will set you up for any onward drive. Better still, settle by the wood burner and enjoy lunch as you admire the lovely range of local photographs taken by Stuart while Kara entertains you with her vocabulary.

The handsome, gabled shop (featured in the hit TV Series *Monarch of the Glen*) stands on a bend in the road where Laggan Bridge crosses the River Spey. Visitors are often on their way to Fort William or Aviemore but there's plenty to divert you here at the edge of the Cairngorms, particularly the Corrieyairack Pass, which leads across the Monadhliath Mountains.

Opening hours
Mon, Tues, Thurs, Fri 8am-5pm
Sat-Sun 9.30am-5pm
Seasonal opening hours apply – please check

Laggan Stores, Laggan Bridge, Laggan PH20 1AH
**WWW.LAGGANSTORES.CO.UK   01528 544737**

# *Hettie's* **TEAROOMS**

JUNCTION PITLOCHRY; 2 MINUTES

Clare named her tearooms after her daughter but was inspired by her granny, Eunice, to honour the family talent for baking and a blether (chat, for the non-natives). Behind the enticing turquoise and pink front, the dog-friendly café rings with the bustle of busy waitresses and happy chatter, especially from twinkly eyed, good-humoured Clare. Hettie's Loose Leaf Teas – all 31 flavours – are blended in-house and have become so popular they're now shipped all over the world. Newer on the scene is the coffee, roasted on the premises in Donnie the roaster, this time named after grandad.

You can lunch on sandwiches (served with pink coleslaw), salads and jacket potatoes, but it's the cake that people really come for. Try the triple-layer signature cake or strawberry tart and be warned that if you let kids loose on the eye-widening ice cream selection, you'll need to take them for a riverside walk (where you can also find free parking) before piling them back in the car.

Opening hours
Mon–Sun 9am-7pm

Hettie's Tearooms, 93-95 Atholl Road, Pitlochry PH16 5AB
**WWW.HETTIESTEAS.CO.UK   01796 473991**

CHOCOLATE HOUSE-EXHIBITION-SHOP

# *Iain Burnett* HIGHLAND CHOCOLATIER

JUNCTION A827; 7 MINUTES

Pull in here if you're hankering after a hot chocolate on your way through Scotland. Iain Burnett has won international awards for his chocolates, notably his smooth-as-silk Velvet Truffles, and this is his factory. You can peer into the workshop to watch the team blend Perthshire cream with cocoa imported from São Tomé to make the sensational (if pricey) chocolates in the shop.

Service in the tartan chocolate lounge is slick, friendly and slightly formal (but don't let that put you off). Chocolate is the star here so expect to gorge yourself on the good stuff. The thick hot chocolate – an espresso-cup full of molten Velvet Truffles – is a regular crowd pleaser, and the chocolate tastings are unmissable: an audio tour from Iain himself will guide you through a flight of gourmet chocolates or the secret art of the chocolatier.

Even non-chocolate lovers will enjoy getting off the highway to drink in the rural scenery, the sweep of the River Tay and the forest carpeting the hills behind.

Opening hours
Mon-Sun 10am-5pm
(11am-4pm Jan-Mar)

Iain Burnett Highland Chocolatier, Grandtully PH9 0PL
WWW.HIGHLANDCHOCOLATIER.COM   01887 840775

CAFÉ-DELI

# *Scottish* DELI

**JUNCTION A923; 1 MINUTE**

A grocer's shop has stood on this spot since 1809 when the Duke of Atholl demanded a village store be built for the new crossroads. Today, behind the elegant façade and preserved signage, the shelves and counters of the Scottish Deli are crowded with an enormous array of artisan products, from oatcakes to smoked meats, haggis, chutneys and an enviable cheese selection. They are carefully selected by owners Sarah and Simon and supplied by producers nearby, wherever the quality is high enough: the smoked salmon and preserves scoop the prize for lowest food miles, made just 30 metres down the road.

Grab a spot at one of the handful of convivial tables scattered through the shop to savour gourmet sandwiches, salads and soups at lunch or the delicious tapas menu in the evening, which you can wash down with a glass of wine. Service is relaxed and friendly, lingering is encouraged, and dogs and children are welcome.

Opening hours
Mon-Sun 9.30am-6pm; 6.30pm-10.30pm
(Sat 9am; Sun 10am)

Scottish Deli, 1 Atholl Street, Dunkeld PH8 0AR
**WWW.SCOTTISH-DELI.CO.UK   01350 728028**

# *Gloagburn* FARM SHOP & COFFEE SHOP

Skirt the duck pond at the entrance to Alison and Ian's working farm to find the solid, timber-clad farm shop. Set in the gently rolling hills of Perthshire, its view is maximised for those inside by the stunning floor-to-ceiling windows. The shop is a treasure trove, warmly lit by woven wicker lights. Browse the range of regional produce, including the farm's own beef and rare breed pork, eggs, jams, gingerbreads, oats and turnips, as well as artisan products such as pottery, art prints, scented candles and homewares. Everything stocked here must pass the family's 'tried and tasted' test before reaching the shelves.

The café and adjoining conservatory are strung with festoon lights and brimming with geraniums. In summer, the glass doors are flung open to let the breeze in, while in winter the wood burner is stoked up to keep the cold at bay. Food is freshly made in the kitchen, from soups and burgers to cheese soufflés and gooseberry tarts. Don't miss the Orkney fudge cheesecake.

Opening hours
Mon-Sun 8.30am-5.30pm

Gloagburn Farm Shop & Coffee Shop, Tibbermore, Perth PH1 1QL
**WWW.GLOAGBURNFARMSHOP.CO.UK   01738 840 864**

# *Another* TILLY TEAROOM

**JUNCTION 11; 4 MINUTES**

The magnificent 13th-century cathedral is reason alone for stopping in Dunblane, a picturesque town on the Allan Water river filled with charming architecture. But it's also home to Scotland's oldest private library, which has some 4,500 books dating as far back as 1500, as well as Andy Murray's famous golden postbox.

Wander the pretty streets before refuelling at the comforting Tilly Tearoom – recently voted the Most Wanted Café in Scotland – where sensational homebaking is the order of the day. Red gingham cloths dress the tables, to which plates of scrambled eggs on toast, homemade panini, and bowls of lentil soup and soda bread are ferried. Cakes are a real highlight – try a slice of hummingbird cake, a fresh meringue or gluten-free millionaire's shortbread – and the fabulous cooked breakfasts are served all day. Tea is served in vintage china cups from pots warmed by cosies made from recycled jumpers. The Belgian hot chocolate will transform a cold rainy day.

**Opening hours**
Mon-Sat 9am-4pm
Sun 10am-4pm

Another Tilly Tearoom, 87 High Street, Dunblane FK15 0ER
**TILLYTEAROOM.CO.UK** 01786 832968

CAFÉ

# *Buttercup* CAFÉ

JUNCTION STOCKBRIDGE: 4 MINUTES

Visitors have been swarming to Doune Castle since it's starring roles in *Game of Thrones* and '*Monty Python*. But even if its silver screen fame doesn't lure you in it's well worth visiting this impressive medieval stronghold, built for the Regent Albany, 'Scotland's uncrowned king'. You can take an audio tour narrated by Terry Jones himself as you explore the wooded grounds, towering battlements, vast banqueting hall and castle kitchens.

When you've had your historic fill, beeline for the Buttercup Café on the high street to fill up on hearty home cooking. The café is airy and warm with diner lights strung over cosy booths and there's a sheltered courtyard out back.

The Buttercup pancake stack is a breakfast to remember; for lunch try the homemade cauliflower soup with sourdough bread, aubergine and potato curry, or salmon and prawn sandwiches. Don't miss out on a slice of the fabulous cakes before you leave.

Opening hours
Mon-Fri 9am-4pm
Sat 9am-5pm
Sun 10am-4pm

Buttercup Cafe, 7 Main Street, Doune FK16 6BJ
**BUTTERCUPCAFE.CO.UK**   01786 842 511

# *The* COFFEE BOTHY AT DEANSTON

**JUNCTION A820: 6 MINUTES**

Set on the banks of the River Teith, the Deanston Distillery occupies an imposing former cotton mill whose cool, humid weaving shed also proved perfect for ageing organic malt whiskey. The waters that once drove the mill's wheel still power the building today thanks to upstream turbines. It's worth lingering for a tour of the traditional whiskey making methods (it's the national drink after all), especially the chocolate pairing.

Whisky drinker or not, you should stop in at the Coffee Bothy. Stocky wooden furniture and green bistro lighting create a warm atmosphere, the food is reliably tasty (try the lentil and haggis soup) and the coffee is great. It's an outpost of the excellent Blairmains Farm Shop down the road and a popular haunt for locals as much as distillery visitors. Old photographs lining the wooden shelves on the wall show the history of the mill. There's plenty of free parking in the distillery car park, and you can buy a bottle of whisky in the shop for when your journey's over.

Opening hours
Mon-Sun 10am-4.30pm

The Coffee Bothy, Deanston Distillery Visitor Centre, Doune FK16 6AG
**WWW.DEANSTONMALT.COM/VISIT-US/°COFFEE   01786 843 010**

# *Smiddy* FARM SHOP, BUTCHERY & CAFÉ

JUNCTION 10; 5 MINUTES

The spacious Smiddy Farm Shop stands on the site of the old village blacksmith's, now transformed into a tantalising local food hub stocking produce from all over Scotland. Browse the shelves for Harris Tweed or artisan ceramics and fill your basket with treats from the deli counter and butchery. The meat is all reared down the road and the game is from the surrounding countryside. Don't leave without picking up one of the Smiddy's steak pies and perhaps some of their home-cured bacon.

In the airy beamed café chefs whip those same ingredients up into delicious dishes (including an outstanding bacon roll). It's busy but staff are smiley and efficient. Grab a pew at the breakfast bar or pull up one of the zingy orange chairs to tuck into panini stuffed with Stornoway black pudding, mature Cheddar and tomato relish, or some homemade banoffee pie or a finger-licking peanut butter slice with a flat white. Don't miss the loos before you head on your way – visitors always remark on the spectacular view.

Opening hours
Mon-Sun 9am-5pm

Smiddy Farm Shop, Butchery & Café, Blair Drummond, by Stirling FK9 4UY
WWW.BLAIRDRUMMONDSMIDDY.CO.UK   01786 235 024

# *Blairmains* FARM SHOP & COFFEE BOTHY

**JUNCTION 10: 11 MINUTES**

Backed by the gorse-strewn slopes of the Ochil Hills and the soaring gothic tower of the Wallace Monument, the unassuming exterior of Blairmains Farm Shop and Coffee Bothy belies the delights within.

Six generations of the Logan family farmed here, before opening a café and farm shop in 2001 (one of Scotland's first). It quickly established itself with a wide range of Scottish produce from local Farm Assured meat and game to fruit, veg and locally brewed beers. The delicious homemade goodies from the Bothy Kitchen are also extremely popular: sausage rolls, quiches, cheeses and pies.

The Coffee Bothy has a selection of daily specials, light lunches and filling soups, all created from the farm shop's fresh produce. Don't forget to satisfy that sweet tooth with a piece of scrumptious Bothy cake or pudding of the day.

**Opening hours**
Mon-Sat 9am-5pm
Sun 10am-4.30pm

Blairmains Farm Shop & Coffee Bothy, Manor Loan, Blairlogie FK9 5QA
**WWW.BLAIRMAINS.COM  01259 762266**

FARM SHOP-CAFÉ
# *Loch Leven's* LARDER
JUNCTION 8: 4 MINUTES

The scenery alone makes a diversion here worthwhile – set between rolling hills the Larder has a panoramic view of Loch Leven. In the food hall, shelves are stacked with a carefully chosen selection of goodies from local producers: cheeses, craft spirits and ales, preserves and confectionary. An artisan bakery creates delicious goods using high-quality local ingredients.

The Larder stands at the heart of the family's farm and crates of vegetables are delivered direct from the fields, where chefs transform them into imaginative seasonal dishes. The informal, family-friendly atmosphere in the café, where visitors can walk straight in from the Loch Leven Heritage Trail, makes it the perfect place to slow down and appreciate fresh local food. If you're in a hurry the Greenhouse Café is designed for express visits.

There's plenty of parking and the 1.5-mile path around the fields is suitable for buggies. There's also a play area, making it a great place to enjoy some fresh air.

Opening hours
Mon-Sun 9am-5.30pm

Loch Leven's Larder, Channel Farm, Kinross KY13 9HD
**WWW.LOCHLEVENSLARDER.COM**  01592 841000

# CAFÉ
# NO.98

**JUNCTION 6; 3 MINUTES**

The Lowlands are often overlooked but take some time to drop in to Kinross on your way through Scotland. Centred on a large loch, the sleepy town is ringed with low-lying hills and is a world leader in cashmere production.

On an islet in the loch is the enchanting Lochleven Castle where Mary Queen of Scots was once held prisoner. Take the ferry out to the castle before meandering over to No. 98, where owners Jim and Jane will indulge you in their love of mouth-watering burgers and fair trade coffee. It's far from a two-trick pony, though: there are also excellent brunches (with meat from the butcher down the road) and a good line in vegetarian and vegan dishes.

Kids will love the pink panther milkshake and crunchie rocky road, while sandwiches such as the pulled brisket with slaw and mustard sauce will keep anyone filled up till the Highlands. Service is attentive and the vibe relaxed. A great place to rest road-weary bodies.

Opening hours
Mon-Sat 9am-4.30pm
Sun 10am-3pm

No.98, 98 High Street, Kinross KY13 8AJ
**WWW.NO98FOOD.COM   01577 862542**

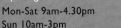

ATTRACTION

# *Archerfield* WALLED GARDEN

JUNCTION HADDINGTON: 13 MINUTES

The Victorian kitchen garden at Archerfield spreads out among the estate's fields and woodland. Step through the archway from the car park into the yard – sometimes host to pop-up street food markets – to find the modern, wood-clad Garden Café.

Fill up on open sandwiches and soup, or treat yourself to one of the kitchen favourites such as the Archerfield IPA battered haggis fritters or king scallop salad with smoked Carluke bacon. Try to keep room for one pastry chef Jean Philippe's delectable daily cakes.

The market alongside the café supplies some of the lovely local produce used in the kitchen (alongside a tempting array of gifts – woollen blankets, artwork, the estate's own craft ale). Kids will love the fairy trail that threads through the woodland, and you can work up an appetite by exploring the estate's footpaths. Four-legged companions are welcome, and the stroll down to the beach at Yellow Craigs is fantastic for a leg stretch before continuing your journey.

Opening hours
Mon-Sun 9.30am-5pm

Archerfield Walled Garden, Archerfield Estate, Dirleton EH39 5HQ
**WWW.ARCHERFIELDWALLEDGARDEN.COM   01620 388588**

# *Fentons* BARN CAFÉ & SHOP

**JUNCTION HADDINGTON; 9 MINUTES**

Originally built to serve the RAF airfield that stood here in the war, the squadron buildings at Fenton are now a fantastic pint-sized shopping village. At the centre is the farm shop, where owner Mhairi thoughtfully manages her trove of Scottish produce and tasteful gifts — cookbooks, kitchenware, cheese, eggs, oatcakes, chocolates and seasonal fruit and veg.

The café at the far end has been remodelled to include an open fire. Food matches the cosy vibe and is home made or locally sourced where possible: quiches, over-filled sandwiches, house-recipe stovies (a Scottish speciality made with meat and potatoes and served with chutney) as well as delicious cakes piled on the dresser. The smoked fish is particularly noteworthy, hooked from the North Sea and smoked down the road. Pick up a cup of freshly made soup to go — the sweet potato, spinach and chickpea is delicious — or try the homemade custard creams or the cheese and chive scones for a tasty snack on the run. We had to prise ourselves away.

Opening hours
Mon-Sun 10am-5pm

Fentons Barn Café & Shop, Unit 16 Fenton Barns Retail Park, North Berwick EH39 5BW
**FENTONBARNSFARMSHOP.COM   01620 850294**

CAFÉ

# *The* LOFT CAFÉ & BAKERY

### JUNCTION HADDINGTON: 5 MINUTES

A lot has changed since Charlotte and Anita took over Haddington Council's former canteen. With an eye for thrifty design they kept the functional stainless steel serving counters and disguised them with piles of food and pallet wood cladding; furniture is second-hand and upcycled. And, with a wave of their wand, they transformed it into a fresh, light-drenched space. A sheltered courtyard in front of the L-shaped, stone building is a fantastic place to pause and unwind on sunny days.

The emphasis here is on good, home-cooked food and there's a strict local sourcing policy for ingredients. Breakfast on shakshuka or pancakes with bacon and maple syrup, lunch on mackerel pâté on homemade oatcakes, pearled spelt salad or the legendary sausage rolls; and indulge in the home-made ice-cream and brilliant cakes – the lime and courgette and bakewell slice are particularly recommended. Coffee is freshly ground and you should try the turmeric latte if you haven't had one before – a cup of golden sunshine.

Opening hours
Mon-Fri 8.30am-4.30pm
Sat 9am-4pm

The Loft Café & Bakery, Peffers Place, Haddington EH41 3DR
**WWW.LOFTCAFEBAKERY.CO.UK   01620 824456**

# *Restoration* YARD

JUNCTION WHITECRAIG: 6 MINUTES

Just outside Edinburgh the 2,000-acre Dalkeith Country Park is a bucolic stop with something for everyone. Kids will love the enormous Fort Douglas Adventure Park and when you've tired them out on the climbing walls, treehouses and slides, head to the stunning Restoration Yard.

Once the stable block for the Duke of Buccleuch's estate and crowned with a stately clock tower, the yard has been given a radical makeover. Browse the beautiful clothing, homewares, books and gifts in the shop, pick up some artisan deli goods in the fine foods store, even stop for a yoga class. You can refuel in the informal coffee bar alongside or grab a table in the slightly more formal Restoration Café with plate glass windows overlooking the river and herb garden.

Dalkeith Country Park is looped with dog-friendly walking and cycling paths, so stretch your legs before getting back in the car. The longest, two-hour trail takes you through woodlands and along the River Esk – look out for roe deer, otters and buzzards.

## Opening hours

Restoration Café: Mon-Sun 9.30am-4.30pm
Store & Coffee Bar: Mon-Sun 9.30am-6pm
Fort Douglas: Mon-Sun 10am-6pm (4pm winter)

Restoration Yard, Dalkeith Country Park, Edinburgh EH22 1ST
WWW.RESTORATIONYARD.COM   0131 322 2572

CAFÉ
# *Soutra* COFFEE HOUSE

JUNCTION FALA VILLAGE; 0 MINUTES

Spectacular views and a counter laden with homemade food make Soutra Coffee House a special place to stop. Take a table on the terrace or at one of the enormous windows to drink in the expansive tableau of hills rolling into the distance. In one direction you can see across the Firth of Forth, in another out to the Bass Rock in the North Sea.

It's the sister café to the gorgeous Carfraemill Hotel just down the road and shares its reputation for great food and warm hospitality. Bacon rolls come with a slice of haggis, sandwiches are hearty, soups are homemade and the cakes are reassuringly indulgent. The chai latte is particularly good.

Parking is plentiful and there's a well-supplied toy corner for keeping children entertained while you enjoy your lunch or coffee. If you fancy a longer stop, stretch your legs in the Lammermuir Hills or visit the nearby medieval hospital at Soutra Aisle before heading on your way.

Opening hours
Mon-Sun 9am-5pm (Apr-Oct)
Mon-Fri 9am-4pm (Nov-Mar)
Sat-Sun 9am-4.30pm (Nov-Mar)

Soutra Coffee House, Blackshields, Fala Soutra Hill, Pathead EH37 5TF
**WWW.HOUSEOFSOUTRA.COM   01875 833795**

# *Cloudhouse* **CAFÉ-GALLERY**

**JUNCTION LAUDER: 9 MINUTES**

Zip over the beautiful moorland road from the A68 to the pretty town of Stow to find the striped awning and glowing windows of the Cloudhouse Café. The building has had various lives as a grocers and bakery (the delivery horse was once stabled in what is now the kitchen), but now it's Caroline's domain where she and her friendly team serve hearty country dishes amid a collection of local artwork. Full breakfasts might come with duck eggs, bread is freshly cooked and vegan dishes are frequently seen on the menu.

The atmosphere is familiar and there's a play area to keep kids entertained. Cushions soften pew bench seats, upcycled tables are painted in earthy tones and on sunny days tables are set out on the pavement next to pots of lavender. Browse the gallery at the back for a souvenir art piece, pick up a trinket from the counter or a holiday read in the book exchange. It's popular with cyclists (thanks to those wavey moorland roads). A bellwether of good cafés if ever there was one.

**Opening hours**
Mon-Thurs 10am-3pm
Fri 10am-4pm
Sat–Sun 10am-3pm

Cloudhouse Café-Gallery, 23 Townfoot, Stow TD1 2QN
**CLOUDHOUSECAFE.CO.UK  01578 730718**

RESTAURANT
# SEASONS

**JUNCTION TWEEDWOOD COTTAGE; 4 MINUTES**

One diner described the cooking here as 'sorcery of the best kind', and it's worth making a little extra time in your journey to pause at this exceptional restaurant. A flat-roofed building with rows of flower boxes, it stands in Gattonside, just outside Melrose, on the banks of the pretty River Tweed.

Firm foodies, Roger runs the kitchen and Bea keeps everything ticking over seamlessly in the relaxed restaurant, and their devotion to seasonal food is in the title.

The lunch menu is reasonably priced and enticing with starters such as smoked fish pâté on buckwheat oatcakes or beetroot and soft cheese salad, and mains such as slow-cooked shoulder of lamb or a tortilla stuffed with foraged mushrooms and spinach. Dinner might be Eyemouth crab with bloody Mary mayo or smoked duck. Everything is delicious and the atmosphere is relaxed and friendly.

Opening hours
Wed-Sun from 6pm
Fri-Sun noon-2.30pm

Seasons, Main Street, Gattonside TD6 9NP
**WWW.SEASONSBORDERS.CO.UK   01896 823217**

SHOP-CAFÉ

# *Abbey* FINE WINES

**JUNCTION RAVENSWOOD ROUNDABOUT; 3 MINUTES**

The lovely border town of Melrose is well worth building into your Scotland itinerary. Abbey Fine Wines is on the square opposite the Trimontium Museum of Roman Scotland (a fascinating insight into the life of Agricola's soldiers who camped here, with the chance to try on Roman armour).

It might sound like a booze shop, and it is, but it also has a fantastic family-run café serving light lunches, scones and good coffee. The cheese board is excellent and owners Malcolm and Ian are extremely knowledgeable about their wines and they'll advise you on the perfect drop to uncork at your destination. Visitors also rave about the selection of single malts.

Come summer, people spill out onto the pavement under the striped green awning to linger in one of the town's people-watching spots. Limited parking is available on the square, and there's a pay-and-display car park round the corner at Abbey Car Park.

Opening hours
Mon-Sat 9am-5pm

Abbey Fine Wines, 17 Market Square, Melose TD6 9PL
**01896 823224**

SHOP-CAFÉ

# *The* MAINSTREET TRADING COMPANY

## JUNCTION ST BOSWELLS; 1 MINUTE

A magical combination of books, gifts and food, The Mainstreet Trading company should be factored into every journey through this part of the Borders. Make time to browse the fabulous bookshop, then refuel on the food that draws inspiration from the cookbooks on its shelves. Try the tomato, cumin and fig soup or hand-cured gravadlax with labneh and bread, or pastrami and leek jam sandwich. Cakes are all baked in-house by a small team: the gluten-free Tunisian cake is particularly good. The café is dog- and child-friendly: we loved the understairs book burrow for kids where they can listen to audio books among the piles of cushions.

In the courtyard out the back, a former barn has been developed to add a home shop and deli. The shop, in the old wine cellar, is stacked to the rafters with woven baskets, enamelware, French soaps and beautifully illustrated stationery; the deli stocks all manner of goodies from independent food producers, with cheese as the star of the show.

Opening hours
Tues-Sat 9am-5.30pm (café 5pm)
Sun 11am-4.30pm (café 4pm)

The Mainstreet Trading Company, Main Street, St Boswells TD6 0AT
WWW.MAINSTREETBOOKS.CO.UK   01835 824087

# *Buccleuch* ARMS

JUNCTION ST BOSWELLS: 0 MINUTES

You'll be instantly restored by the gardens alone at the Buccleuch Arms. The classic coaching inn sits on the roadside between Edinburgh and Newcastle and is a terrific place to break the journey. It has the feel of a welcoming country home with its run of spacious, tastefully decorated rooms, stoked fires and comfy corners to flop into.

The Blue Coo Bistrot restaurant has a more modern air with wooden floors, blue-painted panelling and an oversized basket of logs to feed the crackling wood burner. Tables in the bar are dog-friendly and informal, and there's a small play area in the garden for kids.

The menu is a triumph of local produce and is similar in the Bistrot and the Bar. Dishes are often created with ingredients foraged from the hedgerows or reared in the fields nearby: damsons, crab apples, venison, partridge and the speciality, Aberdeen Angus steaks. Owners Billy and Rachael are of farming stock and ardent supporters of local suppliers.

Opening hours
Mon-Sun 6.45am-midnight

Buccleuch Arms, The Green, St Boswells TD6 0EW
WWW.BUCCLEUCHARMS.COM   01835 822243

GARDEN CENTRE
# WOODSIDE
**JUNCTION ANCRUM: 1 MINUTE**

You may want to bring your camera when you pull into Woodside's south-facing Victorian walled garden, as the sun-warmed microclimate buzzes with wildlife. It's an absolute treat to sip a cup of tea in the Birdhouse Tearoom and watch the birds feeding just outside. On summer days sit at tables in the garden and envelope yourself in the crackles and tweets of the open air; as cold days draw in you can retreat to the cosiness of the wood burner. The close connection to wildlife is what first attracted gardeners Emma and Stephen Emmerson to set up their plant centre here in what was once the fruit garden for nearby Monteviot House.

Food is measured in metres rather than miles in the café; many of the ingredients for the soups, cakes, jams, chutneys and lunches are grown in the garden and taste sensational for it. More than once have the scones been proclaimed the best in the Borders. Every other Friday evening from April to October the café is transformed into the Kailyard Restaurant where delicious vegetarian and vegan food is served based on what is available from the garden.

Opening hours
Mon-Sun 10am-5pm (4pm Nov-Feb)

Woodside, Woodside Walled Garden Ancrum Jedburgh TD8 6TU
**WWW.WOODSIDEGARDEN.CO.UK  01835 830315**

# *Born* IN THE BORDERS

**JUNCTION CLEIKHIMIN; 4 MINUTES**

Riverside walks, farm shop, terrific café, brewery, distillery, ospreys: Born in the Borders is a visitor centre that ticks a lot of pit-stop boxes. There's a tranquillity to its sprawling fields and woodlands, and visitors are encouraged to connect with nature. Choose between the mini beast safari, grass boarding, a spirit-restoring wander along the banks of the River Teviot or the thrill of spotting resident ospreys Sampson and Freya in the skies.

The fields and farms around supply the kitchen with almost all the ingredients it needs for its excellent dishes, whether beef braised in home-brewed beer, hearty sandwiches, local ice cream or marmalade cake. The shop will supply everything you need for an equally delicious picnic – local charcuterie, cheese, bread, honey – and the fields nearby offer fabulous spots for enjoying it. You needn't miss out if you're passing in the evening either: the sister pub in nearby Ancrum is a convivial hub with the same approach to excellent food.

Opening hours
Mon-Sun 10am-5pm

Born in the Borders, Lanton Mill, Jedburgh TD8 6ST
**WWW.BORNINTHEBORDERS.COM   01835 830495**

CAFÉ

# *Hazel's* BUTTERFLY BAKERY

JUNCTION 5; 7 MINUTES

A labour of love for Hazel, the Butterfly Bakery is a brilliant neighbourhood café on Uddingston's high street. Occupying one half of a rose-coloured stone building with a handsome bay window the café is bright and inviting with scrubbed wooden tables and walls decorated with pictures of Hazel's finest creations.

She's been conjuring up celebratory cakes for family and friends for years and now they form the centrepiece of her café – multilayered, multi-flavoured and impressive. Try a slice of maple and pecan or white chocolate and cranberry, or go for a lemon curd cupcake. Confectionary is served alongside tasty breakfasts (including great sausages from the butcher across the street) and home-cooked lunches of soups, toasted sandwiches and baked potatoes.

Plentiful parking is available at the back, where you'll also catch a glimpse of the Tunnock's factory – the production house of Scotland's much-loved snowballs and tea cakes.

Opening hours
Mon-Sat 9am-4pm
Sun 11am-3pm
Last hot food orders 30 mins before closing

Hazel's Butterfly Bakery, Unit 1, 54 Main St, Uddingston G71 7LS
**WWW.HAZELSBUTTERFLYBAKERY.CO.UK  01698 801662**

# *The* OVEN AT OVERTON FARM

JUNCTION 8; 10 MINUTES

By the River Clyde, Overton Farm is a vibrant example of modern agriculture. The Young family have been raising cattle and growing crops in the valley for decades, and have added a farm shop and, more recently, a modern café. They host regular events throughout the year, from the stunning Blossom Day in spring and the fruit celebration in autumn to the popular point-to-point horse races each March. The large car park is regularly turned over to a weekend car boot sale between April and October.

The homely Oven @ Overton café is abuzz with visitors enjoying the robust and generous home cooking. Staff ferry weighty plates to tables, and the powder blue counter groans under the pile of tempting cakes and meringues. Kids can let off steam in an enclosed play area at the rear. Browse the gift shop for eclectic local crafts before you leave – Highlands artwork, whittled walking sticks – and cross the yard to the farm shop to stock up on honey, eggs, fruit, vegetables and farm-reared cuts of meat.

Opening hours
Mon-Sun 9am-5pm
(Drinks and cakes only after 4pm)

The Oven, Overton Farm, Crossford, Carluke ML8 5QF
WWW.FARMSHOPLANARKSHIRE.CO.UK  01555 861214

CAFÉ-DELI

# *Alexander Taylor* **BAKERY & DELI**

JUNCTION 8: 12 MINUTES

It's worth every extra drop of fuel to make the detour to Strathaven (pronounced 'Stray-ven'), a colourful market town set around a traditional square, just south of Glasgow. The castle ruins and independent shops are ripe for exploration while the beautifully manicured park is perfect for a breath of fresh air. Stroll around town before rewarding yourself with a visit to the fantastic Alexander Taylor Bakery, facing the river. It was established here in 1820, and six generations of the Taylor family have been producing a vast range of delicious breads and baked goods on the site ever since.

Buy an organic sourdough loaf, cheese bagel or chocolate éclair to take away, or have a seat in the rustic tea room across the road to enjoy a bowl of Kype-a-leekie soup (made from St Brides free-range chicken and home-grown leeks), crisp cheese toastie or hot bacon roll made with Ramsay's Ayrshire bacon. The coffee is great and best paired with a pineapple tart or treacle crumpet. A hearty pit stop.

Opening hours
Mon–Fri 8am-5pm (8.30am café/deli)
Sat 7am-5pm

Alexander Taylor Bakery & Deli, 10-11 Waterside St, Strathaven ML10 6AW
**ALEXANDERTAYLORBAKERY.CO.UK 01357 521260**

# *Tudor* COFFEE HOUSE

**JUNCTION 8; 9 MINUTES**

Cake lovers will adore the cosy Tudor Coffee House, whose stately black timbers at the head of the town square look fresh out of a fairy tale. The café is daintily decorated with flowery bistro curtains, white linen tablecloths and vintage china. Reasonable prices and excellent baking mean it's often packed, so on fine days you can spill out onto the riverside terrace and watch the world go by in this historic market town.

Breakfasts and sweet treats are the speciality here. The counter is packed with Marianne and her team's home baking under gleaming glass cloches, from lip-smacking strawberry tarts to lemon and ginger scones and homemade chocolate truffles. Hot chocolate is made with proper flakes of chocolate and tea is served in pretty floral china.

Lunches are simple and traditional – including Cajun chicken paninis and vegetable lasagne – but it's the cream and afternoon teas that people rave about.

Opening hours                                            GF  V
Mon–Fri 9.30am-4.30pm
Sat 9am-5pm
Sun 10.30am-4.30pm

Tudor Coffee House, 4a Common Green, Strathaven ML10 6AH
**TUDORCOFFEEHOUSE.CO.UK    01357 529487**

# *Cairn Lodge* SERVICES

The newest relation to Tebay Services and Gloucester Services, Cairn Lodge has settled seamlessly into the family. It too started life as a home-run business when founders John and Aileen MacInnes spotted an opportunity on the then-new M74 motorway in the early 1990s. They named it after the gothic gateway on site, which is all that remains of an abandoned attempt to build anew Douglas Castle in the 1700s.

Westmorland Family over in 2015 and continued the good work with Donna Hodd, daughter of the founders, at the helm as operations manager. After a major renovation, it's now dressed to impress in the Westmorland signature look. It has a brand new Farmshop stocking local gifts and artisan foods and a coffee bar with handy charging points, underneath the soothing leaves of a gargantuan ceiling planter. The loos and showers are lovely, and the new Kitchen is a mellow place to fill up on a hot meal or quick cuppa. They're also proud to have a changing place toilet, one of the first on the Scottish motorway network.

Opening hours
Mon-Thurs 7am-10pm
Fri-Sun 7am-9pm

Cairn Lodge Services, Douglas ML11 0RJ
**WWW.CAIRNLODGESERVICES.COM   01555 851880**

# *The* SCRIB TREE

**M74**

**JUNCTION 11/12; 3 MINUTES**

Cosy and welcoming in a honeycoloured, slate-roofed building by the Douglas Estate, The Scrib Tree is an enthusiastic champion of Lanarkshire farm produce and handcrafted gifts. If you're travelling between Glasgow and the Borders, swing in here for excellent coffee (roasted by hand in Glasgow by the Giambastiani family), great breakfasts, home-baked cakes and delicious lunches. The soups are a particular speciality.

Soak up the sun on the little terrace or eat in the lofty café. Here you can also browse the emporium of fresh produce and crafts – hand-thrown pottery, hand-turned wood and homespun woollens are all made by local artisans. Meat, game and vegetables come from the estate or neighbouring farms. Chefs in the kitchen use the same ingredients so if you're impressed by the flavour, fill your shopping bag before you leave. Parking is plentiful and it's worth popping in to Douglas itself – with origins stretching back to medieval times – to visit St Bride's church whose clock is rumoured to have been a gift from Mary Queen of Scots.

Opening hours
Mon-Sun 10am-5pm

The Scrib Tree, 1-3 Colliers Court, Douglas ML11 0RX
**WWW.THESCRIBTREE.CO.UK   01555 851262**

RESTAURANT-CAFÉ

# *Brodies* OF MOFFAT

JUNCTION 15; 3 MINUTES

Once a spa destination and centre of the wool trade, Moffat is a handsome market town arranged around a broad high street. Quirkily decorated Brodies is tucked behind the museum to the south of the main square. A much-loved family-run restaurant it's a tea room by day and a relaxed candlelit restaurant by night.

Russell is the man in the kitchen and his much lauded food is almost one of the town's tourist attractions. Lunches are light and flavourful; gutsy, slightly posher dishes are on the evening menu. Even if you're not looking for a full meal, the cakes – baked in-house – and afternoon teas are worth seeking out, while non-drivers might want to sample the enviable selection of gins proudly on show in a beautiful drinks cabinet.

If you've got time, head just out of town to the wonderfully named Devil's Beef Tub, a valley once used by members of the Moffat Clan to hoard cattle stolen in raids.

Opening hours
Mon–Tues 10am-5pm,
Wed–Sat 10am-11pm
Sun 10.30am-9pm.

Brodies of Moffat, 1-2 Altrive Place Holm St, Moffat DG10 9EB
WWW.BRODIESOFMOFFAT.CO.UK   01683 222870

# *Pink Flamingo* VINTAGE TEA ROOM

**JUNCTION 17; 9 MINUTES**

Sensational flavours draw the crowds to Pink Flamingo Tea Room. The baking is inventive and outstanding, loading the counter with irresistible goodies such as chocolate orange polenta cake and lemon mascarpone cheese cake with homemade pistachio biscuit base. You can also get a hearty lunch here; try one of their famous naan pizzas or the delicious pasty of the day made with homemade pastry. There's a cosiness to the tearoom with owner Samin's vintage wingback chairs, brightly painted furniture and ornate stove enclosed by whitewashed stone walls. A box of toys and books will keep little ones occupied; keep a lookout for a teddy bear sitting at one of the tables.

Lochmaben itself is a great place to visit, frequently hosting farmers markets where you can stock up on Scottish goodies. Its castle claims to be the birthplace of Robert the Bruce and the Annandale Way, which passes through the town, offers superb walking. This is the perfect stop off on the way to the Highlands.

Opening hours
Mon-Fri 9am-4.30pm (Sat 5pm)
Sun open seasonally;
please check website for winter hours

Pink Flamingo Vintage Tea Room, 6a Bruce St, Lochmaben DG11 1PD
WWW.PINKFLAMINGOVINTAGETEAROOM.COM   01387 810883

# *The* MALTINGS COFFEE SHOP

A sleeping beauty, restored to life after a nearly hundred-year hiatus. Annandale Distillery opened its doors and began filling casks again in 2014 following a £12.5 million restoration. Handsome original sandstone buildings, which opened in 1836, are set around a cobbled courtyard, highlighted by original Johnnie Walker production chimney and Charles Doig pagoda roof. Behind these hallowed walls lies the magical rumblings of a working distillery.

Set in Robert the Bruce and Robert Burns land, the friendly team offer wonderfully informative tours and tastings, (drivers packs available) to reveal the distillery's and region's rich history. Choose between the Classic, Restoration or Technical Tours, and you'll learn all about the site's former life as a Johnnie Walker distillery and farm to being restructured as a working single malt distillery as you are guided through the gleaming copper stills, mash house, kiln, mill and oak barrels of maturing spirit in the 19th-century warehouse.

The dog-friendly Maltings café serves renowned cheese scones made fresh daily, alongside Afternoon Teas, homemade soup and huge, fresh filled sandwiches (try the cheese and haggis, or 8 hour slow cooked pulled beef). The towering home-baked cakes are impressive, with appealing flavour combinations such as courgette and avocado, and cranberry and white chocolate tiffin, as well as some of your favorites; gluten free options are also available. Gainey-edged wood, exposed beams, rosy sandstone walls and iron pillars create a soothing spot; striking triangular tables are ideal for clustering around for a gossip, while weary drivers can kick back in the deep, purple sofas, and to top it all off the log fire sets the mood for the winter months. Coffee is fresh, rich and strong, tea is loose leaf.

In the shop you can buy glassware, 'Rascally' a Clear Malt Spirit, clothing and other gifts. The impressive range of single malts is stunning, from the collector's edition, 2014 production, the first in 100 years from Annandale, to their sherry and bourbon cask bottlings; Man O'Sword is the peated malt named after Robert the Bruce, or there's the un-peated Man O'Words, named after Robert Burns. There's plenty of parking a short walk away in the car park, with closer options for disabled visitors.

The nearby aptly named Devils Beef Tub, a dramatic hollow where devilish thieves hid cattle until the 17th century, is worth a visit for its striking views and unlawful past. Described by Sir Walter Scott as 'A damned deep, black, blackguard-looking abyss of a hole' it can be reached by a clearly signposted, pleasant woodland walk along the stream. Look out for marigolds in the spring and dragonflies in summer.

Opening hours
Mon-Sat 9am-5pm
Sun 10am-5pm

The Maltings Coffee Shop, Annandale Distillery, Northfield, Annan DG12 5LL
WWW.ANNANDALEDISTILLERY.COM   01461 207817

TEA ROOM

# *Lanercost* TEA ROOM

JUNCTION NAWORTH LODGE; 4 MINUTES

When Hadrian ordered his men to build a wall to keep out the marauding Scottish Picts he could have scarcely imagined the attraction it would become. At 73 miles long and built in just over five years, it is a feat of engineering and marked the Roman empire's northerly limit.

Travellers looking for a launchpad for wall excursions or a break from the highway should turn into Lanercost Priory half a mile away and steeped in it's own history. The Hadrian's Wall Visitor Information Centre here has been described as the best place to start your journey along the Wall. The abbey's old farm buildings have been converted into an airy tea room decorated with giant paper pom-poms. Food is prepared to order – including Cumberland sausage sourdough rolls and traditional fish and chips – and the scones are baked in the kitchen each morning.

The fields and riverbanks nearby make Lanercost a popular spot for dog walkers, so there's a dedicated Bark and Brew café by the gift shop where four-legged friends are warmly welcomed.

Opening hours
Mon–Sun 9.30am-5pm
Closing time in winter may be subject to change, please check Nov–Mar.

Lanercost Tea Room, Abbey Farm, Lanercost CA8 2HQ
WWW.LANERCOSTTEAROOM.CO.UK  016977 41267

# *The Coffee House* & BROWN'S LAKESIDE LARDER

**JUNCTION B6342; 2 MINUTES**

Slate roofed and set above a lake in the midst of pastoral Northumberland, it's easy to see how Kirkharle inspired its most famous son, Capability Brown, the 'Shakespeare of Gardening' (the exhibition and lake walking trail will tell you more). Daffodils flourish by the mossy banks of the stream in spring, pots bloom on the patio in summer and the countryside tableau looks like a watercolour. The courtyard has been remodelled into an artisans' hub, where the low-slung outbuildings are home to craftsmen whom you can watch at work as they make sculptures, jewellery, furniture and papier mache art.

There's a farmhouse cosiness to the beamed coffee house, matched by exposed stone walls and panelling, while the food is a cut above your average café fare – think smoked duck breast sandwich with beetroot and orange hummus alongside tea cakes and good coffee. Make sure you visit the new farm shop – Brown's Lakeside Larder – which stocks an array of products from the North East as well as artisan delicacies from further afield.

## Opening hours
Mon–Sun 10am-5pm (4pm in winter)

The Coffee House & Brown's Lakeside Larder, Kirkharle Courtyard, Kirkharle NE19 2PE
**KIRKHARLECOURTYARD.CO.UK  01830 540362**

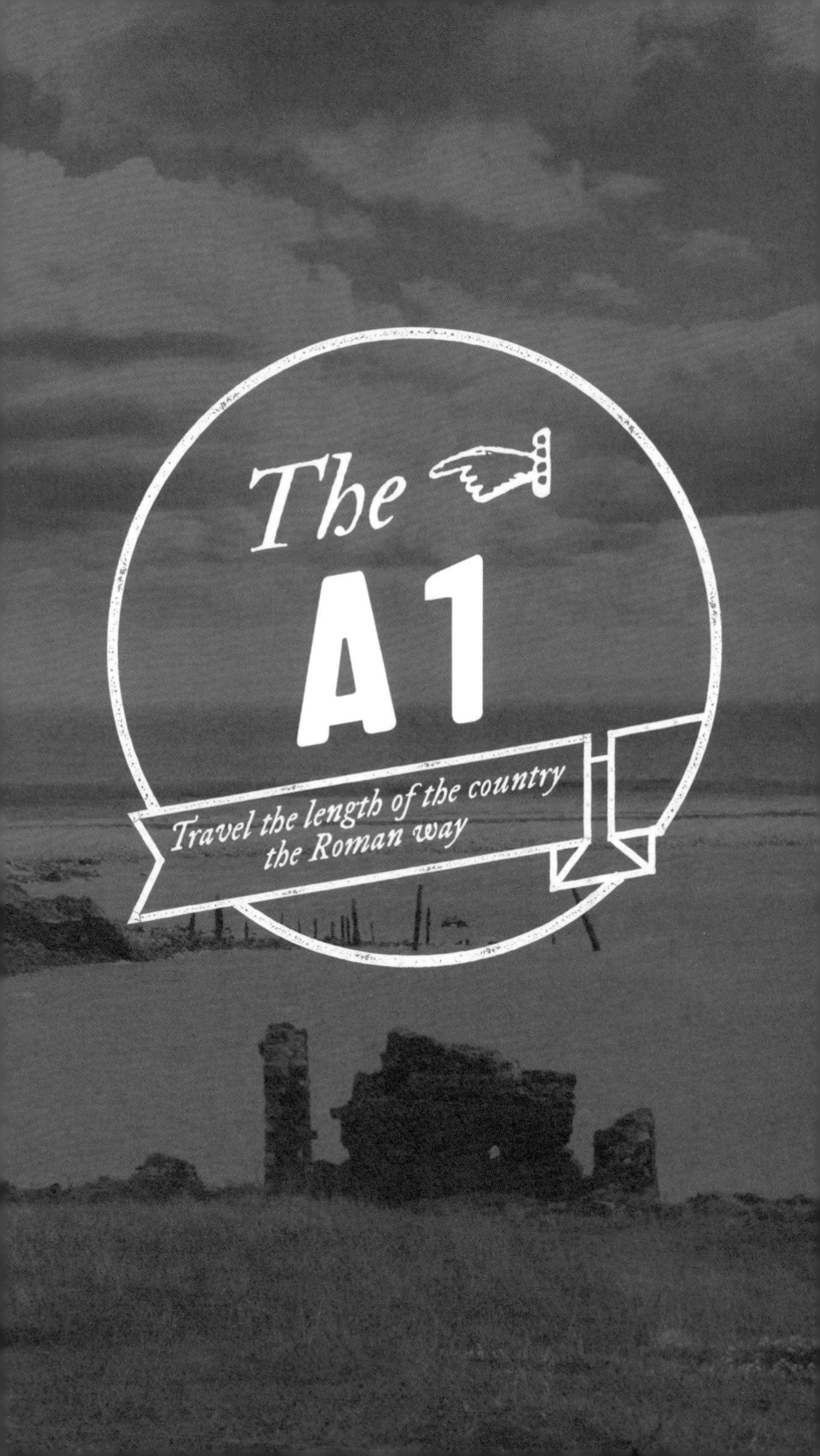

# The ☞

# A1

Travel the length of the country
the Roman way

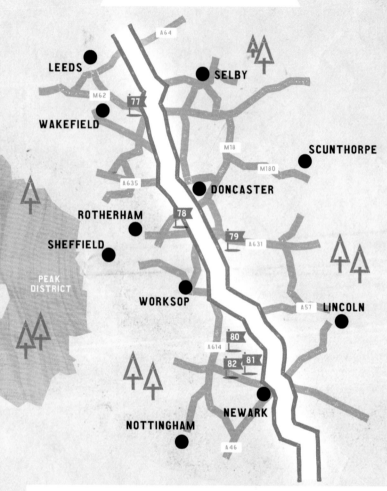

# A1 NORTH

LEEDS

A64

SELBY

M62

77

WAKEFIELD

M18

SCUNTHORPE

M180

A635

DONCASTER

ROTHERHAM

78

SHEFFIELD

79    A631

PEAK
DISTRICT

WORKSOP

A57    LINCOLN

80

A614

82    81

NEWARK

NOTTINGHAM

A46

| | | |
|---|---|---|
| 60 Chain Bridge Honey Farm | 68 Cross Lanes Organic Farm | 77 Farmer Copleys |
| 61 Doddington Milk Bar | 69 Mainsgill Farm | 78 Garden Room Café |
| 62 The Old Stables Tea Room | 70 Shoulder of Mutton | 79 Torworth Grange |
| 63 Barter Books | 71 High Parks Tearoom | Farmshop & Lakes |
| 64 Moorhouse Farm | 72 Lister's Farm Shop | 80 The Hay Barn Café |
| 65 Broom House Farm | 73 Bowe & Co | 81 Newfield Dairy |
| 66 Archers Jersey | 74 Minskip Farm Shop | Ice Cream Parlour |
| Ice Cream Parlour | 75 The Castle Inn | 82 Maxeys Farm Shop |
| 67 Tea with Alice | 76 Tom Foolery | |

# A1 SOUTH

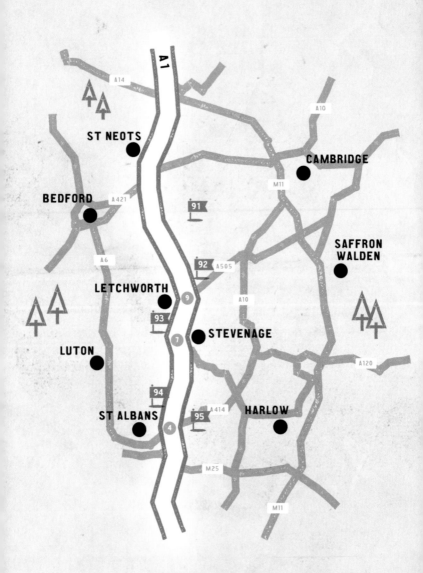

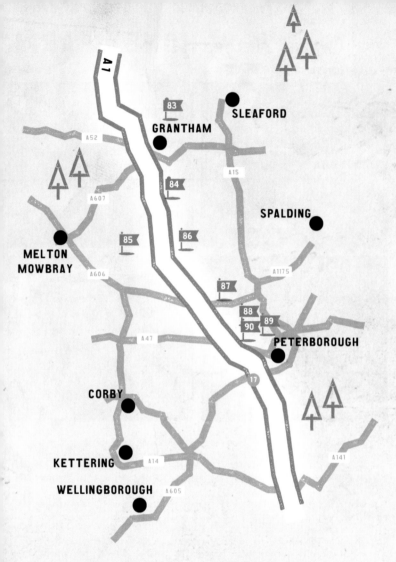

A1

83

GRANTHAM

SLEAFORD

A52

A15

84

A607

SPALDING

85

86

A1175

MELTON
MOWBRAY

A606

87

88
90 89

A47

PETERBOROUGH

17

CORBY

KETTERING

A14

A141

WELLINGBOROUGH

A605

| 83 | The Stag | 88 | The White Hart | 93 | The Rusty Gun |
|----|----------|----|----------------|----|----------------|
| 84 | Easton Walled Gardens | 89 | Willow Brook Farm Shop | 94 | Heartwood Tea Rooms |
| 85 | The Black Bull | 90 | Sacrewell | 95 | River Cottage Kitchen |
| 86 | The Olive Branch | 91 | The Coach House | | at Hatfield House |
| 87 | Café au Chocolat | 92 | Tea at Tapps | | |

# *Chain Bridge* HONEY FARM

### JUNCTION A698: 6 MINUTES

© *Walter Baxter, Creative Commons*

On your travels in Northumberland, you will see W. S. Robson's honey for sale in farm shops. Most outlets stock the solid heather variety; harder to source are tubs of their intensely fragrant and runny flower comb honey. For this sensory delight, you may need to go direct to the source, high above the wooded slopes of the River Tweed.

A short walk from the early 19th-century suspension bridge that gives the farm its name, Mr Robson's shop sells beeswax beauty products, polish, candles – and, of course, honey.

Outside you will see a double-decker bus, now a tea room run by the farmer's daughter, Frances. The interior of this Café Bus will take you back to the 1950s with its gingham curtains and original aluminium-framed bus seats. Farm produce is used wherever it tastes good (try the ham and honey mustard sandwiches over a honey latte). A lady in the local village bakes many of the cakes, including a honey and beer sponge.

Opening hours
Tues-Sun 10am-5pm
(from early April to end October)

Chain Bridge Honey Farm, Horncliffe, Berwick-upon-Tweed TD15 2XT
**WWW.CHAINBRIDGEHONEY.COM  01289 382362**

# *Doddington* MILK BAR

**JUNCTION BELLSHILL; 15 MINUTES**

Ice cream and milkshake lovers, hold your horses here. Painted a shade of powder blue and guarded by a life-size model cow, the cutesy Doddington Milk Bar sells meals and snacks fresh from the Maxwell family's dairy farm. It's a little way off the A1 at the edge of Northumberland National Park, but a fun diversion on the way to or from Scotland.

The interior is decked out like an American diner – baby blue and navy booths, breakfast bar and zingy orange lamps – and service is faultlessly friendly to match. Breakfasts are free range and delicious. Doddington's own cheese goes into the scrumptious lunchtime rarebits – pick up a piece at the small cheese counter if you're seduced.

But it's the ice cream that people (especially little people) really come for. The counter has around ten varieties, such as lemon meringue and caramel and sea salt, that can be served in cones or tubs, or whizzed up into a milkshake and devoured in seconds.

Opening hours
Tues-Sat 7am-5pm
Sun-Mon 9am-5pm

Doddington Milk Bar, 11 South Road, Wooler NE71 6QE
**WWW.DODDINGTONMILKBAR.CO.UK   01668 282357**

CAFÉ

# *The* OLD STABLES TEA ROOM

JUNCTION DENWICK; 1 MINUTE

For travellers looking for a quick pit stop close to Alnwick but don't want to navigate through the town, this friendly, secluded coffee shop is the place. The courtyard outside is a wonderful suntrap in the afternoon and provides guests with views of farmland and the distant A1 (which can be seen but delightfully hardly heard). For the most part the only sounds are the wind in the trees and buzzards calling overhead.

The stone stables that give the coffee shop its name adjoin the courtyard and a small kitchen garden. Inside, the homely farmhouse style café doubles as a little gift shop selling sweet vintage-inspired toys: snakes and ladders, tin cars, Famous Five book sets.

On the food front, there's no escaping the huge cakes on the counter: pistachio, raspberry, lemon and meringue Victoria sponge, coffee and walnut. Sandwiches and soups are served with really good homemade bread. As for the coffee, it's got to be Pumphrey's, a regional favourite.

Opening hours
Weds-Sat 10am-4pm

The Old Stables Tea Room, Broomhouse, Denwick, NE66 2LB
WWW.OLDSTABLESALNWICK.CO.UK   07594 044904

# *Barter* **BOOKS**

JUNCTION A1068; 4 MINUTES

"I wanted it to be a place people could just go and be alone and stay all day," says Mary Manley, the charismatic co-founder of this quirky second-hand bookshop and café housed in Alnwick's former train station.

The Station Buffet in the restored Victorian waiting rooms serves hearty, strongly flavoured and generously portioned lunches: quiches, Northumbrian rarebit, bangers and mash. This is comfort food at its very best. Watch out for the sinfully rich macaroni cheese topped with bacon bits. After a bowl of Barter Books' signature dish by the open fire, you will be forced to abandon your onward journey. Edinburgh by the evening? No chance, my friend.

Breakfasts and the 100+ cakes baked daily on site are equally likely to raise your cholesterol – French toast with syrup, bacon with everything (more or less), egg and chips... You could be good and opt for one of the 'Super Healthy Options', which include avocado toast and porridge.

Opening hours
Mon-Sun 9am-7pm

Barter Books, Alnwick Station, Wagon Way Rd, Alnwick NE66 2NP
**WWW.BARTERBOOKS.CO.UK   01665 604888**

FARM SHOP-CAFÉ

# *Moorhouse* FARM

JUNCTION STANNINGTON; 2 MINUTES

A super farm shop and café on the edge of a 500-acre family farm, where home-grown is the buzzword. "If we don't produce it ourselves, we know somebody local who does," says farmer Ian. The farm shop is well-stocked with Northumberland produce: from fresh bread to home-reared meat, jams, farmhouse cakes and cheeses. Pick up some spicy jalapeno sausages and minted lamb burgers for a delicious BBQ. A convenient click-and-collect service means you can order ahead and whip a bag of groceries away with you.

The coffee shop serves honest, home-cooked food – cooked breakfasts, pie of the day, fresh sandwiches, burgers, sponge puddings with ice cream and lunch boxes for kids. Grab a cup of Rington's tea and a slice of cake, then take in the country views from the terrace. Children will enjoy the free play area, sandpit, ride-on tractors and visits to the animals – catch Ian at the right time and you might even be able to help him hunt for eggs.

Opening hours
Mon-Sat 9.30am-5.30pm
Sun 10am-4pm

Moorhouse Farm, 21 Station Rd, Stannington, Morpeth   NE61 6DX
**WWW.MOORHOUSEFARMSHOP.CO.UK   01670 789016**

# *Broom House* FARM

**JUNCTION 63; 15 MINUTES**

© *Anna Termolaresa*

Broom House Farm sits at the top of a hill looking out over the dip and roll of the countryside towards Durham cathedral. The coffee shop is cosy in winter with a wood burner and gleaming domes of cakes, whilst in summer there is seating outside, overlooking a huge grassy play field and meadows stocked with sheep and cattle. During the warmer months there's nature-based family action in the Forest Adventure (buy a ticket at the coffee shop) — let off some steam here before heading back to the café to enjoy home cooked snacks and freshly ground coffee.

Ingredients sourced from the farm and surrounding area are whizzed into irresistible bites, such as bacon sandwiches, beef burgers and toasties. Traybakes and cakes are summoned daily from the oven. Fill your bags in the farm shop on the way out: our picks include Durham honey and Broom House chutney.

Opening hours
Mon-Sun 9am-5pm

Broom House Farm, Witton Gilbert, Durham DH7 6TR
**WWW.BROOMHOUSEDURHAM.CO.UK  0191 3718382**

# *Archers Jersey* ICE CREAM PARLOUR

**JUNCTION 58: 5 MINUTES**

It was nearly curtains for John and Susan Archer's farm when the foot-and-mouth outbreak of 2001 wiped out their whole herd. But they replaced their stock with 320 productive Jersey cows and turned tragedy into triumph by the power of ice cream.

Today, the girls out in the field make Archers Jersey ice cream a much-loved fixture of the Darlington countryside. Drop into the farm (you may see the cows being herded into the milking parlour) to get the freshest ice cream imagineable in a range of 50 flavours: toffee, pistachio, chocolate, Christmas pudding (in season), tiramisu, crème brûlée, as well as exceptional sorbets. Visit in spring and you might meet a newborn calf.

The parlour has a conservatory to the front, maximising the bucolic, far-reaching views and outstretched trees. There's a play area for kids to bowl about in, and balls can be borrowed from the café for a kickabout; don wellies for the two-mile walk round the farm in summer.

Opening hours
Mon-Sun 10am-6pm
Closed from October-March

Archers Jersey Ice Cream Parlour, New Moor Farm  Walworth Gate, DL2 2UD
**WWW.ARCHERSJERSEYICECREAM.CO.UK    01325 300336**

# *Tea* WITH ALICE

**JUNCTION 58: 2 MINUTES**

"We only use the best ingredients, we give free smiles with every visit, we will always fuss over your children or dog and appreciate your handbag," say Mark and Mary, owners of Tea With Alice. We can't disagree. They set up their friendly neighbourhood café after the arrival of their daughter, Alice, and have devoted boundless energy to making it a haven for travellers. There are toys, games and colouring for kids; bowls of water and biscuits for furry visitors.

The neon sign gleams in the window, colourful vintage furniture fills the café and personal trinkets litter the shelves. In the summer holidays workshops and activities – from pizza decorating to bread making – keep the little ones happy while you enjoy your meal.

Tea is loose leaf and the coffee is excellent. In the kitchen brother-in-law Paul cooks everything from scratch using the best ingredients in Country Durham. Home-made bread and Weardale artisan brie create a cheese sandwich to remember.

Opening hours
Tues-Sat 8am-4.30pm

Tea with Alice, West Park 4 Tilage Green Darlington DL2 2GL
**WWW.TEAWITHALICE.CO.UK  01325 360397**

FARM SHOP-CAFÉ

# *Cross Lanes* ORGANIC FARM

JUNCTION SCOTCH CORNER: 13 MINUTES

Sustainable living is the watchword at the fabulous Cross Lanes Organic Farm, set on the theatrical A66, which links the glorious North Pennines to the Lake District. Owners Peter and Sue have woven eco-principles into the very fabric of the business. Sheep occasionally graze on the meadow-turfed roof, the compost loo is thatched with heather, solar panels heat the water, toilet doors are made from recycled plastic bottles and straw bales line the building.

The restaurant serves a wide range of delicious meals using organic, fresh, wild, local and home-grown ingredients. Home-cured bacon and homemade sausages feature on the breakfast menu; koftas, salads and wood-fired pizzas at lunch; cakes and scones for tea. The shop has a butcher's counter, deli, bakery and a craft section, all focused on local producers and ethical ranges.

Three infamous resident geese will entertain children if they tire of the sturdy, wooden adventure playground.

Opening hours
Mon-Sat 8.30am-5pm
Sun 10am-5pm

Cross Lanes Organic Farm, Cross Lanes, Barnard Castle DL12 9RT
WWW.CROSSLANESORGANICS.CO.UK   01833 630619

FARM SHOP-CAFÉ

# *Mainsgill* **FARM**

JUNCTION SCOTCH CORNER: 6 MINUTES

From the camels – Doris, Delilah and Camelot – grazing in the field to the zip wire and adventure playground there's a lot to love about Mainsgill Farm. Just off the thunderous A66 overlooking the northern edge of the Yorkshire Dales, it's a gargantuan farm shop with butchery, food hall, tea room, gift shop and homewares.

Step through the front door and you come face-to-face with a 28-metre deli counter filled with cheeses, cold meats, pies, antipasti and fresh meats. The vegetable aisle has a picture window giving onto those rolling dales, as if to remind you where it all comes from. Most of the goods on offer have their roots (and hooves) in the Mainsgill family's 500-acre farm; the rest is carefully selected from British and continental suppliers.

The café prides itself on freshly baked cakes, meringues, country breakfasts and award-winning soups. The menu is simple and comforting, the service friendly. A fabulous place to break a journey.

Opening hours
Mon-Sun 9am-5pm

Mainsgill Farm, East Layton, Richmond DL11 7PN
**WWW.MAINSGILLFARM.CO.UK  01325 718860**

PUB

# *Shoulder of* **MUTTON**

**JUNCTION SCOTCH CORNER; 1 MINUTE**

An ideal pit stop at just a minute's drive from the A1, and a cut above your average pub food. Tasty starters (duck spring rolls, black pudding and pulled pork bonbons, moules marinières with fennel, even snails bourguignon) are followed by imaginative mains, from Korean BBQ rump steak to steak pies, asparagus and mascarpone ravioli to the eponymous shoulder of mutton, slow cooked for hours. Among the usual suspects on the dessert menu are sparks of inspiration in the blackcurrant sorbet and poached pear and lemon tart.

There's a cosiness in the dusky lighting, tartan carpets, inviting nooks and open fires in winter. Tables are spread over several levels, a product of 400 years of history, and serving staff ferry plates to them with friendly smiles.

If you're travelling with four-legged friends, there's a surfeit of footpaths and bridleways fanning out from the village where you can glimpse signs of its copper-mining past.

Opening hours
Mon 5.30pm-11pm
Tues-Sat noon-3pm, 5.30pm-11pm
Sun noon-10.30pm

Shoulder of Mutton, Middleton Tyas, Richmond DL10 6QX
**WWW.SHOULDEROFMUTTONMIDDLETONTYAS.CO.UK   01325 377271**

# *High Parks* **TEAROOM**

**JUNCTION 51: 9 MINUTES**

You can't help but be restored by the panoramic views over the Yorkshire Dales from the High Parks tearoom. Grab a table by one of the huge windows or out on the terrace to soak up the rugged scenery as you tuck into the tasty café fare – perhaps a Full Yorkshire Breakfast, Wensleydale and pear toastie or the renowned High Parks Afternoon Tea.

There's plenty to keep you entertained beyond the tearoom too. You'll have to prise kids away from the street-themed play area inside, where they can bake cakes, buy groceries and watch films in the cinema.

Outside, the fort playground throngs with little people on sunny days (and is fenced, so you can watch from the peace of the café) while the farm animals are enduringly popular, particularly Dicky and Lily the miniature Shetland ponies. Everyone will enjoy glimpsing a little magic – or even a goblin – on a walk through the new enchanted fairy woodland.

**Opening hours**
Mon-Sun 9am-5pm

High Parks Tearoom, Newton le Willows, Bedale DL8 1TP
**WWW.HIGHPARKS.CO.UK  01677 450555**

FARM SHOP-CAFÉ

# Lister's FARM SHOP

JUNCTION DISHFORTH; 3 MINUTES

From farm to fork, Lister's is a wonderful place to enjoy a taste of Yorkshire. It's run by the Lister family, with Grace at the helm, third generation farmers who keep Aberdeen Angus cattle, pigs and sheep as well as an arable enterprise. In the farm shop you'll be tempted by counters of home-reared meat, handmade sausages and home-cured bacon as well as a selection of deli goodies, including home-cooked hams, quiches, local cheese, jams and chutneys.

The café has wooden tables topped with posies of flowers where you can enjoy homemade sausage rolls, salads, tray bakes, cakes, toasted tea cakes, grazing boards and filling sandwiches. The breakfasts are award-winning – a plateful of Listers' bacon, sausages, black pudding, tomatoes, mushrooms and eggs will satisfy even the biggest appetites.

Children are very welcome and will love the dedicated play area. They can have the run of the pedal-on tractor course, sandpit, swings and Wendy house and a maize maze in season.

Opening hours
Tues-Fri 8.30am–5.30pm
Sat 9am-4pm
Sun 10am-4pm

Lister's Farm Shop, Leeming Lane, Langthorpe, Boroughbridge YO51 9DE
WWW.LISTERSFARMSHOP.CO.UK   01423 326452

# *Bowe &* **CO**

**JUNCTION 48; 4 MINUTES**

Pretty Boroughbridge is bounded by gently rolling hills and pockets of history. Stretch your legs by the River Ure or walk to the edge of town to find three ancient standing stones, known as the Devil's Arrows and said to have been flung there by Satan. Refuel at Bowe & Co, a relaxed and friendly café-deli on the high street. Lunch is wholesome, generous and freshly made. Regulars rave about the salads, which are served alongside soups (maybe beetroot and horseradish), quiches and frittatas.

The go-to Yorkshire platter is an enormous plate of salads, cooked ham, cheese, crisps and a pork pie; cakes are playful – try the coconut and Malibu, raspberry and amaretto or orange and almond. Coffee is deliciously smooth, the tea – Yorkshire, of course. The deli counter is ripe for the picking – fabulous cheeses, sandwiches (maybe pastrami or local roast beef) and anti pasti.

Opening hours
Mon-Sat 9am-4pm

Bowe & Co, 27 High Street, Boroughbridge YO51 9AW
WWW.BOWEANDCO.COM  01423 323037

# *Minskip* **FARM SHOP**

**JUNCTION 48; 1 MINUTE**

Food miles are so low at the Minskip Farm Shop near Boroughbridge that you can see vegetables growing in the field in front. Chickens scratch around for grubs in the field at the back, supplying golden-yolked eggs to the shop, and you can visit the lambs in spring.

Third-generation pig farmer Ben and his novelist wife Emma took over the farm business in 2017 and have been busy evolving the popular farm shop into a local food hub. They stock a wide range of fresh and store-cupboard products from the local area, 96% of which are sourced less than 30 miles from the door. These goodies include Aga tray bakes and jams from Bessie's Yorkshire Preserves, bread from the village down the road, pork pies from Whixley, pâté and smoked mackerel from Mackenzies Yorkshire Smokehouse. Plunder the selection for a sensational picnic or the makings of a delicious dinner.

Keep an eye out for the café, which is due to open soon and promises good things.

Opening hours
Mon-Fri 8.30am-5.30pm
Sat 8.30am-5pm
Sun 10am-4pm

Minskip Farm Shop, Minskip Road, Boroughbridge YO51 9HY
**WWW.MINSKIPFARMSHOP.COM 01423 329 063**

# *The* CASTLE INN

**JUNCTION 46; 8 MINUTES**

A beautifully updated stone pub in the Yorkshire countryside with 12 very stylish bedrooms. The original bar and pretty dining room have been transformed and extended with the addition of a relaxed courtyard and two private dining rooms. A sliding glass roof, wood-clad walls, wicker chairs and jolly blankets give the whole space a modern breezy style.

Food is freshly prepared and beautifully presented. Begin your day with a brilliant breakfast and from noon enjoy an excellent choice of starters, mains and desserts. Little diners can choose from their own menu and there's a good selection of light bites if you are short of time.

Drop into the free-to-visit Spofforth Castle while you're in the area. Once the family seat of William Percy, a close associate of William the Conqueror, this is reputedly where rebel barons drew up the Magna Carta.

Opening hours
Mon-Sat 7am-11pm
Sun 7am-10pm

The Castle Inn, 35 High Street, Spofforth HG3 1BQ
**WWW.THECASTLEINNHARROGATE.COM   01937 590200**

CAFÉ-BAR
## Tom FOOLERY
**JUNCTION 45: 3 MINUTES**

A light-hearted café-bar on Boston Spa's high street, Tom Foolery is decorated whimsically with umbrella light fittings, John Lennon artwork and metal Tube signs. It's community-focused and informal, so you're as welcome to slump into a sofa with a coffee and raspberry blondie as sit at a table and order the works.

Varied breakfasts will suit all appetites – toasted crumpets with apricot jam, poached eggs and pesto on sourdough and big fry-ups with wild boar sausages, bacon, black pudding and garlic thyme mushrooms. Salads and sandwiches are on the menu at lunchtime – speck ham, mozzarella and sun-dried tomatoes; hummus, roasted courgettes and olives – along with bread baked in house. If you're hungry, burgers and pizzas topped with chorizo, salami feline, nduja sausage and Applewood cheese will more than fill a hole, and kids will love the chocolate and toasted marshmallow pizza on the dessert menu.

**Opening hours**
Mon-Sun 10am–midnight

(GF) (V)

Tom Foolery, 179 High Street, Boston Spa LS23 6BD
**WWW.TOMFOOLERYBOSTONSPA.CO.UK   01937 541500**

FARM SHOP-CAFÉ
# *Farmer* COPLEYS
**JUNCTION 33: 9 MINUTES**

The family has been farming here for over 140 years but Farmer Copleys as it is seen today began 15 years ago and is a fantastic showcase of sustainable agriculture and British food.

You'll struggle to resist the homemade jams, fudge, chutneys and gelato in the farm shop as well as farm fresh fruit and vegetables. Plunder the lovely deli and 10m-long butchery counter for ingredients for your dinner, and peek into the Jam Kitchen to see the cooks at work.

Quirky cow-print lampshades hang from the rafters of the award-winning Moo Café next door, where friendly staff serve home-cooked food from breakfast till tea time. Bread and cakes come from the farm's own bakery; other ingredients from the fields outside.

It's a great place for kids to learn about farming – we didn't know that alpacas keep foxes away! You'll have to peel little ones away from the close-up animal experiences.

Opening hours
Mon-Sat 8.30am-5.30pm
Sun & Bank Hols 8.30am-4pm

Farmer Copleys, Ravensknowle Farm Pontefract Rd, Pontefract WF7 5AF
**WWW.FARMERCOPLEYS.CO.UK  01977 600200**

CAFÉ

# *Garden Room* CAFÉ

**JUNCTION 36; 9 MINUTES**

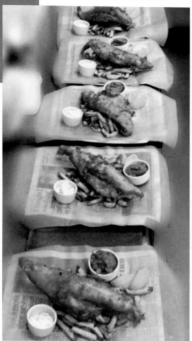

Unpretentious homemade food is the promise from Gina and Stuart at The Garden Room, and that's exactly what you get. Whether you order a healthy breakfast, weighty tuna melt, delicious afternoon tea or gargantuan slice of carrot cake you won't go hungry. Ingredients are sourced from nearby farms wherever possible, and on Fridays you can sample fish 'n' chips made with the daily catch at Filey. Everything is cooked to perfection and the staff are welcoming and efficient.

The café is swamped by blooming plants and shrubs (make the most of the lush courtyard on fine days) and housed in a low stone building. Light pours in from country-cottage windows. Walls are decorated with delicate floral patterns and the wood panelling is painted a soft olive green. You'll find it in a handsome village just south of Doncaster and near Sheffield, so it's a great place to break a long journey north or south.

Opening hours
Tues-Sun 10am-4.30pm

Garden Room Café, High Street, Braithwell S66 7AL
**WWW.GARDENROOMCAFE.CO.UK** 01709 790790

# *Torworth Grange Farmshop* **& LAKES**

**JUNCTION 34: 7 MINUTES**

However arduous your journey the sound of wind rustling through the reeds in the lake at Torworth Grange will calm you down. Farm shop, café, campsite and fishing spot, this family business occupies an idyllic corner of Nottinghamshire and stocks almost everything you could want for your onward journey. Artisan bread, regional cheeses, homemade meat pies, craft beers and ciders – even fresh cuts of ostrich and wild boar.

The decked terrace, looking over the lake, is festooned with lights and flowers for making the most of warmer evenings. Inside is bright and comfortable and quirkily decorated – the front of an old Tata bus, for example, makes a wonderful dresser. Tea is served in vintage cups that Val 'Mother Goose' has collected from charity shops and food is inspired by her own recipe book.

Try the homemade fishcakes, scotch egg platter served with crunchy pickles and coleslaw or a hunk of chocolate and raspberry cake.

Opening hours
Mon-Sun 9am-5pm
(winter 9am-4pm)

Torworth Grange Farmshop, Great North Rd, Torworth DN22 8NY
**WWW.TORWORTHGRANGE.CO.UK  01777 816439**

CAFÉ

# *The* HAY BARN CAFÉ

**JUNCTION CARLTON-ON-TRENT; 10 MINUTES**

For a warm, country welcome look no further than the Hay Barn Café. The genial ladies (and occasionally gent) who work here are interminably friendly and don't bat an eyelid at muddy footwear, muddy paws and messy children. They're expert bakers to boot, and scones are often served warm from the oven (try their cherry and almond variety if you're there on the right day), always with homemade jam and Chantilly cream.

Freshly made quiches, toasted paninis, baps and sandwiches are on the lunch menu. Prices are reasonable, the coffee is smooth and the gravelled, suntrap courtyard is ringed by tall, red-brick walls and filled with bright plants and sage-coloured furniture – a lovely spot for listening to the chirrup of birds over a pot of tea or a full, farm-fresh breakfast.

A rank of shelves at the back harbour local produce to take away such as plum bread, farmhouse fudge, butter bites, pressed juice and Scrumpy Wasp cider made in East Markham.

Opening hours
Mon-Sat 9am-4pm

The Hay Barn Café, Old Hall Farm, Kneesall NG22 0AD
WWW.HAYBARNCAFE.CO.UK   01623 862677

# *Newfield Dairy* ICE CREAM PARLOUR

**JUNCTION NORTH MUSKAM; 10 MINUTES**

With views reaching over the Nottinghamshire countryside and 16 imaginative ice cream flavours, often imaginatively using seasonal fruits (damsons and cream, apple and cinder toffee ripple, liquorice and elderberry), Newfield Dairy has become something of an institution. Try their award-winning raspberry macaroon or ginger and honeycomb ice cream.

The flavours are born in the fields around you, and that farm-fresh ethos applies to excellent café fodder too: a farmer's fuel breakfast, hot steak baguettes and homemade quiches. Coffee is locally roasted and, as you'd expect, the floats and milkshakes are legendary. Gluten-free, skinny and dairy-free dishes are available, as well as yummy sorbets and gluten-free cones.

The breezy café overlooks the fields and a safe play are. It's warmed by the wood burner in winter and has plenty of games to keep everyone amused. Outside there's lots of seating for taking in those views, and a grassy lawn for lolling about in summer.

Opening hours
Mon-Sun 10am-4.30pm

Newfield Dairy Ice Cream Parlour, Caunton Rd, Hockerton NG25 0PN
**WWW.NEWFIELDICECREAM.COM  01636 636600**

# *Maxeys* **FARM SHOP**

## JUNCTION NORTH MUSKHAM: 13 MINUTES

Housed in a purpose-built, wood-clad building at the side of the family farm, Maxey's is a fabulous shop stocking Nottinghamshire's finest produce. The deli counter has a vast selection of English cheeses – some 70 plus – with locally made chutneys and condiments stacked on the dressers to accompany them. The in-house bakery pumps out the tantalising scents of homemade pork pies and impressively fluffy cakes and meringues in an array of flavours.

The farm shop sells homegrown vegetables all year round – from asparagus to brassicas – culminating in the famous pumpkins in October where visitors can literally grab a wheelbarrow and pick their own from the pumpkin patch.

A butchery counter sells local meats (the Lincolnshire sausages are fantastic) and fish. A one-stop shop for a delicious dinner or a BBQ, and there's a small and well-chosen collection of gifts and homewares.

**Opening hours**
Mon-Sat 9am-5.30pm
Sun 10am-4pm

Maxeys Farm Shop, Hockerton Road, Kirklington NG22 8PB
**WWW.MAXEYSFARMSHOP.CO.UK   01636 814566**

# *The* STAG

JUNCTION GONERBY MOOR/A52: 11 MINUTES

A family-run pub roosting on the green in Barkston near Grantham, The Stag is set among the sublime cornfields of Lincolnshire. It's warmly lit and tastefully decorated in cream and mink. and has slate floors, wooden tables, leather wingback chairs and bookshelves filled with homely knick-knacks to give a sense of familiarity.

Nibble on olives and fresh bread in the bright conservatory, sup a hand-pulled pint of ale by the crackling wood-burner or take a coffee to the well-tended patio garden washed by birdsong and country air. The menu is a notch up from pub grub: prawn and crab Thai salad with pickled cucumber or homemade chicken liver pâté with doorstep toast to start; beer-battered salmon or twice-cooked belly pork and roasted apples for mains. Round off with a chocolate-dipped meringue and berry compote, or blueberry sponge with custard. Walk off any excess along a lovely looped route through Belton WOods, and keep your eyes peeled for deer.

**Opening hours**
Mon-Fri 11.30am-2.30pm, 5pm-11pm
Sat noon-11pm (Sun 10pm)

The Stag, Church Street, Barkston NG32 2NB
WWW.THESTAGEBARKSTON.CO.UK   01400 250363

ATTRACTION

# *Easton* WALLED GARDENS

**JUNCTION COLSTERWORTH/B6403; 3 MINUTES**

Once famously described as 'a dream of Nirvana, almost too good to be true' by Franklin Roosevelt, the gardens of Easton were nearly lost forever when the original house, Easton Hall, was demolished in 1951.

Thankfully Ursula and Fred Cholmeley took over the family property in 2001 and have been restoring the 12-acre gardens. There's a turf maze, yew tunnel, meadows, rose garden, orchards and a pickery (Easton's unique term for its cut flower garden). A sweet pea festival is held every July and showcases heritage and modern varieties.

A garden-themed gift shop smells evocatively of English country gardens and is a rich hunting ground for souvenirs. The tea room serves simple but flavourful meals: filled baguettes, cream teas, excellent cakes, a gardener's ploughman's and vegetable soups. Wash it down with hot cups of tea or homemade elderflower cordial in the summer. You'll need to pay the entrance fee even to access the café so make it a leisurely stop.

Opening hours
Wed-Fri, Sun, Bank Hol Mon 11am-4pm
(from March-October)

Easton Walled Gardens, Easton, Grantham NG33 5AP
**WWW.VISITEASTON.CO.UK  01476 530063**

PUB

# *The* BLACK BULL

JUNCTION STRETTON: 6 MINUTES

Serving fresh, made-to-order food in the Leicestershire wilds, the Black Bull is a charming thatched pub overlooking a patch of allotments and the Rutland countryside. A firm village hub, the atmosphere is jolly and down-to-earth: kids, dogs and walking boots are welcome.

Sit at one of the pavement tables to eat your lunch and you can watch red kites wheeling in the sky, or simply sprawl on a comfortable sofa by the fire. Portions are generous and the flavours fresh. Lunch on a filled baguette – perhaps bacon and halloumi or roast beef with horseradish mayo – or try a bowl of vegan chilli or a home-cooked steak and ale pie. The evening menu takes the range up a notch, but remember to save space for pudding – the sticky toffee with butterscotch sauce is unmissable. Dietary requirements are cheerfully accommodated.

You'll find countless footpaths to explore on the doorstep should you need some digestive fresh air.

Opening hours
Tues-Sat noon-3pm, 6pm-11pm
Sun noon-6pm

The Black Bull, 2 Teigh Road, Market Overton LE15 7PW
WWW.BLACKBULLRUTLAND.CO.UK  01572 767677

PUB

# *The* OLIVE BRANCH

### JUNCTION STRETTON; 2 MINUTES

A model country pub with a relaxed upmarket vibe, the Olive Branch is as comfortable as a slipper. The pub was formed in 1890 when three cottages built to house farm labourers were knocked together. Since 1999 it has been lovingly developed by owners Sean, Ben and Marcus. A line of pegged wellies stand at the front door for guests to borrow; there's a help-yourself basket of blankets to stave off evening chills; chestnuts roast on the fire in winter. Outside, a lush lawn is fringed with burgeoning borders beyond the pergola, heaven on summery days.

Great lunches and dinners are crafted by Sean from the best seasonal produce he can lay his hands on, perhaps a grilled carpaccio of sea trout, or beef and wild mushroom lasagne. Cocktails are made with herbs from the paddock. If you like what you taste, loot the dinky shop for local swag including recipe books, restaurant wines, local woodwork and jars of beef dripping.

Opening hours
Mon-Sat noon-2pm, 6.30pm-9.30pm
Sun noon-3pm, 7pm-9pm

The Olive Branch, Main Street, Clipsham LE15 7SH
**WWW.THEOLIVEBRANCHPUB.CO.UK** 01780 410355

# *Café* **AU CHOCOLAT**

**JUNCTION A6121; 4 MINUTES**

The crêpes at Café au Chocolat are to die for – 'as good as in Brittany' one French visitor remarked. Lunch on the savoury varieties, made with buckwheat flour so naturally gluten free, perhaps stuffed with mushroom and spinach or hummus, rocket and sundried tomatoes. Follow up with a strawberry and salted caramel version if you've got a gap for something sweet.

You'll find the sky-blue fronted café tucked up a side street in the pretty Georgian town of Stamford. Vintage furniture, a 17th-century cast iron range and scuffed panelling give a sense of tousled Parisienne chic inspired by owner Krystyna's travels around Europe. That leaning also translates into deliciously straightforward food: rich, single origin coffee, freshly squeezed juices, french-style pâtisseries, not to mention its chocolate namesake, which is present in many forms. The raspberry and white chocolate brownies are noteworthy, as are the orange-scented hot chocolate and luxury French truffles.

Opening hours
Mon-Weds 8.30am-5pm
Thurs-Fri 8.30am-8pm
Sun 10am-4pm

Café au Chocolat, 2 Ironmonger Street, Stamford PE9 1PL
**WWW.CAFEAUCHOCOLAT.CO.UK   01780 437080**

PUB

# *The* WHITE HART

### JUNCTION A47 WANSFORD; 7 MINUTES

A beatific 17th-century country pub where fresh eggs sit on the bar for casual sale, you'll wish The White Hart was your local. Rough stone walls, flagstone floors, vintage signs, salvaged agricultural tools and a mishmash of furniture give a comfortable, lived-in feel.

The menu is seasonal and fresh, and rooted in the fields around. Starters might include poached pear with panko-crumbed brie and walnuts, homemade guacamole on ciabatta crostini with a poached egg or beetroot-cured salmon. Feast on the chargrilled steak for main course or tuck into a red pepper and halloumi burger. Round off with forest fruit fool or white chocolate and elderflower panna cotta. Sandwiches and nibbles are available for lighter bites. Eat by the fire in the bar, grab a table in the luminous orangery or take advantage of the suntrap courtyard garden brimming with petunias.

Opening hours
Mon-Fri 7.30am-9.30am, noon-2.30pm, 6pm-9pm
Sat 8.30am-9.30am, noon-9pm
Sun 8.30am-9.30am, noon-8pm

The White Hart, Main Street, Ufford PE9 3BH
WWW.WHITEHARTUFFORD.CO.UK  01780 740250

# *Willow Brook* FARM SHOP

**JUNCTION A47; 7 MINUTES**

You can't help but be restored by the nourishing views from Willow Brook Farm Shop. Sat on a hilltop, it occupies a converted stone bar with large windows surveying a Cambridgeshire idyll: wildflower-peppered meadows, cattle grazing and red kites wheeling overhead.

In the Granary Tea Room you'll rub shoulders with hikers and cyclists who pop in to refuel with cups of tea and a slice of Jo's teetering home-baked cakes. Food is honest and worthy of the farm table: breakfasts of thick-cut bacon, homemade sausages and eggs are followed by toasted sandwiches, baked potatoes, daily quiches and cottage pies; full roasts are on the menu on a Sunday, rounded off with apple and damson crumble and custard.

The shop sells a an enticing selection of pork pies, cheeses, sausage rolls and homemade haslet (a mix of breadcrumbs, pork and seasoning: excellent with pickles) as well as home produced beef and local meats. The Granary's opening hours differ from the shop so check ahead.

Opening hours
Mon 9am-3pm
Tues-Sat 8am-5pm
Sun 9am-4pm

Willow Brook Farm Shop, Scotsman Lodge, Stamford Rd, Helpston Heath PE6 7EL
**WWW.WILLOWBROOKFARMSHOP.CO.UK   01780 740261**

ATTRACTION

# SACREWELL

**JUNCTION WANSFORD/A47; 4 MINUTES**

This beautiful 550-acre farm is a beacon for nature lovers and agriculturalists. It was established in 1964 to re-state the link between town and country, people and agriculture, and has been educating visitors about farming ever since. Children will adore the farm, with rare breeds of horses, sheep, pigs, goats, peacocks, chickens and donkeys. There is plenty for kids to do: the gargantuan indoor play barn, den building, tractor rides, giant sandpit and the Sacrewell Trec which incorporates all the natural obstacles found on a country walk.

The café is airy and flooded with light. Paninis, jacket potatoes, pasta bakes and shepherd's pies made from locally farmed produce will replenish adults, while children can pick and mix their own lunches from a healthy selection of sandwiches, vegetable sticks and fruit. The farm shop alongside sells the best goodies from the farm and its neighbours. The shops and café are free to visit, and walking routes around the local countryside are ideal for stretching legs and exercising dogs.

Opening hours
Mon-Sun 10am-4pm

Sacrewell, Thornhaugh, Peterborough PE8 6HJ
**WWW.SACREWELL.ORG.UK  01780 782254**

The dinky market town of Potton is arranged around a handsome medieval market square, demonstrating its historic importance as a centre of trading. It's horse market attracted international buyers up until the 1930s. The town was ravaged by fire in 1783, which devastated half the centre, and from the ashes of the Rose and Crown rose The Coach House.

The red-brick, Georgian inn is a handy staging post at the southern end of the A1. It's been comprehensively revamped and is staffed by friendly faces in casual uniforms.

Breakfasts are filling while the lunch and dinner menus features traditional pub dishes with a twist, such as cajun-dusted squid, pea and bean burger or Gressingham duck breast with artichoke purée,. You can, of course, opt for a burger or sandwich if you prefer. And if you're feeling sluggish after feasting, you can stay the night in one of the beautiful bedrooms.

Opening hours
Mon-Thurs 10am-11pm
Fri-Sat 10am-midnight (Sat 9am)
Sun 11am-10pm

The Coach House, 12 Market Square, Potton SG19 2NP
**WWW.THECOACHHOUSEPOTTON.CO.UK  01767 260221**

CAFÉ

# *Tea at* **TAPPS**

### JUNCTION 9; 4 MINUTES

There's always a warm welcome from the resident collies at Tapps, a plant nursery housed in a long barn overlooking a patch of allotments and Hertfordshire countryside. Tea at Tapps is off to the right, a roomy, rustic café with floor-to-ceiling windows, decorated with greenery and local artwork.

Teas are loose leaf, coffee is strong and the atmosphere is relaxed. Owner Louise is a maestro in the kitchen, priding herself on home-cooked food,. She conjures up lip-smacking cakes from the oven every day: warm scones slathered with clotted cream and jam, passion fruit and white chocolate loaf, vegan fruit cake with cherries, macaroons and orange and poppyseed cake.

Lunches are hardy and filling: quiches from the oven, jacket potatoes, stuffed sandwiches and Gardener's lunches. Parking is plentiful and muddy walkers and dogs are welcome, so you can work up an appetite exploring the many footpaths that thread through the fields in front.

Opening hours
Mon–Sat 10am–5pm
Sun 10am–4pm

Tea at Tapps, Wallington Road, Baldock SG7 6RS
**WWW.TEAATTAPPS.COM 01462 896302**

PUB

# *The* RUSTY GUN

**JUNCTION 8; 6 MINUTES**

A superb country pub with a flavour of the Wild West, the Rusty Gun is housed in a grey-painted, clapboard barn. Antique cannons sit sentry on the wall, a sign in the door invites you to feed the piglets and low beams are hung with pelts. There's a lovely garden and a properly roofed shelter with a fire pit, so you can enjoy the fresh air even in cooler months.

The menu is varied with everything cooked from scratch and changing with the seasons. Pub classics such as sausage and mash, filled baps and juicy burgers stand shoulder-to-shoulder with a respectable à la carte selection of roast duck and sea bream with peanut pesto. Save space for the chocolate brownie to finish.

The produce shop alongside the pub has an enticing selection of local crafts and goodies. Expect to be tempted by Hertfordshire honey, traditional sweets, flavoured oils, pickled garlic, English wines, carved wooden bowls and crocheted blankets.

Opening hours
Mon–Sun noon–11pm

The Rusty Gun, London Road, St Ippolyts SG4 7PG
**WWW.THERUSTYGUN.CO.UK  01462 432653**

TEA ROOM

# *Heartwood* TEA ROOMS

### JUNCTION 4; 10 MINUTES

Safely beyond the bustle of the big smoke, Heartwood Tea Rooms in the genteel village of Sandridge provides relief from the A1. There's a welcoming informality to its wibbly beams and exposed brick walls and the busy chatter of other travellers.

Choose from 20 loose leaf teas (served properly in teapots and china cups) and refuel on breakfasts with a twist (such as avocado and spiced pumpkin on sourdough with lemon crème fraîche), thick-cut sandwiches and tempting cakes. The courtyard is a suntrap on good days, not to mention dog-friendly and filled with flowers.

A USB charging socket at the breakfast bar means you can recharge both mind and devices over a coffee if you're in a hurry. If you're not, make time to explore the magnificent Heartwood Forest nearby. The power of volunteers and 600,000 saplings has turned acres of farmland into a forest that blazes with bluebells in spring and many other wild flowers in summer.

Opening hours
Mon-Sun 9am-5pm

Heartwood Tea Rooms, 27 High Street, Sandridge AL4 9DD
**WWW.HEARTWOODTEAROOMS.CO.UK  01727 854711**

# *River Cottage Kitchen* AT HATFIELD HOUSE

**JUNCTION 3; 10 MINUTES**

Built in 1611 by the Earl of Salisbury and once the childhood home of Elizabeth I, Hatfield House is a breathtaking Jacobean mansion, well worth a visit for its rich history, exquisite decoration and tales of Tudor intrigue.

The horses have long since been evicted from the Stable Yard, which is now host to a range of boutiques – gunmaker, dog-grooming salon, goldsmith – as well as a year-round programme of events, from the monthly antiques and farmers markets to face painting and buskers. River Cottage has taken over the coach house restaurant, where large windows give onto the paved courtyard. From either side of the glass, depending on the weather, you can enjoy light bites or full meals, cooked from scratch using the best local ingredients chefs can get their hands on.

Entertain the kids at the farm (you'll need to buy a ticket) where they can play in sand pits, visit animals grazing in the paddocks and enjoy tractor rides, which are free, just like the parking.

---

Opening hours
Tues-Sun 10am-5pm

---

River Cottage Kitchen at Hatfield House, Hatfield AL9 5NB
**WWW.HATFIELD-HOUSE.CO.UK    01707 262030**

# The M1

Our very first motorway
linking North & South

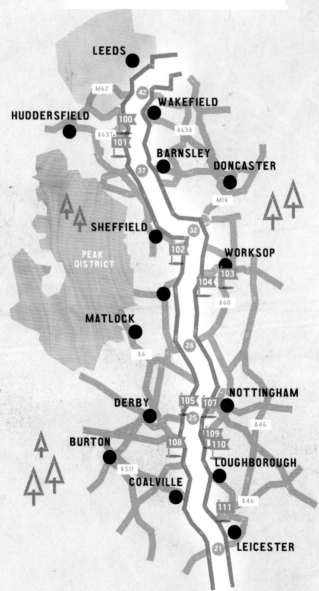

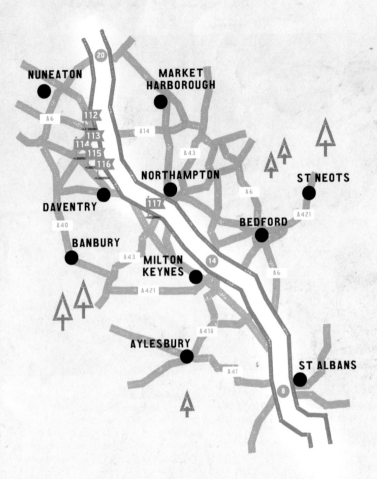

NUNEATON

MARKET
HARBOROUGH

112

113
114
115
116

NORTHAMPTON

ST NEOTS

DAVENTRY

117

BEDFORD

BANBURY

MILTON
KEYNES

AYLESBURY

ST ALBANS

| 100 | Blacker Hall Farm Shop | 107 | Buonissima Aperitivo Bar | 112 | Back in Time for Tea |
|-----|------------------------|-----|--------------------------|-----|----------------------|
| 101 | Cannon Hall Farm | 108 | No. 11 Deli | 113 | The Yard Café Cotesbach |
| 102 | The Café at Renishaw Hall | 109 | The Royal Oak | 114 | The Garden Barn |
| 103 | Welbeck Farm Shop | 110 | Oakley Grange | 115 | The White Swan |
| 104 | The Pump Tea Rooms | | Organic Farm | 116 | Manor Farm |
| 105 | The Old Schoolhouse | 111 | The Forge Inn | 117 | Plantation Café |
| | Deli-Café | | | | |

FARM SHOP-CAFÉ

# *Blacker Hall* FARM SHOP

JUNCTION 39; 2 MINUTES

An Aladdin's cave of delicious West Yorkshire produce (most of it grown or prepared on the farm), Blacker Hall Farm Shop is run by Edward and Cheryl, a hands-on, husband-and-wife team. They pile the shelves high with temptation, from Wakefield rhubarb to Yorkshire ales and Cumbrian charcuterie. Follow your nose to find the in-house bakery making a daily range of bread, cakes, and quiches, or pick up some award-winning roast beef, dry-cured bacon and meat balls from the butchery. Service is friendly and informative – just ask if you'd like some recipe inspiration.

The Barn Café is at the back, through the tantalising shop and past lovely florist and gift concessions in the courtyard. It serves proper farmhouse food, from huge breakfasts to farmer's tasting platters and hunks of cake. Sit up in the airy rafters of the beautiful old barn or grab a table either in the courtyard or on the sun-drenched patio where kids can charge about on the lawn beyond.

Opening hours

Mon-Fri 8.30am-6pm
Sat 8.30am-5pm
Sun 9am-5pm

Blacker Hall Farm Shop, Branch Rd, Calder Grove, Wakefield WF4 3DN
**WWW.BLACKERHALLFARMSHOP.CO.UK  01924 267202**

# Cannon Hall FARM

**JUNCTION 36; 10 MINUTES**

A gargantuan farm attraction in the Pennine Hills, Cannon Hall has something for practically everyone. The lootable shelves and counters of the modern farm shop have everything, from award-winning pork pies (with delicious red-onion marmalade and blue-cheese topping) and sausages to fresh bread, home-marinated olives and even toys and kitchenwares. The White Bull restaurant alongside is modern – exposed brick, timber-framed booths, yellow chairs – and buzzy, selling tasty plates including steaks, curries and burgers. Beeline to the ice cream parlour in the garden afterwards.

Pay your entrance fee and meet hundreds of animals, including llamas, ferrets and reindeer. Specially designed farm buildings offer windows onto the milking parlour, rare breeds' barn and piglet nursery. You'll have to drag kids out of the Hungry Llama indoor play barn (the biggest in the North) and adventure playground, where the tube maze is one of the most popular attractions. A family and foodie heaven.

**Opening hours**
Mon-Sun 9am-5.15pm

Cannon Hall Farm, Bark House Lane, Cawthorne, Barnsley S75 4AT
**WWW.CANNONHALLFARM.CO.UK  01226 790427**

ATTRACTION

# *The Café* AT RENISHAW HALL

JUNCTION 30; 6 MINUTES

Grade I-listed Renishaw Hall, surrounded by award-winning Italianate gardens, has been the Sitwell family seat for nearly 400 years. Not far from the M1 and Chesterfield, the rural grandeur will pacify any road-frayed nerves. Parking is plentiful (you'll need to buy a £1 ticket) and a short walk away from the estate's old stable block. Horses have been hoofed out and the buildings around the cobbled courtyard beautifully renovated to host a range of small businesses, including the Sitwell Museum.

The café is here too, a large, beamed space with dovecote towers at either end and the walls hung with some of the family's collection of art and antiques. Food is seasonal and tasty and the coffee good; you can even have a glass of wine from the Renishaw vineyard. Make a day of it by visiting the idyllic, dog-friendly gardens, which are alive with butterflies and dragonflies and well worth the entry fee. Guided tours of the family home are available every Friday in the season, and weekends in August.

Opening hours
Weds-Sun 10.30am-4.30pm (Mar-Sept)
Fri-Sun 10.30am-4pm (Oct-Nov)
Thurs-Sun 10.30am-4pm (last week Nov-1st week Dec)

Renishaw Hall & Gardens, Renishaw Park, Chesterfield S21 3WB
**WWW.RENISHAW-HALL.CO.UK   01246 432310**

# *Welbeck* FARM SHOP

**JUNCTION 30: 11 MINUTES**

An enormous, traditional estate deep in Robin Hood country Welbeck Farm now hosts a chic and well-rounded community of artisan food producers and entertainments. The large shop sources two-thirds of its produce from the estate, stocking its own meat, raw milk, Welbeck Abbey ales, Stichelton blue cheese, artisan chocolates from in-house chocolatier Shelly Preston and sensational sausage rolls.

Across the courtyard, the Harley art gallery has activities for kids, an irresistible gift shop and contemporary exhibitions alongside the Portland collection. In a building nearby, there's an independent café with a hip, minimalist interior where owner Hilary feeds the hungry hoards with classic fare, delicious daily specials and her unique coffee blend. If you have time to spare, park up, grab some snacks and meander round one of the three downloadable walking routes around the rural estate. Heaven.

**Opening hours**
Mon-Sat 10am-5pm
Sun 10am-4pm

**Welbeck Farm Shop, Worksop S80 3LW**
**WWW.WELBECK.CO.UK   01909 478725**

CAFÉ

# *The Pump* TEA ROOMS

**JUNCTION 29A: 5 MINUTES**

Frequently described as a hidden treasure, The Pump is a captivating tea room alongside the mighty Bolsover Castle. It's housed in a sturdy stone building on the town square and takes its name from the water pump just outside. Inside the vibe is warm and welcoming: tables are clustered with colourful chairs, a stove stands in the original stone hearth and a mural of fields brings a bolt of sunshine to one wall.

For breakfast, lunch and dinner the food is honest and flavoursome (sandwiches, salads, soups; hot meals after dark) and very reasonably priced. Book ahead if you want to try the very popular Sunday roast or build-it-yourself afternoon tea. If you can resist the siren call of the towering cakes and home baking beneath glass cloches on the counter, you're stronger than us.

Do pop into the castle if you have time: far from a defensive stronghold, the 17th-century edifice was built as an indulgent gentleman's retreat and is the birthplace of dancing horses.

Opening hours
Mon-Sun 9am-4pm

The Pump Tea Rooms, 21 Market Place, Bolsover S44 6PN
**WWW.THEPUMPBOLSOVER.CO.UK   01246 827567**

# *The Old Schoolhouse* DELI-CAFÉ

**JUNCTION 25; 4 MINUTES**

A fabulous little café tucked, as you might guess, behind the old school, run by Jo and Wayne who turned their capable hands to the kitchen after careers in the Ambulance Service. It's homely, with bunting and fairy lights strung above the cake-loaded counter – the sort of place you could drop into a sofa with a magazine or do homework at the table.

Breakfasts include scrambled egg on toast and pancake stacks, and the lunch menu may contain jacket potatoes, toasties, crayfish salad and pork and stilton pie. The cakes are killers: from maple and pecan bundt to dairy-free tea loaf and coconut and gooseberry cake. Vegetarians are well catered for, with homemade veggie chilli and 'vork' pie, made with a meat-free alternative and lovable for the name alone. Ask at the counter for free dog treats.

Look at the shelves for a tempting selection of homemade preserves, framed photography, cards and cushions. Take cash: card payments aren't currently accepted.

Opening hours
Mon-Sat 10am-3pm

The Old Schoolhouse Deli-Café, School Lane, Stanton by Dale DE7 4QJ
**0115 930 5699**

# A LITTLE EXTRA

**SOME OF THE PLACES IN THE GUIDE** are kindly offering our readers (that's you!) a little extra: it may be a discount on your bill, a free coffee refill, a complimentary cup of tea when you buy a slice of cake… To redeem offers all you need to do is show your Extra Mile keyring fob at selected venues. The list is on our website and will be updated regularly so make sure you keep checking to snag the latest deals.

---

*Not got yours? Head to*

 **WWW.THEEXTRAMILE.GUIDE**
*and we'll pop one straight in the post.*

---

(While you're waiting for it to arrive you can still take advantage
of the offers by showing your copy of this book.)

# *Buonissima* APERITIVO BAR

**JUNCTION 25; 5 MINUTES**

Turn off the M1 into the old trading station of Stapleford, an unassuming town with red-brick terraces and a long high street, to find Buonissima. The bright bistro, café and bar rolled into one is open and light: wooden floors, red Chesterfields and clusters of tables inviting you to linger. Tables on the wide pavement outside the elegant, charcoal grey frontage are great for people watching and al fresco lunches.

The chef, Pierangelo, is Sicilian and brings that Italian flair for flavours to the menu: homemade tiramisu in individual glasses, frittata with various fillings, antipasti boards served on lovely wooden platters and weekly pasta dishes. Try the pizzas with crispy bases topped with goodies fresh from the deli – accompanied by a glass of Menabrea (possibly Italy's finest lager) or an Aperol Spritz. Pasqualini coffee is imported from Italy, a rich blend that makes for a killer espresso; teas are loose leaf. Service is relaxed and friendly and kids are welcome.

**Opening hours**
Tues 9.30am-3pm
Wed 9.30am-10pm (Thurs-Fri 11pm)
Sat 10am-11pm (Sun 4pm)

Buonissima Aperitivo Bar, 14 Station Rd, Sandiacre NG10 5BG
**WWW.BUONISSIMABAR.COM  0115 939 3256**

# *No.* 11 **DELI**

**JUNCTION 24; 6 MINUTES**

Thousands pass Castle Donington on their way to East Midlands airport or to the well-known Donington Park race circuit, but only a handful of people drop into the village itself. They are well rewarded. The charming high street, farmers' market and Saxon history are well worth a look, even if the castle is long gone.

Refuel for the onward journey at No.11 Deli in the village centre, where Liza and her chipper, friendly team serve nourishing breakfasts (almond croissants, bacon butties, homemade smoothies), tasty sandwiches (hot beef, stilton and red onion chutney, pastrami and sliced gherkin, and cheddar crunch), jacket potatoes and pasta pots alongside an array of salads, pies and cakes. Their famous oinkers, giant sausage rolls, have people queuing down the street.

Scoff your goodies and sip your coffee at the small bar in the window while you decide which deli goods you're going to sweep into your shopping basket.

Opening hours
Mon-Sat 8am-5pm

No. 11 deli, 11 Borough Street, Castle Donington DE74 2LA
**WWW.NO11DELI.CO.UK   01332 813555**

# *The* ROYAL OAK

**JUNCTION 24; 8 MINUTES**

Slip into the Royal Oak and you'll be greeted by a cosy village pub of tartan carpets, high-backed booths, mismatched chairs, inglenook fireplace and locals sipping ale at the bar. It's a gastropub with rooms (housed in outbuildings at the back with a cottagey feel) run by brothers Chris and Alex, but you'd be every bit as comfortable popping in for a coffee and a breather as you would for one of their coveted meals.

Service is excellent and portions generous. Start with a sharing platter for a mouthful of all the flavours: smoked mackerel pâté, chorizo in tomato sauce, soup shots, and halloumi fries with harissa and saffron yoghurt dip. Mains include pub classics, such as fish pie and juicy burgers, as well as more inventive dishes, such as pan-roasted crown of wood pigeon, sea bass with shrimp paella, and chickpea and sultana falafel skewer. Save space, if you can, for the caramelised, rum-soaked pineapple served with coconut sorbet.

Opening hours
Sun-Thurs noon-11pm
Fri-Sat noon-11.30pm

The Royal Oak, The Green, Long Whatton LE12 5DB
**WWW.THEROYALOAKLONGWHATTON.CO.UK 01509 843694**

FARM SHOP-CAFÉ

# *Oakley Grange* ORGANIC FARM

JUNCTION 23; 8 MINUTES

If you love organic food, don't miss this beautiful farm, deli and café. Inger and Richard Mee have been farming the natural way on this 600-acre patch of Leicestershire since 2001. As you walk into a tastefully converted brick barn, a bulging deli counter greets you, touting its tempting fresh bread, chutneys, infused oils, cheeses, chocolates, sugar mice and farm meat, honey, eggs and veg, alongside gifts, jewellery and cards.

Everything in the café is homemade using predominantly organic ingredients: breakfasts of home-cured bacon, Whole Earth beans and artisan bread segue into gourmet sandwiches, farmer's antipasti, mushrooms stuffed with Gruyère cheese and herbs, and chicken and three-cheese pie. Munch cakes, perhaps hazelnut tart or a chocolate brownie, with your coffee.

Service can be slow, but you can drop the pace on a sunny terrace and lawn, and enjoy a cup of tea to the sound of birdsong and the light clink of crockery. Bliss.

Opening hours
Mon-Sun 8am-5pm

Oakley Grange Organic Farm, Shepshed Rd, Hathern LE12 5LL
**WWW.OAKLEYGRANGE.CO.UK  01509 842988**

PUB & RESTAURANT

# *The* FORGE INN

**JUNCTION 22: 11 MINUTES**

Just two minutes from the M1 at Leicester, the Forge is an attractive village pub. It was the first pub in the city's acclaimed Beautiful Pub Collective and founder Sam Hagger has transformed it into a community hub as popular with the natives as it is with those passing on the highway. The décor is eclectic: exposed stone walls next to tartan carpets in the dining room, chunky painted beams and leather Chesterfields in the enlarged bar.

Friendly staff who clearly enjoy their jobs ferry plates of food to busy tables. Dietary requests are seamlessly handled, portions are generous and the menu is wide ranging – try the 'hot hob' filled sandwiches. Grilled cuts of local beef are a speciality and Sunday roasts are the real deal, served with Yorkshires, goose-fat roasties, Sunday papers and Bloody Marys.

Craft beers and real ale are on tap, alongside barista coffees and a good range of non-alcoholic drinks for drivers, including fresh juices and Seedlip's booze-free spirits. A lovely staging post.

Opening hours
Mon-Fri 11am-11pm
Sat noon-11pm
Sun noon-10.30pm

The Forge Inn, Main Street, Glenfield LE3 8DG
WWW.THEFORGEINN.CO.UK   0116 287 1702

CAFÉ

# *Back in Time for* **TEA**

**JUNCTION 20: 3 MINUTES**

Tucked away on an industrial estate at the edge of Lutterworth, this wartime-themed café is a quirky stop. It has chintzy-cool furniture, Union Jacks and memorabilia such as ration books, housecoats, old photographs, tin packaging and teapots. A table made from the front of an old Jeep is a long-standing favourite. The ceiling is hung with an old parachute. Tinkle the ivories on the piano if you're feeling musical. Staff wear 1940s' uniforms and tunes by Vera Lynne or Glen Miller flow constantly from the wireless with a reassuring crackle.

Cakes are delicious: the classic Victoria sponge is faultlessly light. Simple sandwiches are served alongside tasty sausage rolls, pork pies, crumpets and jam tarts inspired by old family recipes. Tea is always served in pots with a mandatory knitted tea cosy. For afternoon tea, stands are burgeoning with time-honoured sandwiches, scones and butterfly cakes. The service is excellent, friendly and sincere. A wonderful, nostalgic stop.

**Opening hours**
Thurs-Sat 10am-4pm
Sun 11am-3.30pm

Unit 22, C&V Business Park, Leicester Rd, Lutterworth LE17 4HE
**WWW.BACKINTIMEFORTEA.CO.UK   07875 087405**

# *The* YARD CAFÉ COTESBACH

**JUNCTION 20; 2 MINUTES**

Delicious, field-fresh food is served in a rustic, wiggly-roofed Victorian stable block. Breakfasts are filling and tasty; the menu changes frequently to take advantage of seasonal produce, much of it organic. Expect homemade soups, quiches (with inventive fillings such as smoked mackerel, beetroot and horseradish), jacket potatoes and generously filled baguettes, which can be washed down with a local beer. Cakes are freshly baked by the in-house chef and feature flavous such as blueberry and marzipan or chocolate orange.

The café is colourful and homely. Furniture is painted bright colours and there's a bookshelf full of games and books to pass the time. Walls are decorated with local arts and crafts, which you can buy along with baked goodies – the scones are highly regarded.

In winter the wood-burner is fired up; come summer the doors are flung open to a peaceful courtyard with pots of flowers and a canopy for shade. Well-behaved dogs are welcome.

Opening hours
Mon-Sat 9am-4pm

The Yard Café @ Cotesbach, Main St, Cotesbach LE17 4HX
**WWW.THESTABLESCOTESBACH.COM   01455 550202**

SHOP-CAFÉ

# *The* GARDEN BARN

JUNCTION 20; 2 MINUTES

Piled with unusual gifts, crockery, homewares, reclamation finds, greetings cards, furniture, plants and garden goodies, the Garden Barn is a veritable emporium comprising a labyrinth of connecting rooms.

The shop began in the mid-1980s as a traditional farm shop and has diversified creatively into a treasure trove – it has an unrivalled collection of Victorian chimney pots, should you need one. It's difficult for even the most hardened minimalists not to walk away with a trinket or two.

In the centre of the action a café offers simple light lunches, rich coffee and sweet treats. The paninis are particularly popular, served with thoughtful extras, such as hummus and crudités or a handful of pistachios. Eat at the open-plan tables by the counter, head for the quieter tea room upstairs with log-burner, reading materials and countryside views, or enjoy al fresco dining in the tumbling gardens during summer months.

**Opening hours**
Tues-Sat 9.30am-5.30pm
Sun 11am-4pm

The Garden Barn, Rugby Road, Cotesbach LE17 4HS
**WWW.GARDENBARN.CO.UK   01455 550900**

# *The* **WHITE SWAN**

JUNCTION 20; 5 MINUTES

You won't be disappointed if you venture off-piste for a bite in The White Swan, an upmarket, country pub tucked into the elbow between the M6 and M1. Drop into a comfortable Chesterfield for a reviving cup of tea or find a table in one of many rooms, depending on your mood – they range from the cosy snug, panelled with scarlet walls and copper lights, to the roomy orangery flooded with light from a sky lantern above. There's a handsome terrace out the front, ringed with roses and sunflowers.

Chef and owner Rory learned his craft at the Connaught, Pollen Street Social and the Berkeley in London, so you can expect top-class food that changes with the seasons. Flavourful dishes include braised beef with wild mushrooms, honey glazed duck breast with parsnip and grape, cod loin with saffron cream, dark chocolate delice with praline and milk ice cream. The fixed-price lunch menu is good value and special diets are skilfully accommodated.

Opening hours
Mon-Sat 11am-11pm
Sun noon-5pm

The White Swan, Main Street, Shawell LE17 6AG
**WWW.WHITESWANSHAWELL.CO.UK   01788 860357**

FARM SHOP·CAFÉ

# *Manor* **FARM**

JUNCTION 18; 7 MINUTES

It's worth skipping off the M1 and up the A5 (you can slink back at junction 20) to find this authentic farm shop, marked out by a red-brick clock tower. Still a working farm, the Grindal family have converted a series of buildings to make space for a farm shop and café. Baskets display fresh produce as you enter. Eggs are collected on the farm; potatoes, asparagus, soft fruit, rhubarb and pumpkins are grown here too; the rest is sourced locally. Also on offer are cheese, jams, treats and Sercombes pork pies from nearby Rugby, and local craft beer, tasty gins and wines are found in the Beer Barn.

The Farmhouse Kitchen out back serves up excellent meals – omelettes, ploughman's platters, baguettes, hot meals and oven-fresh cakes. Refuel in the beamed tea room or take advantage of the small garden outside. Visit the rare breed animals (quails, pigs, sheep and cows) in the large adjoining barn free of charge.

Opening hours
Mon-Sat 9am-6pm
Sun 10am-5pm

Manor Farm, Main Street, Catthorpe LE17 6DB
**WWW.MANORFARMCATTHORPE.CO.UK  01788 869002**

# *Plantation* CAFÉ

**JUNCTION 15A; 7 MINUTES**

You're met at Bell's Plantation by the tinkle of a fountain, a flourish of lilies and glistening goldfish in the raised pond. Once a plant nursery, today it's a complex devoted to outdoor life, with a poultry centre, brewery shop, garden centre and farm shop.

Exposed brick walls, solid wood floors, comfy sofas, covered glasshouse seating, roaring fires and lovely modern loos (important) make the café a cosy stop in the winter. Come summer, visitors spill out onto the lawn to enjoy a full menu of homemade and seasonal food at parasol-shaded tables. Breakfasts are hearty and specials change daily, perhaps fish cakes with a poached egg or pasta bake with homegrown tomatoes.

The chickens that owner Ash and Sheena have kept since the beginning continue to be popular with small visitors, while older guests can browse through calming aisles of seedlings or indulge in a quick massage at the on-site beauty parlour to knead out the road knots.

Opening hours
Mon-Sat 9am-5.30pm
Sun 10.30am-4.30pm

Bell Plantation Garden Centre, Watling St, Towcester NN12 6GX
**WWW.BELLPLANTATION.CO.UK   01327 354 126**

Go the Extra Mile
**COCOES DELI** #138

# EAST ANGLIA

*Criss-crossing the flatlands
of East Anglia*

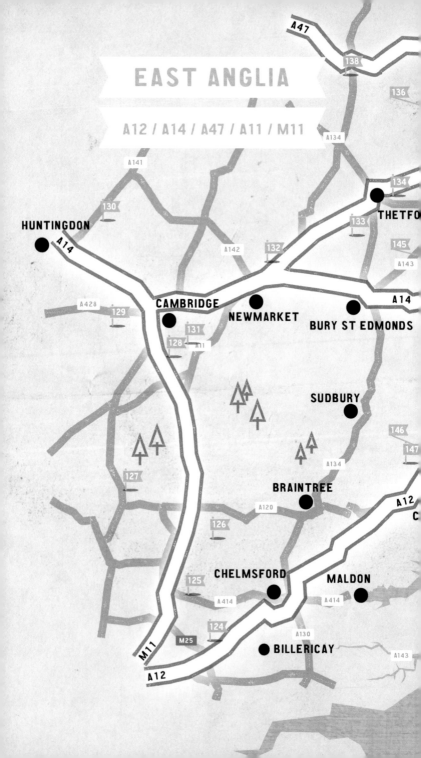

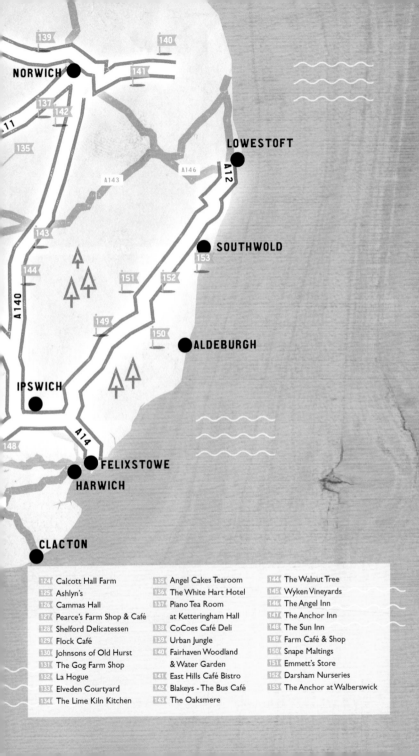

NORWICH

LOWESTOFT

SOUTHWOLD

ALDEBURGH

IPSWICH

FELIXSTOWE

HARWICH

CLACTON

124 Calcott Hall Farm
125 Ashlyn's
126 Cammas Hall
127 Pearce's Farm Shop & Café
128 Shelford Delicatessen
129 Flock Café
130 Johnsons of Old Hurst
131 The Gog Farm Shop
132 La Hogue
133 Elveden Courtyard
134 The Lime Kiln Kitchen

135 Angel Cakes Tearoom
136 The White Hart Hotel
137 Piano Tea Room
   at Ketteringham Hall
138 CoCoes Café Deli
139 Urban Jungle
140 Fairhaven Woodland
   & Water Garden
141 East Hills Café Bistro
142 Blakeys - The Bus Café
143 The Oaksmere

144 The Walnut Tree
145 Wyken Vineyards
146 The Angel Inn
147 The Anchor Inn
148 The Sun Inn
149 Farm Café & Shop
150 Snape Maltings
151 Emmett's Store
152 Darsham Nurseries
153 The Anchor at Walberswick

FARM SHOP·CAFÉ

# *Calcott Hall* FARM

**JUNCTION M25/A1023: 8 MINUTES**

Surrounded by fields and backed by the rearing embankment of the Weald Park hill fort, Calcott Hall Farm is a haven from the crush of the M25 and Dartford Tunnel. The timber-beamed shop, partially powered by solar panels, is a treasure trove of delicacies from cloudy pressed juices and Tiptree gin to Colston Bassett stilton and wild rabbit. Load up your holiday hamper with Essex-grown produce, locally reared meat and sustainably caught fish. Many a variety of fruit and veg are grown on the fields just outside.

The shop stands at the edge of the 120-acre farm where the McTurk family have tended the land for decades. Family is still very much the watchword. Daughter-in-law Niki is behind the latest addition, the Barnyard Café, which serves up farm-worthy breakfasts and tasty lunches – crispy baked potatoes, doorstop sandwiches – alongside devilishly good hot chocolate. Parents can release energetic children into the tractor-themed play area alongside the café. (The farm is not accessible directly from the A12; use A128.)

Opening hours
Tues-Sat 8.30am-5.30pm (Café 4.30pm)

Calcott Hall Farm, Ongar Road, Brentwood CM15 9HS
**WWW.CALCOTTHALL.COM   01277 264164**

# ASHLYN'S

**JUNCTION 7: 5 MINUTES**

It ain't easy being green, said Kermit the Frog, but perhaps he had yet to find Ashlyn's Farm Shop. It's a beacon of organic food and groceries, the shelves groaning with everything from fennel toothpaste to Kentish cherry juice to Ashlyn's own range of honey, jams and pickles. Much of what you see is organic; if not, it's ethically sourced.

In the restaurant – open for breakfast, lunch and sometimes dinner – beautifully lettered signboards tempt you with plates to suit all appetites and pockets, from hearty servings of sausage and mash to a more modest smoked salmon salad. Coax children into a few of their five-a-day with one of the Happy Monkey smoothies, before letting them burn off some energy in the soft play area or farm park outside. Mum or dad can then raid the wine shop or indulge in a massage in the beauty salon. The chirrup of birds is all you're likely to hear on the garden deck if you want a quieter stop, and the Farm Park trail will point out all the local Essex wildlife.

Opening hours
Mon-Sun 9am-5pm (Cafe 3.30pm)

Ashlyn's, North Weald, Epping CM16 6RZ
**ASHLYNSFARMSHOP.CO.UK   01992 525146**

FARM SHOP-CAFÉ

# *Cammas* HALL

**JUNCTION 8; 13 MINUTES**

Cammas Hall, in the beautiful countryside of the Hertfordshire/Essex border, is a family-owned farm that pioneered the pick-your-own movement in the 1960s; large letters at the edge of one field proclaiming 'strawberry fields forever' are a nod to that era.

Collect your own car snacks with a stroll through the fields to pick strawberries, raspberries, cherries, blackcurrants, blueberries and sweetcorn, depending on the season. When little people have had enough, a nature trail, children's playground and maize maze (in the summer) will keep them entertained.

In the Tea Barn you'll find homemade cakes, sandwiches, jacket potatoes, cream teas and fresh smoothies made with ingredients from the farm. There are seats inside and out, and a marquee in the garden. Honey direct from the farm's hives can be bought in the shop, along with other farm produce including fresh eggs, chutneys, meringues and preserves.

Opening hours
Mon–Sun 9am–4.30pm
Open April to October (please check website for dates)

Cammas Hall Farm, Needham Green, Hatfield Broad Oak CM22 7JT
**WWW.CAMMASHALL.CO.UK  01279 718570**

# *Pearce's* FARM SHOP & CAFÉ

JUNCTION 8: 16 MINUTES

Once just a shed in a field selling the family's vegetables, the Pearce's farm shop is now an abundant food emporium and café. Browse the shelves for Hertfordshire honey, fresh fruit and vegetables, smoked meats, artisan cheeses, Granny Pearce's marmalade and fresh cut flowers. Most of the products are from the farm or one of 50 other local suppliers. Stock up on sensational car snacks at the deli counter then settle at a table in the roomy, oak-beamed café. It's been built with the environment in mind and you can watch the family's cows grazing in the fields beyond the floor-to-ceiling windows. When the weather's fine spill out onto the patio terrace and picnic area.

Start the day with a proper farmhouse breakfast, or lunch on chicken, apricot and pistachio terrine. Book ahead for three terrific tiers of afternoon tea. Compostable cups and boxes are available if you want food and drink to go, and if you have time to linger in the summer, sample the raspberries and strawberries in the PYO fields.

Opening hours
Mon-Thurs 8.30am-5.30pm
Fri 8.30am-6pm (Sat 5pm)
Sun 8.30am-4pm

Pearce's Farm Shop & Café, Hamels Mead, Buntingford SG9 9ND
PEARCESFARMSHOP.COM/CONTACT/   01920 821246

CAFÉ & BISTRO

# *Shelford* DELICATESSEN

**JUNCTION 11; 7 MINUTES**

It's easy to see why people flow constantly into the Shelford Deli. Within the walls of the stylish, oak-framed building, the menu is crammed with fresh, tasty salads, soups, frittata and proper artisan pizza – all simple and seasonal. Their homemade cakes are irresistible, perhaps carrot, chocolate mocha with hazelnut, or on Fridays the famous Deli doughnuts including honeycomb and salted caramel, washed down with excellent coffee.

Owners Drew and Nikki have been part of the UK's food revolution since 1999, and founded their kitchen on the simple premise of offering Cambridgeshire delicious food made from sustainable, tasty ingredients. It's gone from strength to strength, growing from a tiny shop to the current, purpose-built café and bistro. There's a warming wood burner for colder months and a beautiful sunlit garden for summer with a wooden playhouse for children, but to get there you'll need to pass a gauntlet of temptation: pick up some artisan bread, coffee, salads or gifts.

Opening hours
Mon-Sat 8.30am-4.30pm

Shelford Delicatessen, 8a Woollards Lane, Great Shelford CB22 5LZ
**WWW.SHELFORDDELI.CO.UK   01123 846129**

# *Flock* CAFÉ

**JUNCTION 12; 2 MINUTES**

Just two minutes off the motorway yet protected from the thrum, Burwash Manor is a wonderful complex of independent shops and cafés housed in converted farm buildings on a 400-acre working organic farm. Flock Café is at the heart of it, serving sumptuous homemade food from the old stables; a sunny patio outside is good for al fresco dining.

Owner Lindsay is ardent about using fresh local ingredients to conjure up imaginative feasts. Avocado and halloumi on sourdough with Portobello mushrooms and eggs is one of Flock's most fêted breakfasts. Lunch might be carrot and ginger soup with crème fraiche, turmeric-roasted cauliflower tart or sweet potato, kale, quinoa and lime salad. Cakes are irresistibly good, from gluten-free carrot cake to almond and ricotta. Stop off at the weekend for an amazing sourdough pizza, cooked in a wood-fired oven outside. To ice the cake, there's plenty of free parking, a children's play area and three signposted farm walks.

Opening hours
Mon-Sat 9am-5pm
Sun 10am-4pm

Flock Café, Units 1 & 2, Burwash Manor, New Rd, Barton CB23 7BL
**WWW.FLOCKCAFE.CO.UK   01223 263100**

FARM SHOP-CAFÉ

# *Johnsons* OF OLD HURST

JUNCTION HUNTINGDON; 12 MINUTES

A sign at the entrance to this modest farm complex reads 'Beware of the Crocs'. It's no idle warning: this farm is home not only to a peaceful tea room, fabulous farm shop and lip-smacking steak house, but also a crocodile farm. The Johnson family rear the reptiles alongside more traditional animals; you're welcome to say hello from the public viewing area (but no smiling).

Don't tell the kids, but you can also buy crocodile meat from the butchery counter where 80 per cent of the produce is home reared. A quick raid of the farm shop, set around a beautiful, covered courtyard in the old cattle shed, should restock your cupboards in full with pork pies, pasties and bread from the bakery, local fruit and veg, 50 varieties of cheese, home-cooked meats, antipasti, scotch eggs and corned beef.

The bright, flower-fringed tea room has a run of arched windows overlooking the children's play field where little ones can burn off the excitement on toy tractors and in the play fort.

Opening hours

Tues-Fri 9am-6pm (4pm Sat)
Sun 10.30am-4pm
Check website for steakhouse opening hours

Johnsons of Old Hurst, Church Farm, Church St, Oldhurst PE28 3AF
**WWW.JOHNSONSOFOLDHURST.CO.UK   01487 824658**

# *The* GOG FARM SHOP

**JUNCTION 11; 12 MINS**

The Gog shares its name with one half of a pagan wicker giant duo, Gog and Magog, who also lend their names to the run of low chalk hills on which the farm shop stands. Its position on the outskirts of Cambridge means it enjoys delightful views over the city and the sunsets are spectacular. The shop is stuffed with seasonal produce, an enviable cheese counter and an amazing butchery – recently voted Butchers Shop of the Year. Fill your basket with everything you could want for the store cupboard or pack yourself a finger-licking picnic.

Dog walkers and cyclists flock to the grey-painted, beamed café, often after enjoying the rural idyll and country lanes on the doorstep. Beneath felt clouds hung from the ceiling, chunky wooden tables are plied with deliciously simple fare prepared daily. Try a proper farmhouse breakfast, varied sharing platters or the award-winning cheese scone made from Montgomery's cheddar. If you prefer you can take a seat outside in the covered Shack to catch the breeze: blankets are laid out for keeping knees warm. A great stop on the way to Cambridge.

Opening hours
Mon-Sat 9am-6pm
Sun 9.30am-5pm

The Gog Farm Shop, Heath Farm, Babraham Rd, Stapleford CB22 3AD
**WWW.THEGOG.COM   01223 248352**

FARM SHOP-CAFÉ

# *La* HOGUE

**JUNCTION B1085; 4 MINUTES**

Naval battles don't usually lend their names to farms but then battleship timbers are not usually re-used to build farmhouses. La Hogue takes its moniker from a 17th-century sea brawl between Britain and France: the British won and hauled the timbers of the burned-out ships back home. Today, the bucolic farm shop and café sit alongside a working arable farm and if you are lucky you may see the owners' fold of Highland cattle grazing alongside the café. Owners Chris and Jo Reeks have used their farming knowledge to stock the shop with the very best of British produce. The butchery counter is a source of particular pride and if you're planning a BBQ, the farm's own sausages should definitely feature.

You can taste them first in the café, in the excellent cooked breakfast. Light lunches, quiches, and jacket potatoes are on the menu during the day, best enjoyed on the terrace if the weather allows. Kids can canter about on the lawn and pedal around on toy tractors while parents admire the view down to the Newmarket gallops.

Opening hours
Mon-Sat 9am-5pm
Sun 9.30am-4pm
No hot food after 3pm & no hot drinks 30 mins before closing

La Hogue, Chippenham nr Newmarket Ely CB7 5PZ
**WWW.LAHOGUE.CO.UK   01638 751128**

# *Elveden* COURTYARD

**JUNCTION B1106; 2 MINUTES**

A few minutes' drive off the A11, onto the B1106 and left again down the wooded drive to a huge car park, with the Courtyard set in the middle of the former stable block. Elveden is the former home of the Maharajah Duleep Singh and the current home of the Guinness family.

Foodies won't be disappointed with the range of goods in the Food Hall; both local and exotic, this is an epicurean Aladdin's Cave. The adjacent restaurant's menu serves meals from breakfast to tea and everything in between. Much of what's served is sourced on the Elveden Estate (look out for shot in your game dish!)

The Tea Room 'Teapots & Post' offers light lunches as well as tea and coffee and delicious homemade scones and cakes. Uniquely it is also the home of the village Post Office. After eating, browse the Home & Garden shop which has an array of gifts and home wares or treat yourself to handmade chocolates or macarons..

**Opening hours**
Mon-Sat 9.30am-5pm
Sun 10am-5pm
(Post Office closes at 2pm on Weds)

Elveden Courtyard, Off Brandon Road, Elveden IP24 3TJ
**WWW.ELVEDENCOURTYARD.COM   01842 898068**

GARDEN CENTRE

# *Lime Kiln* KITCHEN

**JUNCTION A1075; 2 MINUTES**

Within spitting distance of the A11 is the Lime Kiln Kitchen. If weather permits, head out to the deck overlooking the reed beds and Kilverstone Estate – you'll feel like you're in a nature reserve. Inside, the decor is eclectic and there's plenty of seating and a wood-burner for colder days; dogs are treated to their own area with water, biscuits and even a bed if needed.

A wide menu serves breakfast (including pancakes!), a huge array of sandwiches, salads and daily specials such as hand-battered fish and chips. There's a lavish afternoon tea and the scones are particularly highly regarded, often with a weekly feature such as iced coffee and walnut. Children have their own menu and there's a wide range of gluten-free, vegetarian and vegan dishes including cake, so everyone will be happy. Everything is freshly made and the service is excellent.

Don't miss an opportunity to feed the koi in the pond – or send the kids off to feed them while you relax over coffee and discuss how many plants you can fit in the car.

Opening hours
Mon-Thurs, Sat 9am-5pm
Fri 9.30am-7.30pm
Sun 10am-4pm

The Lime Kiln Kitchen, Thetford Garden Centre, Kilverstone IP24 2RL
**THETFORDGARDENCENTRE.CO.UK   01842 763267**

# *Angel Cakes* TEAROOM

**JUNCTION ATTLEBOROUGH: 13 MINUTES**

New Buckenham is lucky to have the enterprising Stacey and her family-run Angel Cakes Tearoom. After ten years' as a cake-making hobbyist, supplying friends and family with enviable edible creations, she took the plunge and opened a community-spirited café. And it's not just afternoon tea on offer – full English breakfast is also available, as is full American complete with pancakes and syrup. Stacey makes all the cakes upstairs where she also runs baking classes and hosts events.

Downstairs, the double-fronted shop windows lend a relaxed airy feel to the spacious café. Tables, chairs and sofas are set out in front of a counter displaying the days' wares. Cakes change regularly, often reflecting whatever seasonal event is closest, and showing great culinary imagination. Who could resist a cheese and bacon scone or homemade cherry Bakewell? Kids will be wowed by unicorn cupcakes and skeleton gingerbread men for Halloween. Parking is easy, right on the street outside.

Opening hours
Mon–Sat 10am-4pm

Angel Cakes Tearoom, King St, New Buckenham NR16 2AF
**01953 860008**

# *The* WHITE HART HOTEL

### JUNCTION ATTLEBOROUGH; 9 MINUTES

If you want to see a really prime English village, take a little diversion to Hingham, Norfolk. It has not one but several village greens, more handsome Georgian houses than you can shake a stick at, and a really proper country hotel in the middle. Welcome to The White Hart, which, despite the grandness of its appearance, strives to provide something for everybody in its community and at prices lower than you'd expect too. The stylish yet relaxed interior will put it straight up your list of must-revisit-and-maybe-stay-the-weekend places – particularly when you realise the dog can come too.

If you've got time for more than a sandwich, then the monthly changing menu might feature local treats such as Norfolk Mardler, Gressingham duck or a tarte tatin of local Hingham apples. Pub classics like ham and eggs, fish and chips and burgers are available for a less formal meal, and the children's menu can't fail to satisfy. Do admire the architecture of this Austenesque spot before you get back on the road.

Opening hours
Mon-Thurs 8am-11pm
Fri-Sat 8am-midnight
Sun 11am-10.30pm

The White Hart Hotel, 3 Market Place, Hingham NR9 4AF
**WHITEHARTNORFOLK.CO.UK   01953 850473**

# *Piano Tea Room* AT KETTERINGHAM HALL

JUNCTION WYMONDHAM: 6 MINUTES

Set in 30 acres of woodland, Ketteringham Hall is ideal for dog walkers, ramblers and families. Park among the trees and follow the path around to the back of house to find the timeless Victorian Piano Tea Room, set in the elegant orangery. On sunny days you can grab an organic ice cream or indulgent candyfloss and satisfy that urge to walk down to the lake, or find a seat on the large terrace; a perfect spot for those just wanting to sit and look at the surroundings.

When it's chillier, settle inside at a linen-laid table and look out of the beautiful windows across the lawns. Cakes, pastries, soups, sandwiches and salads are all freshly made and tea is by the pot, small or large – loose leaf, of course – along with the full range of good coffee. For the official Afternoon Tea, phone ahead, but don't worry if you didn't as there are plenty of other tempting tea items.

Opening hours
Tues-Fri 11am-4pm
Sat-Sun 10am-4pm

Piano Tea Room at Ketteringham Hall, NR18 9RS
WWW.PIANOTEAROOM.CO.UK   01603 812000

DELI

# *CoCoes* CAFÉ DELI

JUNCTION SWAFFHAM; 2 MINUTES

Hidden in plain sight, CoCoes is easy to miss despite its town centre location. Look out for a tiny alley off Lynn Street and at the end of it is a beautiful courtyard hotel reminiscent of rural France. This is Stratton's, luxury and boutique, and CoCoes is the bright, modern café for hotel guests and passers-by alike. The interior is refreshing, cool and stylish with long, bright yellow banquettes. Al fresco seating is available for warmer days and those with dogs. The latter, incidentally, are welcomed as hotel guests so long as they don't chase the resident cats.

The menu is especially good for vegetarians (vegeree, veggie rolls, meze) and presents a challenge for deciding what to eat – a conundrum that can be solved by buying additional deli items and homemade patisserie for eating later (who can resist the rosewater and raspberry meringues, or the fudgy nut slice?). Menus change daily and all dishes are made on-site using as much Norfolk produce as possible.

Opening hours
Mon-Fri 7.30am-5pm
Sat-Sun 8.30am-5pm

CoCoes Café Deli, 4 Ash Close, Swaffham PE37 7NH
**STRATTONSHOTEL.COM/COCOES-CAFE-DELI/ 01760 723845**

# *Urban* JUNGLE

**JUNCTION A1074; 7 MINUTES**

This is not your average garden centre: you're about to experience a mini-break in the tropics! Banana trees, giant ferns, bamboo, succulents, cacti, climbers all thrive in this extraordinary Norfolk jungle. They invade the glasshouse café too, where scrubbed tables and a pretty assortment of chairs and large, floppable sofas nestle among tropical branches.

Children will vanish into the thick vegetation while you relax among cushions to peruse the enticing menu. It's all gluten free and either homegrown or ethically sourced, and includes cakes through to frittatas, toasties and salads with a definite Middle Eastern vibe (the harissa chicken and slow-cooked pulled lamb are mouth-wateringly delicious). Tea is loose-leaf (hurrah!) and coffee carefully sourced from single estates and served in a cafetiere.

This place is a one off – well, a two off, if we include its other, equally exotic, branch in Beccles.

**Opening hours**
Mon-Sun 10am-5pm (Café 4.30pm)

Urban Jungle, Ringland Lane, Old Costessey NR8 5BG
**WWW.URBANJUNGLE.UK.COM   01603 857196**

# *Fairhaven* WOODLAND & WATER GARDEN

**JUNCTION B1104; 6 MINUTES**

© *Jamie Bass Photography*

Naturalists, twitchers and garden lovers may insist on making a day of it to explore the stunning 130 acres of Fairhaven Woodland & Water Garden. Stretch your legs on four miles of pathways or take a 20-minute boat trip on Fairhaven's private broad, and look out for the 95 different bird species found here.

For those with less time the tearoom and shop are available without paying entry. Park in the field and head over to the low wooden buildings containing the shop and café. If you're early in the day, try the Great Norfolk breakfast. If you're too late for that treat, don't worry – light lunches, homemade specials and fresh local cakes can't fail to satisfy. Luxury ice cream – Ronaldo's, the local favourite – shouldn't be missed either. On warmer days head to the large outdoor area – dogs are welcome here and will find water bowls ready filled and waiting. This is a beautiful spot that feels remoter than it actually is. Grab some local jams and chutneys as you leave through the shop.

**Opening hours**
Mon-Sun 9.15am-5pm (Garden 10am) Mar-Sep.
Weds, May-end Aug, open until 9pm
Mon-Sun 9.15am-4pm (Garden 10am) Oct-Feb

Fairhaven Woodland & Water Garden, School Rd, South Walsham NR13 6DZ
**WWW.FAIRHAVENGARDEN.CO.UK   01603 270449**

# *East Hills* CAFÉ BISTRO

**JUNCTION BRUNDALL; 7 MINUTES**

Set above a chandlery in Brundall Bay Marina, this café area was once the preserve of yacht club members only. Now the pretty Norfolk Broads location is open to all in the friendly East Hills Café Bistro run by local Sophie Hodgkinson. Drive down Station Road, over the level crossing and just as the road is about to peter out, turn left and park. Head up the stairs outside the building and, if it's fine, take a seat on the café's covered veranda.

Dog beds arranged among the tables say everything necessary regarding pet policy. If it's less clement, there's ample room inside. Afternoon tea laid out on cake stands looks like the real deal. Italian handmade pizza and crispy fish and chips are on offer daily too.

Looking out over the riparian scene in this quiet spot you can feel yourself unwinding. Enjoy life in the slow lane for a while before pulling back out into heavy traffic.

**Opening hours**
Mon-Weds 9.30am-4pm
Thurs-Sat 9.30am-11pm
Sun 9.30am-6pm

East Hills Café Bistro, Brundall Bay Marina Riverside, Brundall NR13 5PN
**EAST-HILLS.CO.UK   01603 951850**

# *Blakeys* THE BUS CAFÉ

JUNCTION SWAINSTHORPE; 6 MINUTES

If you have a child who's transport mad you'll be prepared to drive across East Anglia to have tea in a converted Bristol Lodekka bus. But even without a tiny bus-spotter you would be mad to miss this place if you're anywhere to the south west of Norwich.

It's hugely popular with locals so there is extra seating outside the bus in case the top deck is full. Sam and Rachael are the owners; Rachael is known locally for her impressive bespoke cakes. Gingham and vintage china make for perfect décor inside the 1950s double decker where sandwiches, jacket potatoes and afternoon tea are served. Children can have a special bus box meal, and it's probably worth investing in the Blakey's Bus children's book to keep them occupied when you're back in the car.

Mulbarton is a village with an enormous green just across the road from the bus – a lovely place to walk off that afternoon tea and give the dogs a runaround.

Opening hours
Mon-Fri 9.30am-4pm
Sat 9.30am-3.30pm

Blakeys – The Bus Café, Mulbarton NR14 8AE
**WWW.BLAKEYSBUSCAFE.CO.UK   07426 533608**

# *The* OAKSMERE

**JUNCTION BROME; 1 MINUTE**

Crunch down a lime-tree lined driveway to find the Oaksmere, a laid-back but elegant country hotel set in 17 acres of parkland. An hour from Norwich and less than two from London, it's a good place to pause en route for a proper refuel.

The restaurant has been newly extended and reaches out into those lovely grounds, part of a careful programme of renovations that are restoring the hotel to its former glory. It hums with life from residents as well as travellers stopping for lunch and dinner. Seasonal produce is whipped up into flavourful dishes such as home-smoked bresaola, crispy beef salad and charred halloumi burgers. For lighter bites, try the Suffolk tapas, which draws on the best flavours from East Anglia and the hotel gardens. Service is attentive and friendly, if unrushed.

For a quicker refuel, have a coffee and slice of fresh cake on the terrace to drink in the parkland view, or else warm up beside the fire in the beamed Tudor bar.

Opening hours
Mon-Sun 10am-late

The Oaksmere, Rectory Road, Broome IP23 8AJ
**WWW.THEOAKSMERE.COM   01379 873940**

# *The* WALNUT TREE

JUNCTION THWAITE; 0 MINUTES

Vegetarians and vegans, hold your horses here. Chef Jan Wise, way ahead of the curve, has been impressing vegetarians and carnivores alike with her creative plant-based dishes for a decade. The whole of Suffolk wailed in dismay when the doors to her debut restaurant, The Veggie Red Lion, closed. Thankfully it was only to make way for a bigger and better brother – The Walnut Tree at Thwaite.

The pub has been lovingly refurbished without losing the traditional pub vibe, but it's the food that really sings. Jan and chef Simon know their flavours inside out and aren't afraid to experiment with flavours from around the world. Try the Wellington with mushrooms and Suffolk blue cheese, and the infamous vegan peanut butter and Oreo torte, or see what they're cooking up on the specials board. Have the full plant experience by taking lunch outside to the secluded, shrub-fringed garden. If you're travelling between Norwich and Ipswich, you don't want to miss it.

Opening hours
Tues-Sat 11am-3.30pm, 5.30pm-11pm
Sun Noon-4.30pm

The Walnut Tree, Norwich Road, Thwaite IP23 7ED
WWW.THEWALNUTTREETHWAITE.COM   01449 766003

# *Wyken* VINEYARDS

JUNCTION 43 OR 44: 15 MINUTES

A Suffolk stalwart, Wyken Vineyards has been showcasing local and seasonal food for over 20 years. Shetland sheep graze the patchwork of fields and the vineyard produces award-winning wines. Formal gardens crammed with topiary, herbs, roses, fruit trees and meandering peacocks, guinea fowl and chickens surround an Elizabethan manor house.

In a huge 17th-century Suffolk barn you'll find the Country Store selling Wyken's wine, hand-crafted pottery, Irish and Scottish woollens, beautiful books and unusual cards. The renowned Leaping Hare restaurant serves truly local dishes, such as Wyken venison (wild, not farmed) with carrots, celeriac gratin and granola, with an emphasis on flavours and the seasons.

Try the café for lighter and less formal fare. Breakfast eggs come from Wyken's chickens and crab salad or lobster brioche roll use Norfolk seafood. A farmers' market, held here every Saturday morning, sells local bread, cheese, apples and meat.

Opening hours
Sun-Fri 10am–6pm
Sat 9am–6pm

Wyken Vineyards, Wyken Road, Bury St Edmunds IP31 2DW
**WYKENVINEYARDS.CO.UK   01359 250 287**

PUB

# *The* ANGEL INN

JUNCTION 30; 10 MINUTES

Snuggle up by the open fires in the oak-beamed bar or settle down to a meal in the lofty double-height dining room known as the Well Room, which takes its name from a 60-foot-deep well in the corner. The Angel Inn is a traditional country pub in the heart of Constable country, but within easy reach of the A12 down pretty green lanes.

This 17th-century coaching inn has been tastefully restyled by Suffolk Country Inns (who also run the The Anchor at nearby Nayland). It's open all day every day, serving breakfast, lunch, afternoon tea and dinner. You'll find a daily changing menu that offers traditional pub dishes, such as butcher's sausages and mash, cod and chips, as well as modern European dishes, such as baked burrito with spiced bean goulash, and seasonal puddings, including elderflower mousse with gooseberry ginger ice cream. Afternoon teas of finger sandwiches, scones and home-baked cakes are a real treat (but you must book ahead).

Opening hours
Mon–Sun 10am–11pm

The Angel Inn, Polstead Street, Stoke by Nayland CO6 4QP
**WWW.ANGELINNSUFFOLK.CO.UK  01206 263245**

# *The* **ANCHOR INN**

**JUNCTION 28; 10 MINUTES**

Beside the River Stour at Nayland (not to be confused with Stoke by Nayland a few miles away), a plaque marks the Nayland Horse Watering Hole, an area of common land used since medieval times by villagers and travellers to water their horses. We may not travel by horse today, and our taste in 'watering holes' has become a bit more sophisticated, but the village's Anchor Inn still offers refreshment and a warm welcome.

A traditional village pub serving craft beer and good pub food, it has a pretty garden and plenty of tables on the river bank, perfect for outdoor dining on warm evenings. In its smokehouse the chefs cure and smoke local meat, fish and cheese. Smoked fish and meat feature in seasonal platters and smoked cheese tops the Anchor burger and fish pie. The Little Plates menu, such as local pork terrine or deep-fried monkfish cheeks, is great for a light lunch or for sharing. The Clean Raw Salads menu ensures plenty of choice for vegans and gluten-free diners.

Opening hours
Mon–Sat 11am–11pm
Sun 11am–10pm

The Anchor Inn, Court Street, Nayland CO6 4JL
**WWW.ANCHORNAYLAND.CO.UK   01206 262313**

PUB

## *The* **SUN INN**

JUNCTION 30; 5 MINUTES

A 15th-century coaching inn located in the quintessentially English village of Dedham the Sun Inn has an oak-panelled bar and lounge that boast big fires and plenty of comfy sofas and armchairs. It's the perfect place for a relaxed drink or lunch with views of grand St Mary's Church. The airy dining room looks out on to the terrace and a large garden.

Both the service and menu are relaxed and unpretentious. Friendly staff serve food featuring local produce with a Mediterranean twist, which benefits the pub's proximity to the Essex coast. Try grilled mackerel, octopus and chickpea salad, or black pork belly with clams, samphire and butterbeans.

The Sun Inn is deep in Constable country. The artist went to school here and Flatford Mill is close by. You can borrow bikes from the pub or take a boat trip down the unspoiled River Stour. With so much to do locally, you may just have to stay a night at the inn.

Opening hours
Mon-Sun 11am-11pm

The Sun Inn, High Street, Dedham CO7 6DF
WWW.THESUNINNDEDHAM.COM   01206 323351

# *Farm* CAFÉ & SHOP

JUNCTION : 0 MINUTES

A favourite with families, the Farm Café has benefitted from recent improvements by new owners to transform it from a roadside caff into a local food destination. Refuel on hearty breakfasts of local bacon and sausages or healthy porridge or granola.

For lunch, find a table in the garden overlooking fields and tuck into Blythburgh free-range pulled pork burgers, Pinney's Smoked Kippers or choose from a selection of sandwiches or paninis. Children's portions are available and if you haven't got time to stop for hot drinks, sandwiches and homemade cakes are available to take away. You can even phone ahead to order to save you having to wait.

If you enjoyed your food here, pick up some ingredients in the shop. It stocks local meat, veg, chutneys and jams; there's also a range of the café's popular dishes, such as cottage pie, soups and puddings, both fresh or frozen, and ready to warm up when you reach your destination.

Opening hours
Mon-Sat 7am-4pm (shop 8.30am-5pm)
Sun & Bank Hols 8am-4pm (shop 8.30am-5pm.

Farm Cafe & Shop, Main Rd, Marlesford IP13 0AG
**WWW.FARMCAFE.CO.UK   01728 747717**

# *Snape* MALTINGS

### JUNCTION FRIDAY STREET; 7 MINUTES

Located on the banks the River Alde, this vast complex of old Victorian maltings looks out over a breath-taking expanse of swaying reed beds. It's well worth a visit to see the world-famous concert hall founded here by Benjamin Britten and enjoy the independent shops, cafés and galleries. If you want to stock up on Suffolk produce, the Food Hall and Pantry will provide everything you need, and if you're passing on the first Saturday of the month make the most of the farmers' market too.

For sit-down meals, you're spoiled for choice. Lunch with a panoramic view can be found on the Concert Hall Café, which serves mains such as homemade bacon frittata and hot smoked salmon with healthy salads – birdwatchers, don't forget your binoculars. Café 1885 is great for coffee and cake, as well as a seasonal menu inspired by the farmers' market. For a more traditional tea room, The Granary Tea Shop offers the best sandwiches, baked potatoes, cakes and scones.

Opening hours
Mon-Sat 10am-5.30pm
Sun 10.30am-4.30pm

Snape Maltings, Snape IP17 1SP
**SNAPEMALTINGS.CO.UK   01728 688303**

# *Emmett's* STORE

**JUNCTION YOXFORD; 6 MINUTES**

Emmett's has been trading on the same site in the pretty village of Peasenhall since 1820 and has a worldwide reputation for its locally sourced ham and bacon. The shop retains some original fittings and is packed with beautifully presented produce. You'll find abundant displays of fresh fruit and vegetables, farmhouse cheese, Sri Lankan chutney and Suffolk apple juice. There's a distinctly Hispanic feel too, with Spanish chocolate, olive oil, almonds and honey.

The small café showcases Emmett's produce and makes a perfect breakfast stop. Don't miss the home-cured ham, free-range bacon and egg or the Spanish equivalent – egg, picante chorizo, tomato and orange. For lunch the generous English, Italian and Spanish charcuterie or the cheese platters are perfect for sharing over a glass of wine. Excellent coffee, tea and cakes are served all day. When the sun shines you can savour the sweet smoke wafting from the smokehouse in the pretty cottage garden.

**Opening hours**
Mon-Fri 9.30am-5pm
Sat 8am-5pm

Emmett's Store, The Street, Peasenhall IP17 2HJ
**WWW.EMMETTSHAM.CO.UK   01728 660250**

# *Darsham* NURSERIES

**JUNCTION DARSHAM: 0 MINUTES**

Step out of the car after a long journey and you'll instantly be revived by the scents of roses and other shrubs sold at Darsham Nurseries. Yet this isn't just another garden centre. The beautiful shop sells a carefully curated collection of ceramics, candles, vases, unusual plant seeds and designer garden tools, as well as stationery, books and cards.

The stylish café wouldn't look out of place in founder David Keleel's native California. with it's white wood walls, a checkerboard floor and colourful flowers from the garden – which also supplies the kitchen with salad, vegetables, fruits and herbs.

Menus are driven by the seasons; the chefs work with the garden team to produce vegetable-led dishes, such as pea potager fritti misti. Local fish and meat feature – try streaky bacon with house brown sauce for breakfast or Sutton Hoo Chicken leg with leek and potato hash for lunch. For tea, try their cakes and pastries with some intriguing flavours.

Opening hours
Mon-Sat 8.30am-5pm
Sun 10am-4pm

Darsham Nurseries, Main Road, Darsham IP17 3PW
**WWW.DARSHAMNURSERIES.CO.UK   01728 667022**

# *The* ANCHOR AT WALBERSWICK

**JUNCTION BLYTHBURGH; 7 MINUTES**

It's true that Walberswick is busy year round, but you'll always find a spot in this large, bustling yet cosy village pub. Whether you've just finished a chilly winter walk through the reed beds, or are in need of après-crabbing refreshments in the summer, The Anchor's changing menu will have just the thing – along with tea or hot chocolate by the fire or a pint of Adam's in the garden overlooking the dunes. Local foods such as Lowestoft smoked fish, Blythburgh ham and Baron Bigod brie are used alongside homegrown vegetables from the allotment in a menu that balances food miles with quality. Bread is baked on site daily.

If you want to work up an appetite or walk off lunch, pick up some local information in the porch. There are many walks around Walberswick that take in a surprising variety of scenery in less than an hour. Or take the rowing boat 'ferry' across the harbour to Southwold and walk back to Walberswick across the Bailey Bridge.

Opening hours
Mon-Sun 8.30am-11pm

The Anchor at Walberswick, Main St, Walberswick IP18 6UA
**WWW.ANCHORATWALBERSWICK.COM  01502 722112**

# The ☞ M25 & M20

*Circle the city and explore the garden of England*

| | | | | | |
|---|---|---|---|---|---|
| 158 | The Secret Garden | 164 | Nest | 170 | The Gatehouse Café |
| 159 | The Potting Shed | 165 | Crockford Bridge Farm | 171 | Norpar Barns |
| 160 | Woodstock Café | 166 | The Bread House | | |
| 161 | Riverside Tea Room | 168 | Coffee House & Deli | | |
| 163 | Priory Farm | 169 | Fred & Ginger Coffee | | |

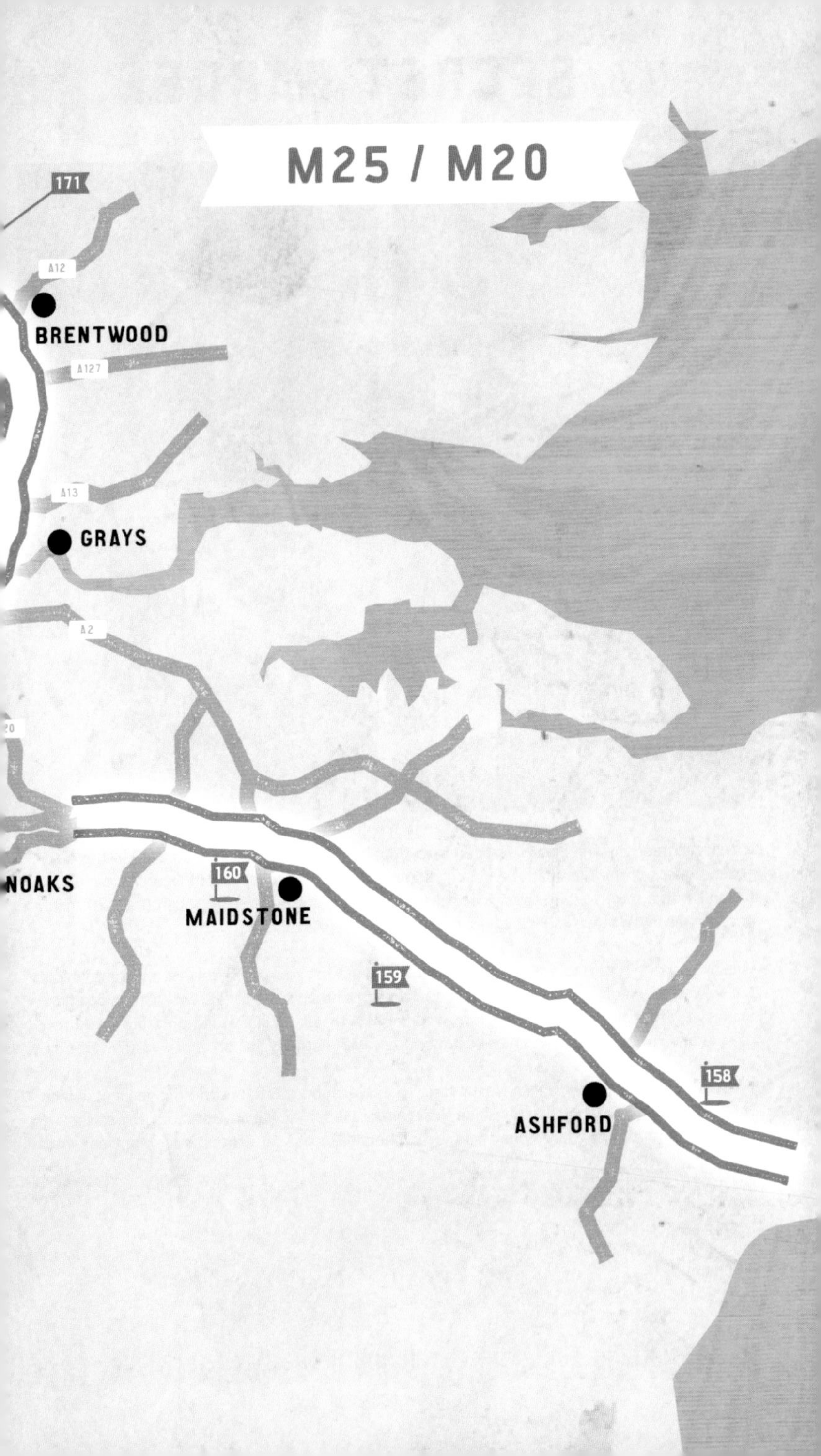

# M25 / M20

171

A12

● BRENTWOOD

A127

A13

● GRAYS

A2

20

NOAKS

160
● MAIDSTONE

159

158
● ASHFORD

CAFÉ

# *The* SECRET GARDEN

JUNCTION: 19; 5 MINUTES

It's easy to see why The Secret Garden is so popular with brides. Squirreled away in the old coach houses of the Mersham Le Hatch Estate, the rambling collection of Victorian buildings, topped with a stately clock spire, are adrift a sea of gorgeous gardens. Though the M20 thrums past not far away, remarkably it can barely be heard.

Luckily you don't have to wait to tie the knot to see it for yourself. Breakfast and light lunches are served seven days a week (when wedding parties haven't invaded), transforming produce from the garden and Kentish fields into wedding-worthy plates. It's worth booking ahead to have an afternoon tea in the dining room flooded with natural light or on the shady veranda.

If you're not in a rush for a ferry, make time to explore the estate beyond the gardens, which has been in the Knatchbull family since the reign of Henry VII. Public footpaths thread through the woodland passing a large deer park, ornamental lake and some impressively ancient trees.

Opening hours
Mon-Sun 10am-6pm

The Court Yard, Mersham-le-Hythe Business Village, Hythe Road, Ashford TN25 6NH

**WWW.SECRETGARDENKENT.CO.UK   01233 501586**

# *The* POTTING SHED

JUNCTION: 8; 8 MINUTES

If you're looking for a quick pit stop on your way to or from Dover, The Potting Shed is it. Spacious and down-to-earth it has plenty of room for the whole family. Walk through the bar and past the decadent leg of Spanish jamon to find the breezy dining room. Felt clouds hang from the lofty vaulted ceiling, above a mismatch of brightly coloured chairs.

Watch the chefs at work in the open kitchen as they prepare the flavourful menu. It's a notch up from pub grub, offering tapas, Lebanese platters and wood-fired pizzas alongside Sunday roasts and burgers.

The sunny terrace is shaded by awnings on sunny days, and deck chairs are set out on the large lawn. History buffs should not depart before heading to the magnificent, if confusingly-named, Leeds Castle. The Norman stronghold is exactly as a castle should look – moated and crenelated – and was used by Henry VIII and his wife Catherine of Aragon.

Opening hours
Mon-Thurs 8am-11pm
Fri-Sat 8am-11.30pm
Sun 8am-10.30am

The Potting Shed, Sutton Road, Langley ME17 3LZ
WWW.ELITEPUBS.COM/THE-POTTING-SHED   01622 862 112

# *Woodstock* CAFÉ

**JUNCTION: 5; 4 MINUTES**

Invisible from the road and a new addition to the family's other businesses (garden furniture, fire and stove shop, cattery), the Woodstock Café is a hidden gem. Tony, Lisa and the team are unfailingly cheerful and their wide smiles make the café a brilliant place to unwind when the grind of the M20 gets too much.

The café occupies a modern wooden cabin made almost entirely, and very impressively, from recycled and reclaimed materials. Its run of bifold doors make it bright, even in winter, and leads onto an outdoor terrace to enjoy on sunny days.

The chiller is full of sandwiches and drinks for the onward journey, or you can pull up a chair to enjoy one of the delicious plates summoned from the kitchen. The smashed avocado on sourdough with chilli, lime and a poached egg is the house special breakfast, popular with devoted regulars. The pancake menu is mouthwatering too, and the coffee and cake is excellent.

**Opening hours**
Mon-Fri 8.30am-4pm
Sat 9am-3pm

Woodstock Café, The Hermitage, Hermitage Lane, Maidstone ME16 9NT
**01622 727900**

# *Riverside* TEA ROOM

Riverside Tea Room sits overlooking the ford in pretty Eynsford, its window boxes brimming with flowers. Reminiscent of childhood sweet shops, it has a pastel pink door and leaded windows strung with bunting. Breakfast might be eggs Benedict with local honey-roasted ham, lunch could be a jacket sweet potato or filled baguette and if you're lucky you'll catch the afternoon scones warm from the oven. Dietary requirements are cheerfully accommodated and ingredients are sourced as locally as possible.

Business and family life intermingle here, with owner Lizzie's kids often found doing their homework at tables after school, wading in the stream or kicking a football around outside. The kids' menu shows that she knows how to get small children eating!

Visitors often drop in after visiting the heavenly lavender farm up the road. Pre-book Riverside's Vintage Afternoon Tea for a princely Kentish stop.

**Opening hours**
Mon-Fri 9am-4.30pm
Sat-Sun 9.30am-4pm

Riverside Tea Room, 2A Riverside, Eynsford DA4 0AE
**WWW.RIVERSIDE-TEAROOM.CO.UK  01322 861551**

The Surrey Hills are a popular escape for London's hikers and cyclists, offering glorious views over the countryside from the top. Just to the south, where the M25 intersects with the Brighton-bound M23, is the fantastic Priory Farm Shop, owned by the Shinner family since 1957.

The vast barn-like store offers a cornucopia of artisan food and drink, much of it from Surrey. Solar panels on the roof add to its eco-credentials. The shelves are stocked with produce and flavours that you won't find in the supermarket, and regular tastings encourage you to discover the unknown. Pack yourself an unrivalled picnic from the deli counter's amazing selection of pies, homemade quiches and salads; pick up a coffee in the plant nursery's café next door.

The year-round programme of events encourages you to take time out from your journey: go or pumpkin picking in autumn, or enjoy the discovery walk past Hungerford Lake to the Big Friendly Giant's Chair and pirate ship.

Opening hours
Mon-Sat 9am-5.30pm
Sun 10.30am-4.30pm

Priory Farm, Sandy Lane, Nutfield, Redhill RH1 4EJ
**WWW.PRIORYFARM.CO.UK 01737 823 304**

Large Dickensian bay windows stand either side of the front door, one piled with an enticing and eclectic range of antiques, ceramics, tableware, books and gifts, the other a window onto the goodies in the café within.

Breakfast on almond croissants baked that morning, lunch on sandwiches, frittata and salads – perhaps quinoa with feta, mango and pomegranate – or pep up your afternoon with a Green and Blacks hot chocolate and a slice of home-baked pistachio and lemon drizzle cake. You can sit at one of the tables inside among the trinkets and fresh flowers or grab a pew on the sunny terrace at the front (though you'll have to beat the cyclists to it; Nest is a popular mid-ride stop). Blankets are provided for world-watching on cooler days.

Dogs are very welcome and there are great walks around this pretty town for wearing them out before browsing Nest's exquisite antiques and enjoying its Italian coffee.

Opening hours
Mon-Fri 9am-5pm
Sat 9am-5.30pm

Nest, High Street, Ripley GU23 6AQ
WWW.NEST-HOME.COM/  01483 211111

# ATTRACTION

*Crockford* **BRIDGE FARM**

**JUNCTION: 11; 6 MINUTES**

When the kids have had enough of M25 traffic jams, Crockford Bridge Farm offers perfect respite. Open from Easter to December, there's a large play area alongside fields of fruit and veg. The pick-your-own fields are open for asparagus in spring and fruit in summer; there's a huge pumpkin picking festival in October and in December you can visit Santa in his woodland grotto before cutting your own Christmas tree.

The Tea Shack and Ice Cream Parlour are housed in cute sheds with brightly painted gables and serve snacks and light meals from a firmly local list of suppliers. Coffee is strong, tea is loose leaf, hot chocolate velvety smooth and chilled glasses of Pimm's are served on hot days; lemonade made with the farm's fruit is available for the designated driver. The gelato in the Ice Cream Parlour and jam for the cream teas also uses home-grown ingredients. If you don't fancy doing the harvest, the farm shop alongside stocks a full range of farm-grown veg and artisan products, including the farm's own honey.

**Opening hours**
Mon-Sat 10am-6PM (Sun 5pm) Mar-Dec

Crockford Bridge Farm, KT15 2BU
**WWW.CROCKFORDBRIDGEFARM.CO.UK   01932 846611**

CAFÉ
# *The* BREADHOUSE
JUNCTION: 17; 12 MINUTES

There's a cheery welcome and a real sense of community at the Breadhouse, encouraged by lovely initiatives such as scrapbooking workshops, guided walks, art exhibitions and seminars. Set in the town's central marketplace, it's a hub for Chalfont St Peter. Step through the door and you're greeted by a beautiful cherry-wood counter laden with home baking, from sausage rolls and banana loaf to chocolate mud cake.

It's family friendly and kids will be kept occupied by the play area in the corner, though with tables spread over two levels, it's easy to find a peaceful spot too.

A roll of brown paper hung on the wall displays the often-changing specials, ranging from Moroccan porridge to sautéed asparagus with poached egg and bacon, mini roast pumpkin stuffed with puy lentils and smoked mackerel salad. Lots for vegans and vegetarians here as well, and the best almond coffee near the M25!

Opening hours
Mon-Sat 8.30am-4pm,

The Breadhouse, 8 Market Place, Chalfont St Peter SL9 9EA
WWW.BREADHOUSE.CO.UK   01753 885371

# A LITTLE EXTRA

**SOME OF THE PLACES IN THE GUIDE** are kindly offering our readers (that's you!) a little extra: it may be a discount on your bill, a free coffee refill, a complimentary cup of tea when you buy a slice of cake… To redeem offers all you need to do is show your Extra Mile keyring fob at selected venues. The list is on our website and will be updated regularly so make sure you keep checking to snag the latest deals.

*Not got yours? Head to*
**WWW.THEEXTRAMILE.GUIDE**
*and we'll pop one straight in the post.*

(While you're waiting for it to arrive you can still take advantage
of the offers by showing your copy of this book.)

Friends Georgie and Tina joined their coffee and floristry forces in the Coffee House and Deli to create a cosy community-focused café in the London suburb of Croxley Green. Bouquets may be thin on the ground but Tina puts her knowledge to excellent use in the nutritional menu.

You can expect to see herby poached eggs, salads, pastries and delicious sugar and butter-free flapjacks (dark arts if ever we saw it) on the menu and countertop. Open sandwiches are a particular speciality (the prawn and avocado comes highly recommended) and scarcely more expensive than a meal deal, while kudos for the cakes largely belongs to local cakesmith Victoria. The duo hold the slow-roasted Vascobelo coffee beans in the highest regard, so import all their coffee from Antwerp and the baristas have added inventive twists such as a beetroot latte.

Choose a superfood smoothie if you're feeling health conscious, or swap cake for a Medjool date energy ball.

Opening hours
Mon-Fri 7.30am-4.30pm
Sat 9am-4pm (Sun 3pm)
Bank Hol Mon 10am-3pm

Coffee House and Deli, 141 New Road, Croxley Green WD3 3EN
COFFEEHOUSEANDDELI.CO.UK   01923 510995

# Fred & Ginger COFFEE

**JUNCTION: 20; 2 MINUTES**

© Russell Mount

The handsome charcoal front of Fred & Ginger Coffee stands on Kings Langley's high street illuminated by filament bulbs and cheery faces and a-buzz with enthusiasm for great coffee. It's a popular local haunt and it's easy to see why: the space is bright and welcoming – decorated with vintage pictures, brass light fittings and soothing palms – and the food delicious.

Whether you're stopping in for an expertly made flat white, a flaky almond croissant or a plateful of sumptuous house salads, you won't be disappointed. Vegan options such as pesto, tomato, courgette and onion filo slices stand alongside crisp sausage rolls, teriyaki salmon and a sea of colourful salads in enamel bowls. When the sun is shining sit at the Parisian tables outside to watch the world go by.

Juices freshly squeezed on site and soya milk chai lattes will pep you up for the onward journey. Parking outside is free for an hour.

**Opening hours**
Mon-Fri 8am-5pm
Sat 9am-5pm
Sun 9am-4pm

Fred & Ginger Coffee, 38c High St, Kings Langley WD4 9HT
**FREDANDGINGERCOFFEE.CO.UK   01923 262420**

# *The* GATEHOUSE CAFÉ

JUNCTION: 25; 8 MINUTES

Tucked in a quiet corner of Waltham Abbey, the Gatehouse Café has enviable views over the town's eponymous church and comes into its own in summer when tables and chairs are set out beneath the trees. Frothy hanging baskets are strung up above the tables on the pavement tables, and inside there's a warmth to the dark grey panelling, wooden floors and pretty sash windows.

The steady stream of regulars is testament to the warm welcome on offer from Aurelia, Sean and their team. Aurelia brings flavours of her native Italy to the cuisine: gnocchi, panini, sundried tomatoes and pesto served alongside full breakfasts, warm quiches and chocolate vegan cake.

Make time to visit the Norman church, gardens and moat next door. This site has been a place of worship since 600 AD and it's thought to be the final resting place of Saxon King Harold. You can pick up an informative leaflet to guide you round.

Opening hours
Mon-Fri 7.30am-5pm
Sat-Sun 9am-5pm

The Gatehouse Café, 2-4 Highbridge St, Waltham Abbey EN9 1DG
07971 800727

Hidden down a winding tree-lined track, Norpar Barns is a vision of old-country farming. Its medieval clapboard doors were first opened to the public in 1969, selling dried flowers as a diversification to the family's traditional farming.

Today the dried flowers have been replaced by a sensational seasonal emporium of rustic homewares and decorations. Each Easter, summer, autumn and Christmas the whitewashed barn is transformed by a new theme. December is a particular highlight with a woodland, Father Christmas, wreath workshops, pork roast and mulled punch, carol singing and a separate blacked-out Christmas light barn. Individuality and fair trade are celebrated. You'll struggle to resist leaving without at least one gorgeous glass bauble or garland, whatever the season. In spring and summer tea and cake is served in a spectacular 14th-century oak barn with wibbly beams decorated with old farm tools, willow boughs and flowers. Don't miss the home-grown apple juice, available to take away.

Opening hours
Tues-Sat 10am-5pm (Sun 11am)
Open Mon when Christmas & Easter Barns are open
Closed January

Norpar Barns, Navestock Hall, Shonksmill Rd, Navestock RM4 1HA
**WWW.NORPAR.CO.UK   01277 374969**

# The M40 & M42

## Chilterns, Cotswolds & canals in the heart of England

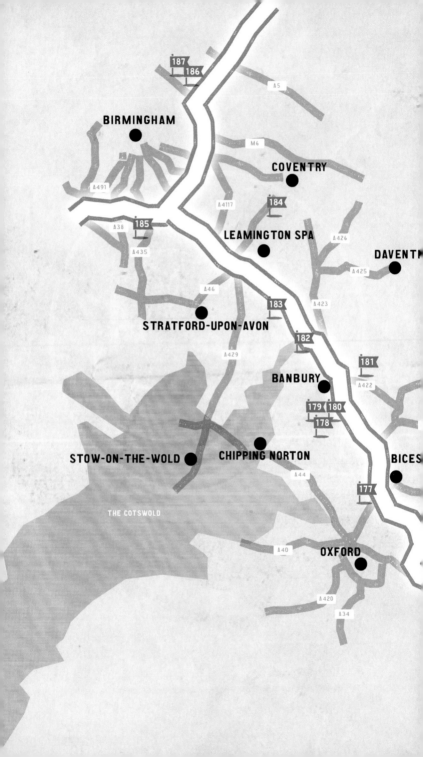

# M40 / M42

- 176 The Royal Oak
- 177 The Milk Shed
- 178 The Yurt at Nicholsons
- 179 Foodies
- 180 The Duke
- 181 Limes Farm
- 182 The National Herb Centre
- 183 Lighthorne Pavilion Café
- 184 Farmers Fayre
- 185 Gin & Pickles Ltd
- 186 Middleton Hall & Gardens
- 187 Forage at Coppice

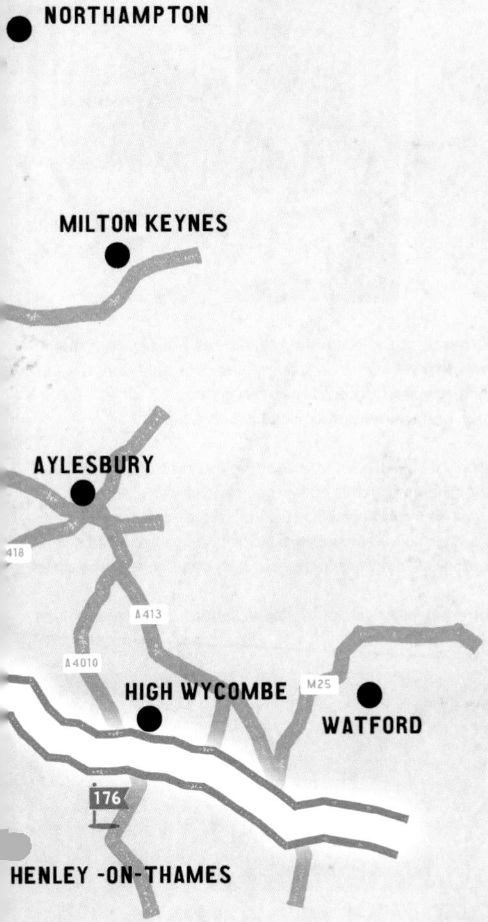
NORTHAMPTON
MILTON KEYNES
AYLESBURY
418
A413
A4010
HIGH WYCOMBE
M25
WATFORD
176
HENLEY -ON-THAMES

PUB

# *The* ROYAL OAK

JUNCTION: 4; 10 MINUTES

A cracking country pub, the Royal Oak stands at the edge of the Chilterns, not far from the Thames-washed town of Marlow. It's informal yet stylish with rugs flung over tiled floors, scrubbed pew seats and dogs asleep by the wood burner. The garden is beautiful for games of petanque and slothful lunches in summer. Keep a lookout for red kites overhead.

There's a wonderful sense of a local economy here: bees bob about in the garden to make the pub's honey, ingredients are foraged from the hedgerows or swapped with local allotment holders, and garden furniture is made from recycled drinking straws. Food is uniformly excellent and moves with the seasons – try the wild mushroom arancini or pan-roasted sea trout with bulgar wheat. And there are dedicated menus for vegan, dairy-, and gluten-free diets.

Before you depart take a stroll through the beech trees of Marlow Common, where you'll find trenches used for practice during the First World War.

Opening hours
Mon-Thur Noon-9.30pm
Fri-Sat Noon-10pm
Sun Noon-9pm

The Royal Oak, Frieth Rd, Bovingdon Green, Marlow SL7 2JF
**WWW.ROYALOAKMARLOW.CO.UK  01628 488611**

# *The* MILK SHED

**JUNCTION: 9; 2 MINUTES**

Don't be put off by its location on an industrial estate. The Milk Shed is one of the best cafés in Oxfordshire. One customer said the ice creams alone are worth a visit, and we agree. They're made on site by Lucie and Dan using only natural ingredients: vanilla pods, lumps of fudge, meringues and mashed-up bananas. Try the grown-up banana split if you want a taste of the divine, or douse a ball of vanilla in locally roasted coffee for a supreme affogato pick-me-up.

The rest of the menu is simple and expertly executed with fine ingredients. People rave about the scrambled eggs on toast, club sandwiches, generous salad bowls and cheese and bean toasties. Lucie indulges her love of cooking in preparing the daily specials, such as smoked haddock chowder or pulled lamb salad with freekeh, garlic yoghurt and pomegranate.

If you're wooed by the flavours, you can fill the car with snacks from the deli counter, from homemade tarts to cured meats and olives.

Opening hours
Tues-Fri 9am-4pm
Sat-Sun 9am-3.30pm,
last food orders an hour before closing time

The Milk Shed, Manor Farm, Northampton Rd, Weston on the Green OX25 3QL
**WWW.THEMILKSHEDSTORE.CO.UK   01869 351387**

GARDEN CENTRE

# *The Yurt* AT NICHOLSONS

JUNCTION: 10: 11 MINUTES

Follow the winding paths through the leafy garden centre to find the luminous tent that houses Nicholsons' café, keeping your eyes peeled for wildlife (we spotted the green flash of a woodpecker). The enormous Mongolian yurt is a blissful sanctuary from the road: in winter it twinkles with fairy lights; come summer the canvas roof glows above tables decorated with large boughs of greenery. This is the perfect al fresco dining for a British climate.

The food has an ethically driven vegetarian and vegan focus and is reliably delicious. Try mushrooms served on potato rosti for breakfast; pan-fried spiced mackerel with beetroot salsa for lunch, or a confit duck leg with red cabbage purée. A slice of the 'cake of the month' – elderflower, lemon and pistachio in May, blueberry, lime and lemon thyme in August – will set you up for the onward journey.

The coffee is strong and the hot chocolate, made from Mexican cocoa, is mindblowing.

Opening hours
Mon-Sat 8.30am-4.30pm

The Yurt at Nicholsons, The Park, North Aston OX25 6HL
**WWW.THEYURTATNICHOLSONS.CO.UK   01869 340342**

# FOODIES

JUNCTION: 10; 13 MINUTES

The honey-coloured Oxfordshire village of Deddington has a bustling market square at its heart. Foodies stands proudly in front of the church with wisteria entwined around the door. White iron tables sit on the terrace outside, a suntrap on summer days; inside feels like a traditional grocer's crossed with a country cottage. At the flower-topped tables you can enjoy light bites such as teacakes, baguettes (don't miss the bacon, brie and chilli jam) and baked potatoes, as well as a chat with friendly owner Sam. Carol makes the cakes and it's nearly impossible to choose between the Guinness and chocolate and her secret-recipe fudge flapjacks. There's a take-away counter down the corridor if you're in a hurry.

If time permits, take a look at Deddington's castle, an 11th-century motte-and-bailey castle that was once the English base of Odo of Bayeux, half brother of William the Conquerer. The ramparts are 15m high in places.

Opening hours
Mon-Sat 8:30am-4:30pm

Foodies, Tuckers House, Market Place, Deddington OX15 0SA
**01869 337470**

PUB, HOTEL, CAMPSITE

# *The* DUKE

JUNCTION: 10; 9 MINUTES

With handsome sandstone walls and thatched roof, the Duke at Clifton is the cornerstone of this Oxfordshire hamlet. Just minutes from the M40, it's a great stop for travellers too. Lovingly refurbished only recently, the 17th-century inn is now an inviting modern pub and hotel but still cosy, with low beams, flagstone floors and sturdy mismatched furniture. Scooter the pub dog is in charge of greetings. A freehouse, it stocks a variety of local ales. In cooler months you can warm up by the open fires; come summer, tables are set out on the lawn under the trees.

The menu is a notch up from your standard pub fare and uses ingredients sourced within a 10-mile radius wherever possible. Vegetarians will be pleased to see a dedicated section of the menu. Snack on stuffed jalapeno peppers or deep-fried whitebait, or order mains such as honey-glazed ham and lamb rump if you need to refuel. If you can't peel yourself away from the mellow tenor and village vibes, book one of the five rooms upstairs or the Shepherd's Hut in the pasture. You can even pitch your tent in the small but well-serviced campsite at the rear.

Opening hours
Mon 5pm-11pm
Tues-Sat Noon-11pm
Sun Noon-9pm

The Duke, Main Road, Clifton OX15 0PE
**THECLIFTONDUKE.CO.UK  01869 226334**

A bastion of traditional farming, the fields around Limes Farm supply the shop and tearoom with lovingly grown and reared produce. The family have been tending the land here for 200 years and eschew chemicals in favour of a more organic approach, which more than shows in the flavour of the meat and vegetables. The tearoom and pared-back farmshop are housed in an old medieval barn. The ancient oven was discovered during renovations and stoked back up to bake bread, cakes and tarts daily. There's a warm homeliness to the low beams, terracotta floor tiles and scrubbed wooden tables.

Service from Peter and his team is convivial and welcoming. They transform the farm's field and hedgerow bounty into a toothsome selection of breakfasts, lunches and snacks. Kids will go crazy for the loaded chocolate brownies, which they can burn off with a visit to the animal petting area. Grown ups can leaf through books in the bookshop over a smooth coffee and slice of courgette and avocado cake.

Opening hours
Mon-Sat 9am-5pm
Sun 10am-5pm

Limes Farm, Main Road, Fartinghoe NN13 5PB
**WWW.LIMESFARM.COM/SHOP/ 01295 711 229**

Drink in the views over three counties from the National Herb Centre, a charming enterprise camped on a lofty ridge. It is so much more than just a garden centre. Depending on the time of year, you will find herb plants to delight the chef, intrigue the gardener and fascinate anyone with an interest in herbal remedies. Stretch your legs and explore the nature trails winding down through the valley. You might even see buzzards, deer and foxes.

Breakfast, lunches and afternoon teas in the Bistro & Coffee Shop are freshly prepared from seasonal locally sourced ingredients. Ice cream, coffee and cake will revive everyone on a quick stop. On fine days enjoy your treats outside and soak up the sun in this glorious rural location.

There's a natural playground for kids and a well-stocked gift shop. If you have time, maximise the breathtaking views by taking a stroll along the Edge Hill escarpment.

Opening hours
Mon-Sat 9am-5.30pm
Sun & Bank Hols 10.30am-5.30pm
Closes at 5pm in winter

The National Herb Centre, Warmington, Banbury OX17 1DF
**HERBCENTRE.CO.UK   01295 690999**

# *Lighthorne Pavilion* **CAFÉ**

JUNCTION: 12; 5 MINUTES

Your shoulders drop as soon as you arrive at the Pavilion Café, a wood cabin perched at the side of the cricket pitch in the sleepy Warwickshire village of Lighthorne. Run by owner Ben, the café's relaxed informality, friendly welcome and countryside setting are instantly soothing. Staff ferry plates of steaming comfort food to tables and sofas by the wood burner or out to the terrace, where parents can watch kids run around on the green when there's no match on. Bare wood shelves are stacked with books and magazines to encourage you to linger.

People rave about the breakfasts and afternoon teas (especially popular after working up an appetite on the country paths nearby), and cups of tea are best paired with the homemade cakes, perhaps coffee and walnut or black cherry.

There's ample parking, dogs are welcome outside and a little gift shop at the rear stocks locally made crafts and goodies.

**Opening hours**
Tues-Fri 7.45am-4.15pm
Sat-Sun 8am-4.30pm

Lighthorne Pavilion Café, Chesterton Rd, Lighthorne CV35 0AD
**07768 195882**

FARM SHOP-CAFÉ

# *Farmers* **FAYRE**

**JUNCTION: 15; 14 MINUTES**

People rave about the breakfasts and Sunday roasts at Farmer's Fayre, but whether you stop in for an early bacon sandwich or for a slice of cake at tea time, you'll be impressed by the flavours. Lunches include delicious combinations such as soured and scorched mackerel salad with beetroot, red cabbage and watercress, or mushroom, garlic, mozzarella and spinach tart. Many are cooked on the in-store Aga and you can relax over your coffee next to the cosy wood-burning stove.

The airy, family-run farm shop and restaurant is found on the sprawling National Agricultural Exhibition Centre at Stoneleigh Park (don't be put off by the barrier and cheery security guards), underlining its commitment to good local ingredients from nearby farms. If you like what you taste, pick up some of the produce in the adjoining farm shop, which stocks produce from more than 40 local suppliers: chutneys, home-baked cakes, cheese and regional delicacies alongside a range of tempting homewares and antiques.

Opening hours
Mon-Sat 7.30am-5.30pm
Sun 8.30am-4.30pm

Farmers Fayre, Stoneleigh Park, Coventry CV8 2LZ
**WWW.FARMERSFAYRE.CO.UK   024 7669 2844**

It's the warm reception and personal service that regulars to Gin and Pickles praise so highly. What started as a simple penchant for gin and pickles has turned into a winning deli-café combination that's hugely popular with the locals.

Zoe behind the counter is an ardent supporter of local producers, from the artisan bread to the eye-widening cheese selection, salted caramel brownies and English charcuterie. The menu mainly features finger food, but you're bound to find something to stave off the hunger pangs, whether a slice of blueberry and violet loaf, a lunchtime deli board or a portion of chilli cashews. At weekends almond croissants and custard chocolate twists are served warm from the oven, and kids love the chocolate popcorn. If you like what you taste, fill a basket from the shelves of the deli – great for snacks, holiday groceries and a tipple on arrival (sample one of the range of small batch gins) – and coffee can be made to go.

Opening hours
Tues-Thurs 9am-5pm
Fri 9am-8pm

Gin and Pickles Ltd, 21 The Square, Alvechurch B48 7LA
WWW.GINANDPICKLES.CO.UK   0121 445 6769

# *Middleton Hall* & GARDENS

**JUNCTION: 2; 11 MINUTES**

The glorious Middleton Hall was saved from ruin by a team of volunteers who have slowly restored the moated, timber-framed building over nearly four decades. Today visitors to the 42-acre estate can explore the its 950-year history, visit the formal gardens (including one of the earliest examples of a heated walled garden in the country) and stroll around the adjoining RSPB Middleton Lakes Nature Reserve. Follow its three miles of winding paths and you may spot kingfishers and herons on the wetlands.

Mind and body restored, head to the Tudor courtyard, which plays host to a small shopping village. Lose yourself for a moment in the second-hand bookshop or head to the tearoom for a friendly welcome and tasty food; it's open every day throughout the year. The paninis are held in high regard and the coffee is very smooth, best paired with a slice of their inventive cakes. Kids will love the unicorn hot chocolate. There is a small car parking charge and an admission charge to enter the Hall and Gardens but there is no admission charge for the Courtyard..

Opening hours
Sun-Thurs & second Sat each month 11am-4pm
(31 Mar to 8 Sept)
Please see website for winter opening

Middleton Hall & Gardens, Middleton, Tamworth B78 2AE
**WWW.MIDDLETON-HALL.CO.UK   01827 283095**

# *Forage* AT COPPICE

JUNCTION: 9; 8 MINUTES

Marooned in a sea of gorgeous shrubs and surrounded by emerald lawns, Fig and Olive restaurant is a world away from the frenetic M42. You can find it in a former growing shed at Coppice Garden Centre, washed with the soothing sounds of birdsong and scents of the garden.

You won't be disappointed by the food on offer, rustled up from carefully sourced ingredients. Try the halloumi chips with red pepper hash, salmon teriyaki with steamed coconut rice, or a steak from the grill if you're famished. Sandwiches and coffee are also served, and better still, you can take your lunch outside to the terrace on summer's days to eat among the flowers.

Alongside the restaurant is Forage Food Hall selling a cornucopia of delicious produce. The shelves heave with homemade pâtés, Fruits of the Forage jams and cordials (made with fruit foraged from abandoned orchards) and incredible macaroons alongside a well-stocked deli counter, butchery, bakery and fresh veg barrows.

---

Opening hours
Mon-Fri 9am-7pm
Sat 9am-5.30pm
Sun 10am-4.30pm

GF V P

Forage at Coppice, Coppice Lane, Middleton B78 2BU
**COPPICEGC.COM   0121 308 7197**

# The M3 & A303

*Capital to country,
the gateway to the South West*

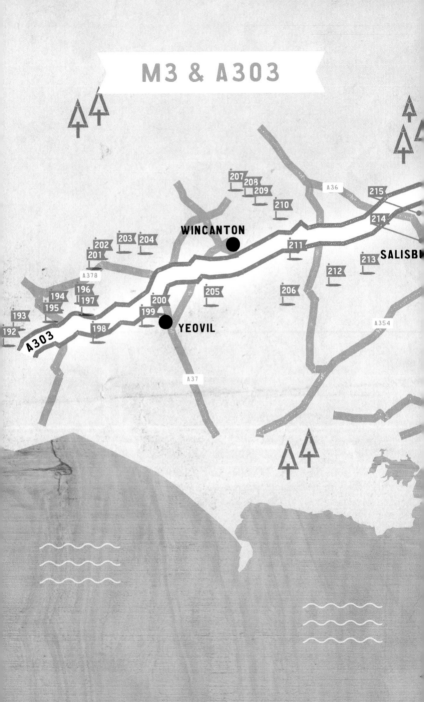

**ANDOVER**

**BASINGSTOKE**

**FARNBOROUGH**

**FARNHAM**

**WINCHESTER**

**SOUTHAMPTON**

**NEW FOREST**

**PORTSMOUTH**

PUB
# *Flintlock* **INN**

**JUNCTION MARSH: 2 MINUTES**

The good-looking village of Marsh hugs the A30 so it's a mere twist of the steering wheel to land at the Flintlock Inn, a characterful country pub hung with traditional lanterns and filled with countryside antiques. Log-burners and low, beamed ceilings combine with a smiley welcome from long-time owners Meryl and Paolo to create a warm atmosphere; a well-tended garden (where dogs are welcome) draws the crowd on fine days. There's bags of space for children to run around, plus a climbing frame to keep them out of mischief.

When it comes to food The Flintlock doesn't cut corners. It's big on flavour: chicken and leek pie, pork tenderloin marinated in cider, or salmon cooked in dill, lemon and cream. The homemade puddings are wide-ranging and excellent, perhaps walnut and treacle tart or strawberry and hazelnut roulade. Portions are substantial, bread is fresh from the oven and lighter bites are available at lunchtime. If you need to stretch your legs, there's a worthwhile walk towards the twinkly River Yarty.

Opening hours
Tues-Thurs, Sat noon-2pm, 6pm-9pm
Fri Noon-2.30pm, 6pm-9.30pm
Sun Noon-2pm, 6.30pm-9pm

Flintlock Inn, Marsh, Honiton EX14 9AJ
**01460 234403**

# The CANDLELIGHT INN

**JUNCTION BISHOPSWOOD; 2 MINUTES**

Landlords Simon and Mike abandoned their high-flying management jobs in banking to take on the Candlelight Inn on the Devon–Somerset border. It was a gargantuan career leap, but they knew what they were doing. Camped in the stunning Blackdown Hills, it's a beautiful country pub – flint walls, beamed ceilings and inviting fireplaces – just moments away from the A303. The welcome is hospitable and informal and staff clearly enjoy being part of the team. The crowd of locals at the bar in the evenings is proof of the convivial atmosphere.

There's a romance to the dining room, with candles (obviously) on every table and a blazing fireplace. Many ingredients for the impressive plates are sourced from the countryside around and the fresh catch down at Lyme Regis, so you can expect anything from hand-picked crab sandwiches to ham hock terrine and cheddar-stuffed chicken. The range of very local ciders is also very tempting – non-drivers should try them out.

Opening hours
Tues-Thurs noon-2.30pm
Fri 5pm-11pm
Sat noon-11pm (Sun 7pm)

Ⓥ Ⓟ

The Candlelight inn, Bishopswood, Chard TA20 3RS
**WWW.CANDLELIGHT-INN.CO.UK   01460 234476**

CAFÉ
# *Monks* YARD

JUNCTION HORTON CROSS; 0 MINUTES

Fresh from its move to swanky new premises, Monks Yard has gone up in the world. Converted cow shed has been swapped for high-ceilinged industrial chic; courtyard for generous gardens – which you're welcome to explore – and ample parking.

One thing that hasn't changed is the unswervingly friendly service, nor the counter loaded with imaginative cakes – apricot and cranberry sponge, perhaps, or coffee amaretto. Ingredients are sourced from the community garden and around Somerset, and transformed into simple but tasty sandwiches, soups and paninis. Breakfasts are brilliant.

Specials change frequently and may include pan-fried mackerel with lemon and rocket, grilled peach salad, battered goat's cheese with beetroot salad, or a picnic platter with individual pork pie, tartlet and Scotch egg. Organic, fair-trade coffee is roasted nearby and teas are loose leaf. Monks Yard is literally metres from the fast food joints and a million miles better.

Opening hours
Mon-Sat 9am-5pm

Monks Yard, Horton Manor, Horton Cross TA19 9PY
WWW.MONKSYARD.CO.UK/EAT/  01460 200020

# *Kitchen* **AT JORDANS COURTYARD**

### JUNCTION ILMINSTER; 1 MINUTE

The brand-new smarter sister of the wonderful Kitchen at the Wharf in Langport, Kitchen at Jordans Courtyard stands conveniently close to the A303 at Horton Cross. Like its counterpart, the food here is wholesome, nourishing and made on site from scratch using seasonal ingredients. A varied menu of old favourites and modern classics include homemade banana bread with cinnamon butter, a wonderful full English and a just-as-good veggie version, homemade sourdough pizza with fennel salami and caramelised onions and salmon gravlax and avocado salad. Puds such as homemade Belgian waffles with ice cream and maple syrup await those with a sweet tooth.

Light spills into the café from a long run of windows and on fine days you can sit at a table on the wide terrace. Jordans Courtyard – an inviting collection of converted hamstone and clapboard barns – is also home to a spa, nail bar and gift shop bursting with Somerset artisan produce, so there's plenty to delay your onward journey if you need a longer break.

Opening hours
Mon-Sun 8.30am-3pm

Kitchen at Jordans Courtyard, Horton Cross Farm, Ilminster TA19 9PT
**WWW.JORDANSCOURTYARD.CO.UK   01460 298 608**

# *Barrington* COURT (NT)

**JUNCTION SOUTH PETHERTON; 10 MINUTES**

© National Trust Images/paul Mogford

Fabulous gardens radiate out from the Tudor manor house like sunbeams, melting at the fringe into a deer park and lush, green fields. The gardens are laid out in 'rooms' where you can idly wander, taking in the brick-pathed pergolas, wiggly-spined stables, dragonfly-laden moat, rose garden, extensive orchards and walled kitchen garden, which still supplies the café. The enormous plot of champagne rhubarb, for example, is put to good use in season for lip-smacking crumbles, and rhubarb and almond cakes.

Stop for tea or lunch in the Strode tea rooms in the main house – where you can munch delicious homemade food in a panelled room with views over the countryside – or in the somewhat grander dining room, which overlooks the lawns and pond through arched, leaded doors. Dogs are welcome in certain parts of the garden (a map tells you which). Fresh water bowls and dog treats are available at reception, where you'll also find a second-hand book barn, fabulous gift shop and ice cream shop.

Opening hours
Mon-Sun 10.30am- 5pm (Feb-Nov)
Check website for winter opening hours

Barrington Court (NT), Barrington, nr Ilminster TA19 0NQ
**WWW.NATIONALTRUST.ORG.UK/BARRINGTON-COURT  01460 241 938**

# *Dennis* CHINAWORKS

**JUNCTION HAYES END ROUNDABOUT: 7 MINUTES**

The squeak and whirr of potters' wheels provide a calming accompaniment to a stop off at the Dennis Chinaworks, as do the pretty gardens. Housed in the old gothic rectory of Shepton House, the pottery has been producing richly coloured earthenware pots since 1993. Inspect the displays of exquisitely decorated plates, vases and tiles or ask staff for a quick tour of the workshop to see the potters in action.

The tearoom is in a cosy outhouse opposite the workshop, surrounded by flowers and cascading greenery and filled with rustic furniture. It faces a delightful courtyard where you can sup a cold lemonade on warm days. The house allotment is behind, a colourful forest of home-grown produce stretching down the slope, most of it destined for your plate. It very much dictates the menu – perhaps courgette, caramelised onion and Cheddar cheese tart; pea and mint salad; blueberry Victoria sponge – but vegan and gluten-free diets are always catered for.

**Opening hours**
Thurs-Sat 10am-4pm
Seasonal opening hours; check website in advance

Dennis Chinaworks, Shepton House, Ilminster TA19 0JT
**WWW.DENNISCHINAWORKS.COM   01460 240622**

FARM SHOP-CAFÉ

# Pip's Railway Carriage CAFÉ

JUNCTION SOUTH PETHERTON; 1 MINUTE

You won't find a quirkier place to stop for a bite than an 1880s railway carriage and old double-decker bus. Now transformed into a café, the train carriage with its communal tables is joined by an ivy-strewn marquee to the double-decker bus, which offers sunny table upstairs, cosy corners below and spectacular countryside views. Outside, there are picnic benches for summer months and plenty of grass for little feet to run around on.

Menus change daily depending on what can be harvested from the fields, which means abundant organic salads in summer, and warming comfort foods with a twist in the colder months.

Don't leave without stocking up at the award-winning Trading Post farm shop next door. It offers a cornucopia of local fare and natural whole foods: pickles, smoked fish, eggs, cheese, homegrown veg, organic wine and fresh-cut flowers.

Opening hours
Mon-Sat 9am–4pm
Fri 5pm-8pm (in summer)

Pip's Railway Carriage Café, Lopenhead TA13 5JH
WWW.PIPSRAILWAYCARRIAGE.COM  07729 685412

# *Montacute* HOUSE (NT)

**JUNCTION A3088; 5 MINUTES**

© National Trust Images/John Miller

Montacute House is a grand example of Gothic-Renaissance Elizabethan architecture – soaring turrets, ornate obelisks and detailed stone masonry – built from warm limestone in 1601 for Edward Phelps, a wealthy and important lawyer who made the opening statement for the prosecution in Guy Fawkes' trial. It's set in acres of beautifully maintained gardens into which parents can safely unleash children to explore. Swings in the garden and thoughtful touches such as extra nappies and wipes in the toilet tell you that kids really are welcome.

Four-legged friends are welcome on leads, provided they stick to paths and don't scare the livestock. Biscuity rewards for obeying the rules can be collected from the Courtyard Café (accessible without paying entry to the house), which has a well-rounded menu including jacket potatoes and gluten-free flan. The savoury cream tea makes a scrumptious antidote to cake and scones, though there are plenty of those available too.

Opening hours
Mon-Sun Mar-Dec please check website for opening times
Wed-Sun 11am-4pm (Jan-Mar)

Montacute House (NT), Middle St, Montacute  TA15 6XP
**WWW.NATIONALTRUST.ORG.UK/MONTACUTE-HOUSE  01935 823289**

# *The* CROWN & VICTORIA

JUNCTION TINTINHULL; 2 MINUTES

The Crown and Victoria is a friendly village pub burrowed in the peaceful Somerset countryside. The broad-smiled welcome is as toasty as the open fires, and there's a large garden filled with flowers, birdsong and picnic benches out front, with an orchard with a waste-disposal pig lies just beyond.

Owners Mark and Isabel focus more on the atmosphere and food rather than the interior design (which is well-maintained but charmingly 90s). Food is organic or free range, locally sourced and excellent. As a result, the menu changes regularly, but might include starters of devilled whitebait and chunky tartare or homemade terrine on toasted granary bloomer, perhaps chargrilled pork loin with haricot cassoulet, or wild mushroom wellington for dinner. Roasts on Sundays are generous and very popular, with fish and vegetarian alternatives. For a breath of fresh air after feasting, explore a footpath from the doorstep and the beautiful Tintinhull Garden nearby.

Opening hours
Mon-Sat 9am-3.30pm, 5.30pm-11pm
Sun 9am-4pm

The Crown & Victoria, 14 Farm Street, Tintinhull BA22 8PZ
**WWW.THECROWNANDVICTORIA.CO.UK  01935 823 341**

CAFÉ
# *Kitchen* AT THE WHARF

JUNCTION PODIMORE; 13 MINUTES

Langport belongs to Somerset's trendy renaissance. It's a pretty town with a lively art scene and a raft of independent shops. Kitchen is at the top of the high street, in a hefty-timbered Victorian warehouse at Great Bow Wharf, once used for trading salt and corn along the waterways.

The roomy café is a popular spot for locals and visitors, especially cyclists. Bare floorboards and white walls often ring with merry voices as people catch up over yummy pastries: sausage rolls, cheese and pesto swirls, and croissants that would make the French blush. Lunches are filling and seasonal, perhaps a BLT with basil mayonnaise or mezze platter with puy lentils, chickpea and quinoa served with Asian salsa.

There's a toy box for kids and treats for four-legged friends. Spill out through a wild flower border, up red-brick steps and on to the rope-bound terrace overlooking the river for beautiful walks.

Opening hours
Mon-Sun 9.30am-3pm

Kitchen at The Wharf, Bow Wharf, Bow Street, Langport TA10 9PN
**WWW.KITCHENLANGPORT.CO.UK   01458 254 354**

# *Art* TEA ZEN

**JUNCTION PODIMORE: 13 MINUTES**

A comforting, bohemian café painted sky blue in the pretty market town of Langport. Find a table (if you can) among the natives habitually found strewn across the place gossiping and languidly reading papers – this is a real community hub.

The breakfasts are generous – crushed avocado on toast with a poached egg, or toasted crumpets with lashings of butter for example – and lunches deliciously homemade. The sweet potato fritters are well regarded, as are the quiches and chicken and avocado toasties. Sweeter treats extent to naughty milkshakes and a fabulous chocolate Guinness cake.

Beyond the bustling counter you'll find a large family room with polished concrete floor, squidgy sofa, piano to tickle and bookshelf stacked with toys and reading materials. Large windows look out onto a dinky, gravelled courtyard where you can enjoy fresh air among local artwork on Parisienne garden furniture.

Opening hours
Mon-Sat 9am-5pm

Art Tea Zen, 105 Cheapside, Langport TA10 9PW
**WWW.ARTTEAZEN.CO.UK   01458 250635**

# *Pitney* FARM SHOP & CAFÉ

JUNCTION PODIMORE; 15 MINUTES

One for the eco-minded, Glebe Farm is a rustic, Soil Association-approved organic farm in the Somerset Levels. Rob and Lizzie tend 90 acres of mixed arable and livestock land, so you'll see Saddleback sows, Mule ewes and Bodmin Brown chickens roaming among fields of carrots, potatoes and onions.

The shelves of the shop, named after the nearby village, are filled with fabulous seasonal produce. You'll find homemade sausages, dried, cured Italian-style meats, Mendip Moments ice cream, locally pressed apple juice, handmade chocolates, Somerset cheeses and organic pork, beef and lamb. It's an ideal pull-in for a picnic or to stock the holiday larder with goodness.

The café is a charming wooden hut run by the lovely Lily. The focus is on vegetarian food – stews, soups, curries – with one or two daily changing meat dishes. Grab a seat on the veranda and breathe in the country air over a hot tea and a slice of ginger loaf with lemon drizzle.

Opening hours
Mon-Sat 9am-5.30pm (farm shop)
Wed-Sat 9am-4pm (café)

Pitney Farm Shop & Café, Glebe Farm, Woodbirds Hill Lane, Pitney TA10 9AP
WWW.PITNEYFARMSHOP.CO.UK   01458 253002

 203

PUB

# *The* WHITE HART INN

JUNCTION PODIMORE; 7 MINUTES

A handsome, 16th-century country pub at the edge of Somerton's octagonal market square, the White Hart is breezy yet cosy with whitewashed walls, stripped floorboards and patchwork tiles, log burners and antler chandeliers. A courtyard garden bursting with olive trees and lavender bushes stands beyond the conservatory dining room.

Broad skylights and sash windows fill the bar with light and in the evening locals often gather for a pint. Shadowy nooks with low-slung lights and chinks of stained glass provide enticing havens for kicking back and unwinding with a paper.

The menu, devised by ex-River Cottage chef Tom Blake, shows seasonal West Country cooking in its best light. Lunch and dinner includes delights such as falafel with baba ganoush, slow-cooked Creedy duck leg, grilled Cornish mackerel and wood-fired pizza. People rave about the breakfasts.

Opening hours
Mon-Sun 9am-11pm

The White Hart Inn, Market Place, Somerton TA11 7LX
WWW.WHITEHARTSOMERTON.COM  01458 272273

# *The* QUEENS ARMS

**JUNCTION SPARKFORD; 9 MINUTES**

A large blackboard outside advertising film nights and game supper evenings underscores the community feel of this friendly country pub. It's lively and welcoming, with a comfortable, eclectic style, from the boater-wearing bison head to faded rugs flung over flagstones and deep sofas. Muddy paws and sticky fingers are welcome, and rooms are fab should you want to stop the night. The rear courtyard looks over the fields, a good place to soak up the rays or start a walk.

Order a homemade pork pie in the bar and mix with pint-drinking regulars reading leisurely papers and friendly locals catching up on the gossip. Step through to the dining room for delicious, uncomplicated meals – seared wild sea trout, rosary ash goat cheese and roast peach salad, treacle-cured salmon and pineapple salsa or lamb and anchovy butter. Food provenance is 'measured in metres, not miles'; some ingredients come from the pub's own smallholding, some bartered with neighbours in exchange for meals.

**Opening hours**
Mon-Thurs 8am-11pm
Fri-Sat 8am-midnight
Sun 8am-10.30pm

The Queens Arms, Corton Denham DT9 4LR
**WWW.THEQUEENSARMS.COM   01963 220317**

# *Udder* FARM SHOP & CAFÉ

**JUNCTION BOURTON; 13 MINUTES**

You can do your weekly grocery round in Udder Farm Shop, which has a deli, fishmonger, gift, booze and freezer sections (farm produce, rather than crispy pancakes) and butchery – and that's the point. Farmers Jane and Brian Down opened their vast, modern shop to offer a low-mileage alternative to supermarkets and support British agriculture. Eyes peeled for special treats such as gooseberry vinegar and Cerne Abbas giant shortbread.

Breakfasts are farm-filling (full English, porridge with honey, poached egg on muffins); lunchtime cottage pies and burgers are generous and made with meat reared in the fields over yonder. Home-baked cakes, fluffy meringues and scones will tide you over the afternoon munchies. Children will be absorbed by the outdoor play park where parents can supervise from the patio while admiring views across Blackmore Vale. If you're in a rush you can grab hot drinks, pasties, frittata and slices of quiche to go from the deli.

**Opening hours**
Mon–Fri 9am–6pm
Sat 8.30am–6pm
Sun 9am–4pm

Udder Farm Shop & Café, Manor Farm, East Stour SP8 5LQ
**WWW.THEUDDERFARMSHOP.CO.UK   01747 838899**

# *At the* **CHAPEL**

© *Jon Hancock*

The town set love Bruton, an arty enclave of galleries, bohemian boutiques and antique shops tucked away in Somerset. At the Chapel is a converted 17th-century chapel, transformed with whitewashed, minimalist delicacy into a destination with contemporary bedrooms, restaurant, bar, bakery and winestore. The atmosphere is relaxed but buzzes all day with visitors and you're as well to drop in for a coffee and pastry, warm from the oven, as you are to explore the menu at lunch and dinner. Expect dishes like chargrilled Cornish sardines and ham hock with soft-boiled egg and pizzas (making full use of the bakery's wood-fired oven) at lunch and an enlarged menu at dinner. Puddings could include limoncello Eton mess or salted chocolate fondant, so save space.

Book a table in the calming dining room or spill out onto the south-facing terrace accented with the scent of jasmine. At weekends families arrive en masse to read papers, brunch and sip Bloody Marys after a country walk.

**Opening hours**
Mon–Sun 8am-9.30pm

At the Chapel, High Street, Bruton BA10 0AE
**WWW.ATTHECHAPEL.CO.UK   01749 814070**

# *Roth* BAR & GRILL

JUNCTION WINCANTON: 10 MINUTES

This well-heeled corner of Somerset is well-supplied with lovely eateries and cafés, but Roth Bar and Grill still manages to stand out. Sitting within the site of world-class art gallery Hauser & Wirth Somerset, it's vivacious and achingly cool. Roughly whitewashed walls are decorated with contemporary art and a bar made of scavenged materials.

Food is seasonal and simple, with a menu that changes daily. Highlights include the famous homemade merguez sausages, superfood salads, Lyme Bay scallops and Somerset cheeses. Coffee is organic and smooth; tea is served with a tranche of cakes in the afternoon.

Durslade is a working farm and supplies the restaurant with beef, pork and lamb after it's been dry-aged in the Himalayan salt-lined hanging room. It's on the pricey side, but ever so civilised.

Opening hours
Tues-Thurs 9am-5pm
Fri-Sat 9am-11.30pm
Sun 9am-5pm

Roth Bar & Grill, Durslade Farm, Dropping Lane, Bruton BA10 0NL
**WWW.ROTHBARANDGRILL.CO.UK   01749 814700**

PUB

A303

# *The* BULL INN, BRUTON

**JUNCTION B3081; 10 MINUTES**

You'll find The Bull Inn just outside the trendy Somerset town of Bruton. A handsome building with white stone walls and slate roof, it was recently taken over by the owners behind the stunning Hauser and Wirth gallery and Roth Bar & Grill. They've added to The Bull's traditional pub vibe (horse brass by the fire, a stuffed pheasant, blue and white farmhouse crockery, pewter tankards) with a delicious new menu.

Pub classics are given a new twist by the chef: slow-cooked shepherds pie, fennel-fried chicken with chips and coleslaw or local river trout with new potatoes, hazelnuts and a poached egg. This is not a gastropub, it's a local pub with great food, so you can still drop in for a ploughman's lunch or soup and a sandwich.

If you're just planning a fleeting stop, bar snacks of sausage rolls and skin-on chips will fill a hole. In summer you can take them outside to the large garden for a game of boules.

Opening hours
Weds-Sat 11am-11pm
Sun noon-4pm

The Bull Inn, Bruton, Hardway, Kingsettle Hill, Bruton BA10 0LN
**THEBULLINN-BRUTON.COM   01749 812200**

ATTRACTION

# STOURHEAD (NT)

**JUNCTION MERE (B3092); 2 MINUTES**

© National Trust Images/Arnbel de Serra

Wonderful gardens drew crowds to Stourhead when they first opened in 1740 (described as a living work of art) and they still do today. The Arcadian design centres around a lake and is overlaid with all manner of finery: temples, thatched cottage, lofty spires, bridges, cascades, mature shrubs and a child-pleasing grotto: come autumn it's a riot of colour. Dogs are welcome but access areas are restricted during summer – check the website.

Rest weary legs in the café where you can feast on honeyed-pork one-pot, sausage rolls, soups, bacon sandwiches and fresh cakes. Eggs come from the estate, many of the vegetables from the kitchen garden. Lunchboxes are available for kids and there's an great play area in the corner.

Before you leave, visit the Stourhead Farm Shop, which is blissfully oblivious to the passage of time: you can pick up wild roe deer venison, fresh pasties, smoked bacon, yoghurt, cheeses and local produce. Nibbling encouraged.

Opening hours
Mon-Sun 9am-5pm
please check website for seasonal variations

Stourhead (NT), High Street, Stourton BA12 6QF

**WWW.NATIONALTRUST.ORG.UK/STOURHEAD  01747 841152**

# *Visit* HILLBRUSH

**JUNCTION MERE (B3092); 1 MINUTE**

Not the most obvious of stops but this brush factory – yes, brush factory – is a fantastic place to pull in if you're travelling on the A303. Hillbrush has been making brushes in Mere since 1922 but it only recently opened a visitor centre and fantastic café alongside. The museum is colourful, tactile and surprisingly kid-friendly, and there are plenty of appealing gifts in the shop, from shaving kits to quirky hedgehog door stops. With the factory producing nearly 3,000 different products for export there's every brush you can imagine here.

In the bright, modern café, cakes from the Lavender Blue Bakery tempt you from beneath gleaming glass cloches. Busy tables are plied with steaming breakfasts, lunches and afternoon teas, from a selection of delicious burgers, salads and main dishes, including their popular beer battered fish and chunky chips with homemade tartar sauce, as well as special Sunday roast dinners and a bespoke themed evening menu every third Friday of the month. Dogs are welcome on the sunny, south-facing terrace.

**Opening hours**
Mon-Sat 8am-6pm
Friday 8am-9pm
Sun & Bank Hols 8am-4pm

Visit Hillbrush, Norwood Park, Mere BA12 6FE
**WWW.VISIT.HILLBRUSH.COM   01747 860494**

CAFÉ-RESTAURANT

# *Pythouse* KITCHEN GARDEN

**JUNCTION A350; 9 MINUTES**

An utterly idyllic spot in Wiltshire where you can malinger from dawn to sundown. The café and restaurant are centred around a sublime, 18th century walled garden where all manner of surprising produce grows, including kiwis, apricots and artichokes.

Inside you'll find a light-flooded conservatory which has a colourful shabby chic style, antique furniture intermingled with scuffed white walls, wood burning stoves, a corrugated iron bar, and bright, upcycled chairs. An old ladder hung above the bar is twisted with willow branches and foliage. In the summer the doors to the garden are thrown up, parasols popped and visitors invited to spill out into the scented calm of the terrace. There's a Wendy House and treasure trail, as well as runabout space, to keep little folk entertained. Slump onto a French day bed next to the fire in winter. Drop in for lunch to enjoy fire pit salmon, courgette and broad beans with cow's curd, homegrown summer tart and pulled shoulder of lamb. Save space for gooseberry fool and lemon verbena posset. Dinner is served on a Friday and Saturday and draws seasonal menu inspiration from what's growing in the beds.

Opening hours
Sun-Thurs 10am-4pm
Fri-Sat 10am-11pm

Pythouse Kitchen Garden, West Hatch, Tisbury SP3 6PA
**WWW.PYTHOUSEKITCHENGARDEN.CO.UK   01747 870444**

# *Howard's* **HOUSE**

JUNCTION COW DROVE; 6 MINUTES

Teffont Evias is a gorgeous Wiltshire backwater where the pace is unhurried, the river burbles and even the bus stops are thatched. It's in the gorgeous Nadder Valley so you can stride out into the fields before retreating to Howard's House, a serene country hotel open all day for restorative coffees and drinks, as well as for breakfast, lunch and dinner.

Chef Andy Britton cut his teeth with Albert Roux and his grade-A experience really shines through in the flawless dishes, as do the flavours cultivated in the veggie patch at the top of the garden.

The terrace is a canopied oasis surrounded by beautiful borders and a croquet lawn to the front. It's a beautiful spot for a long, cold drink in summer, serenaded by birds. You can also enjoy a tiered afternoon tea here or in the cosy sitting room inside, where the fire is stoked up on cooler days (pre-booking essential). It's a posher stop but a very worth-while one.

Opening hours
Mon-Sun 8am-9pm

Howard's House, Teffont Evias SP3 5RJ
**WWW.HOWARDSHOUSEHOTEL.CO.UK   01722 716392**

# *Bird & Carter* FARM SHOP & CAFÉ

JUNCTION WYLYE; 9 MINUTES

Once a stables, a carpentry workshop and then a percussion school, this long, slate-roofed farm building has had a varied history. Today it's metamorphosed into a super delicatessen and café: brick walls are painted cream, bunches of garlic hang from the rafters and a run of deli counters peddle smoked fish, Wiltshire ham, antipasti and some of the best scotch eggs around. Ask nicely and smiley owner Joff will slice and smear them with mustard. Shelves are loaded with goodies and groceries, from spelt flour to fresh pasta, jars of preserves and crocks of sweeties.

Café seating is found at the far end, a room with a bank of antique drawers, wood-burner and large windows looking out to the paddocks. There are plenty of high chairs and a surplus of toys and books for little ones. The doors are thrown open at breakfast, serving eggs, locally reared bacon and sausages. Sandwiches, quiches and pies are tasty, cakes temptingly moist – such as chocolate Guinness, ginger or lemon meringue.

Opening hours
Mon-Sat 8.30am-5.30pm
Sun 10am-4pm

Bird & Carter Farm Shop & Café, Chilhampton Farm, Warminster Rd, Wilton SP2 0AB
**WWW.BIRDANDCARTER.CO.UK   01722 744177**

# *The* BOOT INN

**JUNCTION BERWICK ST JAMES; 1 MINUTE**

A crackling fire, cascading hanging baskets and cosy nooks: The Boot is the sort of charismatic pub where help-yourself roasties are left on the bar on a Sunday afternoon. It's housed in a 17th-century, ivy-dressed building in the handsome village of Berwick St James, itself the kind of village where home-grown veg and honesty boxes stand by front walls.

Travellers, many fresh from visits to Stonehenge up the road, rub shoulders with ale-drinking locals and day-tripping families. Children fly out into the lawned beer garden where there are picnic benches for al fresco dining and plenty of space for spontaneous games.

Lunches of stilton hummus, platters of home-smoked meats or gin-cured salmon are followed by tasty dinners of rabbit leg casserole, lamb chops and potato salad with Cornish lemon sole and cockles. Save space for one of Giles's lip-smacking desserts, perhaps rhubarb fool with pink peppercorn shortbread or chocolate ale cake.

Opening hours
Mon 6pm-8pm
Tues–Sat Noon-3pm, 6pm-11pm
Sun Noon-3pm, 7pm-10.30pm

The Boot Inn, High Street, Berwick St James SP3 4TN
**WWW.THEBOOT.PUB   01722 790243**

# *Cholderton* FARM SHOP & CAFÉ

JUNCTION A338; 1 MINUTE

You'll breakfast like a king at Cholderton Farm, a convenient halfway point between the south west and London. It's a working farm so chickens and cockerels scratch around in the yard and tractors park up outside the beautiful flint and red-brick farm shop.

The homely welcome in the café more than makes up for the simple surroundings, not to mention the grade-A bacon butties. Shelves ring the room, laden with store cupboard essentials – bread, vegetables, chutneys – and the fridges are full of free-range meat, local cheese and a range of deli treats that will more than supply you for your destination.

The coffee is barista standards and staff deliver plates of crisp jacket potatoes, amply filled toasties, huge ploughmans' and homemade quiches to tables scattered about inside. To get a real taste of the country, take a picnic table in the covered barn outside or a parasoled one on sunny days.

Opening hours
Tues-Sat 9am-4.30pm
Sun 10am-4pm

Cholderton Farm Shop & Café, Tidworth Rd, Cholderton SP4 0DR
**WWW.CHOLDERTONFARMSHOP.CO.UK   01980 629894**

# *The* TEA COSY

**JUNCTION A343 ANDOVER: 11 MINUTES**

A friendly welcome awaits you in this village tearoom, once you have located it behind the car showroom and convenience store. Retro tables and chairs are painted in bright hues, a sofa area invites the weary to put their feet up. Cheery staff serve tables with a constant stream of light bites, afternoon teas and simple lunches. Seasonal salads, breakfast favourites and selection of sandwiches and paninis, are all on the menu along with homemade milkshakes, made from clotted cream ice cream. There is also a children's menu for smaller guests.

But it is the cakes that have people queuing up here, particularly on a Friday when the 'cake of the week' is revealed. Friday or not, there is always a counter full of creative cakes to tempt you, best washed down with one of the 24 loose leaf teas served in teapots with hand knitted novelty tea cosies. Customers can also indulge in a glass of prosecco or one of The Tea Cosy's specialty, tea-infused gins.

**Opening hours**
Wed-Sun 9.30am-5pm

The Tea Cosy, The Dene, Hurstbourne Tarrant SP11 0AS
**WWW.THETEACOSYHAMPSHIRE.COM   01264 736644**

# *Newlyn's* FARM SHOP & CAFÉ

**JUNCTION 5; 2 MINUTES**

Skirt round a lush field, past the shack selling freshly laid eggs via an honesty box, down a concrete farm track and you'll see the large red-roofed barns of Newlyn's Farm. Friendly Roger the butcher prepares the meat that the family have been producing here (four miles down the road, in fact) for four generations, alongside a heaving deli counter of olives, chicken liver pâté, fresh loaves, Hampshire cheese and fine pressed oils. The spacious farm shop sells locally grown produce and a covetable range of foodie gifts.

The large, bright café with picture windows leads onto a patio terrace where you can breakfast on home-cured bacon with soft poached egg, or on rolled porridge oats with cream, fruit and Hampshire honey washed down with freshly squeezed juice. For lunch, pick from burgers, triple-stacked sandwiches and piggy platters. Cookery courses show you how to use the farm's produce to best advantage throughout the seasons; if you'd rather someone else do the work, you'll find dinner-party worthy ready meals using the farm's ingredients in the freezer section.

Opening hours
Mon-Fri 8am-6pm
Sat 8am-4pm
Sun 9am-noon

Newlyn's Farm Shop & Café, Lodge Farm, North Warnborough RG29 1HA
**WWW.NEWLYNS.COM   01256 704128**

# *Courtyard* **CAFÉ**

**JUNCTION 5: 8 MINUTES**

Tucked away at the back of an antiques shop in the historic village of Hartley Wintney, the Courtyard Cafe is a hidden haven serving fresh, high-quality food made with the best local ingredients. A run of bi-fold doors in the garden room crumple back to lead onto a flourishing courtyard where the fountain trickles and birds nest. A gate leads out to the village cricket green where owner Laura recommends taking a turn with restless babes to lull them to sleep.

Grab a newspaper and enjoy a slice of the chef's artful cakes (think ombre, gluten-free blueberry and vanilla cake decorated with fresh flowers) or treat yourself to a healthy breakfast of homemade granola or waffles with berries.

Though the lunch menu changes regularly according to the season, you can expect such delights as parmesan and truffle gnocchi, saffron trout fillet or well-stuffed sandwiches, and wash it down with a civilised glass of wine. A real gourmet stop.

Opening hours
Mon-Sat 9am-5pm
Sun 10am-4pm

Courtyard Café, 63 High Street, Hartley Wintney RG27 8NY
**WWW.COURTYARDCAFE.COM  01525 842616**

CAFÉ

# *The Hobo.Co* **IN THE SHED**

### JUNCTION 5; 10 MINUTES

Tucked in a peaceful corner of the award-winning Hortus Loci plant centre, the humble Hobo in the Shed creates some serious magic. Seasonal salads, homemade soups, toasted paninis, delicately flavoured cakes and hearty hot meals emerge from the serving hatch. Expertly made coffee and homemade soft drinks too – lemonade in summer and spiced winter berry juice in winter. Don't miss the courgette, lime and pistachio cake or the famous gluten-free triple chocolate brownies.

Comfy chairs, magazines and hanging seats on the cosy veranda offer an indulgent pause enveloped by blooming boughs and perfumed plants. There's even a bureau nook – complete with WiFi and antique books – should you want to set up office for an hour or so. In cooler months, heaters, blankets and hot water bottles are provided to keep you toasty in the fresh air.

Opening hours
Mon–Sat 9am–5pm
Sun 10am–4pm

The Hobo.Co in the Shed, Hortus Loci, Hound Green, Hook  RG27 8LQ
**WWW.THEHOBO.CO  07894 150290**

# *The* COURTYARD

**JUNCTION 3; 8 MINUTES**

The Courtyard is a new venture for Ashley and Ben, who have created a chic and relaxing bistro. Drawing on their extensive experience they've devised a menu that has something to suit all with hearty salads, light bites and soup as well as daily-changing cakes and sweet treats and freshly-made smoothies and baguettes. The Signature Fries and Salt Beef Ciabatta are the heroes of the menu and a must for the hungry. There are plenty of vegetarian, vegan and gluten free options – the gluten-free walnut brownies are divine!

The Courtyard is decorated with beautiful plants inside and out with plenty of seating in the garden for sunny days; well behaved dogs are always welcome too. Just outside the London Orbital motorway, this is a perfect place to pause and soak up village life or take a moment for yourself before heading into the city. Parking is available just behind the bistro, with Ascot and Windsor Great Park nearby if you need to fill your lungs with fresh air and stretch your legs before your onward journey.

Opening hours
Mon-Sat 8am-5pm

The Courtyard, I Chapmans Courtyard, Sunninghill SL5 9NF
**WWW.THECOURTYARDSUNNINGHILL.CO.UK  01344 627687**

# The ☞

# A30 & A38

*Moors, beaches &*
*lashings of clotted cream*

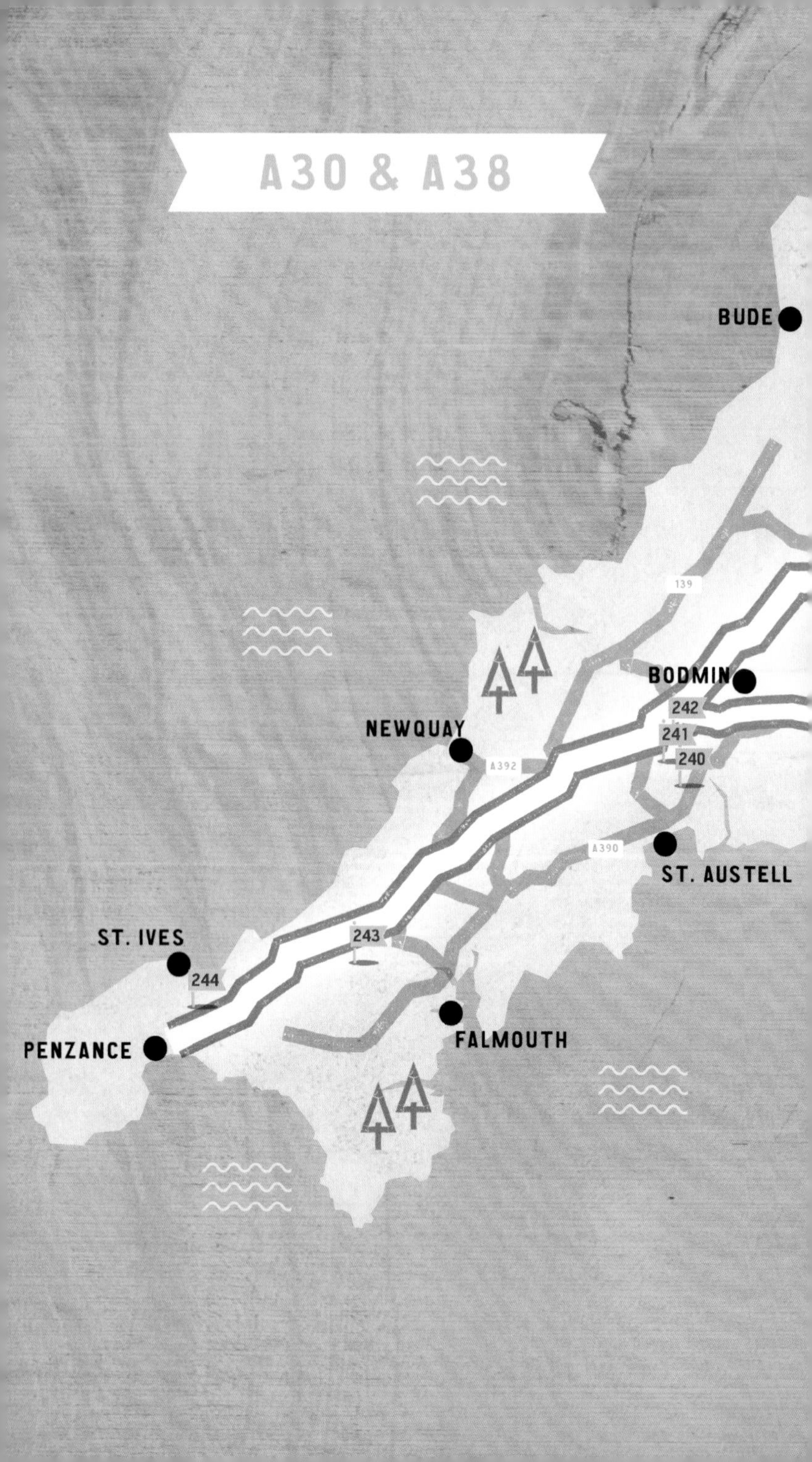

A30 & A38

BUDE

139

BODMIN

242
241
240

NEWQUAY

A392

ST. AUSTELL

A390

ST. IVES

243

244

PENZANCE

FALMOUTH

**OKEHAMPTON**

**EXETER**

A 386

246

245

232

233

DARTMOOR
NATIONAL
PARK

234

235

237

TORQUAY

A380

247

226 227

229
228

230

M5

239

238

PLYMOUTH

SALCOMBE

| | | | |
|---|---|---|
| **226** The Potting Shed, Olives Et Al | **233** Ullacombe Farm | **241** Lanhydrock (NT) |
| **227** Martyrs Inn | **234** Riverford Field Kitchen | **242** Woods Café |
| **228** River Cottage Canteen | **235** The Almond Thief | **243** Miss Molly's Tea Rooms |
| **229** Millers Farm Shop | **237** The Curator Café & Kitchen | **244** Scarlet Wines |
| **230** The Coffee Factory | **238** Saltram (NT) | **245** Lifton Farm Shop |
| **231** The Seven Stars | **239** Heskyn Mill Restaurant | **246** Hog & Hedge |
| **232** The Ridge | **240** Duchy of Cornwall Nursery | **247** Quicke's |

# *The Potting Shed,* OLIVES ET AL

JUNCTION:A37; 1 MINUTE

Just seconds from the main road this cosy deli is a proper treat. It's located in the intriguing town of Poundbury, an experimental development built on Duchy of Cornwall land. The architects' aim was to combat post-war suburban sprawl and create a town with real character. They certainly succeeded.

Olives Et Al sits on the edge of the beautiful central square. The architectural detail of the streets transports you to the continent – as do the contents and decor of the deli and café. The menu is a homage to the Mediterranean, often with a modern twist, such as fig and goats cheese tart served with pomegranate molasses or feta, aubergine and honey pie. The coffee is the 'the best in Poundbury' according to locals and if the smell as you enter is anything to go by, they're right. The deli counter will provide anything you need for a quick pit stop, and you can take away your coffee too. Parking is plentiful outside on the square

Opening hours
Mon-Fri 8.30am-5pm

The Potting Shed, Olives et Al, 81 Poundbury Farm Way, Poundbury DT1 3RT
**WWW.OLIVESETAL.CO.UK    01305 216788**

# *The Martyrs* INN

**JUNCTION: AFFPUDDLE ; 2 MINUTES**

At the heart of a rural community this characterful pub is just a stone's throw from the A35. Tolpuddle is a picturesque village steeped in history. The namesakes of this charming inn – the Tolpuddle Martyrs – were arrested in 1833 for swearing an oath to a 'secret workers' society', which many consider to be the early sketches of a trade union.

Inside it's modern and inviting with comfy chairs, long bars and dining areas surrounding brickwork chimney breasts. There's chatter from locals and friendly staff to greet you. For food, it's pub classics all the way, with a pinch of local influence. The Dorset mushroom risotto, steak and ale pie or Dorset lamb hot-pot won't disappoint. If you need to wear off your meal, take a stroll through the village where references to the martyrs' history can be found in every direction. If you don't fancy that and the weather prevails, there's plenty of seating out the front of the pub, where you can observe the comings and goings of the thatched village.

Opening hours
Sun-Thurs 11am-11pm
Fri-Sat 11am-midnight

The Martyrs Inn, 49 Main Rd, Tolpuddle DT2 7ES
**WWW.THEMARTYRSINN.CO.UK  01305 848249**

CAFÉ

# *River Cottage* CANTEEN

JUNCTION: A358: 3 MINUTES

Waste warriors and organic crusaders will need no introduction to Hugh Fearnley-Whittingstall's River Cottage Canteen in Axminster. It's just down the road from the famous River Cottage HQ, and three minutes off the A35, the trunk road across the English Riviera.

Hugh spotted an opportunity in the high street's shuttered pub and turned it into an informal, dog-friendly eatery. Light spills from the ceiling lantern into industrial-edged dining room at the back, once the town's dance hall; floorboards are stripped; tables scrubbed and set with fresh flowers and linen napkins. A well-stocked deli counter runs the length of the front room, stacked with a host of picnic temptations (show your meal receipt to get 10% off), while locals regularly convene for a natter and languorous coffee.

The food is wholesome and inventive – breakfast, lunch and dinner served with a smile by staff in smart aprons. Very much worth any extra minutes on your journey.

Opening hours
Mon-Sat 9am-9pm
Sun 9am-4pm

River Cottage Canteen, Trinity Square, Axminster EX13 5AN
**WWW.RIVERCOTTAGE.NET/RESTAURANTS/AXMINSTER 01297 631715**

# *Millers* **FARM SHOP**

JUNCTION: KILMINGTON; 0 MINUTES

A family run farm shop brushing the A35, Millers has a snug café and enough country fayre to fill your larder with flavour. Malcolm and his family have been serving hungry travellers and locals for more than 30 years. The Teapot Café is a charming timber nook, flooded with daylight and instantly inviting. It has a selection of home-made cakes, small treats and light, seasonal dishes. If it's a long journey then a proper full English might be in order or a sausage buttie, all sourced locally, of course; there's freshly ground coffee and traditional Devon cream tea if you just want a pit stop.

The shop is a mine of farming delights – earthy veggies, spring greens, wonky veg that's full of flavour and no plastic in sight. It's also full of tasty French produce as Malcolm and wife Angela travel to France each week to scour the markets for the country's best food and drink. If you fancy a tipple at the end of your journey, don't leave before browsing the impressive wine selection.

**Opening hours**
Mon-Sat 7.30am-6pm (9am-5pm café)
Sun 8am-1pm (9am-1pm café – seasonal)

Millers Farm Shop, Gammons Hill, Axminster EX13 7RA
**WWW.MILLERSFARMSHOP.CO.UK   01297 35290**

229

CAFÉ

# *The Coffee* **FACTORY**

JUNCTION: SHUTE; 4 MINUTES

An unsuspecting country lane leads you to this truly fortuitous find: a coffee lover's paradise in the middle of the countryside, over the yard from the Lyme Bay Winery. The smell of freshly ground beans guides you in from the forecourt to find a vibrant, modern café at the heart of this artisan factory.

Coffee lovers nationwide have roasted beans despatched from here to their doorstep, such is their renowned quality. Inside, the traditional mechanics are laid bare and the industrial chic offers a clear view of how much care and attention goes into roasting every bean. For food it's just light bites, but a selection of delectable cakes and sweet treats from the Exploding Bakery nearby – including apricot flapjacks, carrot cake and salted caramel brownies – will leave you smiling. There's plenty of parking directly outside and after tasting one of these artisan coffees you're sure to be leaving with a bag of very freshly roasted beans.

Opening hours
Mon-Fri 10am-3.30pm

The Coffee Factory, Unit 3 Samurai Buildings, Seaton Junction, Axminster EX13 7PW
**THECOFFEEFACTORY.CO.UK   01297 551259**

# *The* SEVEN STARS

**JUNCTION: KENNFORD; 3 MINUTES**

You'll wish the Seven Stars was your local. Good ales, farmhouse cider, and tasty food at a reasonable price. Natives chatter at the bar and shoot pool, whilst couples and families fill the dining-room tables. A cinema club and weekly quiz reinforce community links and open-door policy. The interior is quirky-rustic: leather chesterfield next to the log-burner, a table fashioned from an old pub mirror, metro tiles behind the bar and a grandfather clock in the corner. At the back there's a wonderful secret garden with sheltered wooden booths, deck chairs and AstroTurf lawn.

Food is a couple of notches up from pub grub, brought forth from the kitchen by smiley staff: perhaps a hand-pressed burger, pan-fried fillet of hake with crispy pancetta, wild venison with gratin potatoes and celeriac purée, or goats cheese, beetroot and spinach risotto, rounded off with fruit crumble or crème brûlée. Pizzas are some of the best (and biggest!) in Exeter and are available all day to eat in or takeaway.

Opening hours
Mon 3pm-1pm
Tues-Thurs noon-11pm
Fri-Sat noon–midnight (Sun 10.30pm)

The Seven Stars, Kennford EX6 7TR
**WWW.SEVENSTARSKENNFORD.CO.UK   01392 834887**

CAFÉ

# *The* RIDGE

JUNCTION: HALDON FOREST; 3 MINUTES

There's no more idyllic location for a pit-stop. Haldon Forest offers spectacular views across the glorious Devonshire countryside with Dartmoor to the west and the Exe Estuary to the east.

The Ridge Cafe is quaint and calming. Décor is wood-heavy (to reflect its surroundings), rustic and charming. There's enough outdoor seating to catch some rays, and as Haldon is high above sea-level, a light dusting of snow can be seen on crisp winter mornings.

Options for lunch change regularly and include fresh salmon salad, proper cheesy nachos and pork and apple sauce rolls. Home-baked cakes are likely to tempt you, alongside the amazing flapjacks and brownies. The coffee is second to none and service always with a smile. The forest paths are buzzing with energy: this a renowned spot for cycling and a regular haunt for four-legged friends. If you're lucky you may spot the elusive green woodpecker.

Opening hours
Mon-Fri 10am-5pm
Sat-Sun 9.30am-5pm

The Ridge, Bullers Hill, Kennford EX6 7XR

**WWW.FORESTRY.GOV.UK/HALDONFORESTPARK   01392 833268**

# *Ullacombe* FARM

**JUNCTION: COLDEAST; 8 MINUTES**

Carved into the hillside this quaint farm shop and café will fill your lungs with Dartmoor air. The décor is reminiscent of a log cabin in the mountains, just as cosy but without the jetlag. Outdoor seating is plentiful, accompanied by the rural soundtrack of sheep gently bleating, and there's a secure play area for little guests to run around.

Classics fill the lunch menu and always use locally sourced meats. The homemade 'Barn Burger' reliably pulls in locals and the roasted chili salmon is a tasty alternative if you fancy something lighter. Cream teas are all homemade and the coffee will revive you. If you're lucky enough to be passing on Sunday, the roasts are something of a local secret and non-drivers can even wash their spuds down with a glass of Prosecco. Stock up on fantastic local produce in the shop and, should you have the time, drive a little further to Haytor just up the road: the famous granite outcrop offers unrivalled views of South Devon.

Opening hours
Mon-Sun 8.30am-5pm

Ullacombe Farm, Haytor Road, Bovey Tracey TQ13 9LL
**WWW.ULLACOMBEFARM.CO.UK   01364 661341**

RESTAURANT
# *Riverford* **FIELD KITCHEN**

### JUNCTION: BUCKFASTLEIGH; 6 MINUTES

The Riverford field kitchen is a cornucopia of delights based on the family's organic farm, so you can be assured that the food will be free of any contaminants. There's just one sitting (lunch every day and supper most), tables are shared and the whole restaurant eats at the same time. The food is fresh from the fields, the atmosphere light-hearted and convivial, and the cooking superb. Vegetables are the main focus here, served in all manner of creative guises and varied daily depending on what's in season. Portions are generous and if you've got room, puddings are every bit as delicious as the mains.

Make time, if you can, for a field to fork farm tour. It will certainly work up an appetite for lunch! Check the website for dates. If there's no tour when you visit, borrow some wellies and roam the fields with a free map and MP3 audio guide – narrated by Riverford's founder, Guy Singh-Watson. People come from far and wide to eat here and it's worth every drop of fuel.

Opening hours
Every day for lunch, most days for supper.
Lunch 12.30pm, Supper 7pm
Booking essential. Check availability online

Riverford Field Kitchen, Wash Farm, Buckfastleigh TQ11 0JU
**WWW.THERIVERFORDFIELDKITCHEN.CO.UK   01803 762074**

# *The* **ALMOND THIEF**

JUNCTION: SOUTH BRENT; 12 MINUTES

Incongruously located on a small industrial estate, the Almond Thief has earned a fearsome reputation for its quality baked goods. There's no cutting corners here, only traditional techniques and the finest ingredients. Watch the bakers at work as you sup a cuppa. The café is starkly minimalist and on-trend, with wooden trestle tables and benches, vintage chairs, polished concrete floors and holly boughs decorating the walls. There's a small play corner for kids.

The menu is small, made from scratch and perfectly formed. Bread features prominently, naturally: perhaps Bob's biodynamic poached eggs on toast served with home-smoked salmon, house granola with raspberry compote and yoghurt, leek and goat's cheese frittata, or red lentil, lemon and ginger soup. Coffee is great and accompanied by princely Semla buns, flakey almond slices and caramelised egg custard tarts.

Don't, whatever you do, forget to pick up a loaf on your way out.

Opening hours
Mon-Sat 9.30am-4pm

The Almond Thief, Unit 3/4 Webber's Yard, Dartington TQ9 6JY
**WWW.THEALMONDTHIEF.COM    01803 411290**

# Sawday's

'More than a bed
for the night…'

Britain
France
Ireland
Italy
Portugal
Spain

www.sawdays.co.uk

Self-Catering | B&B | Hotel | Pub | Treehouses, Cabins, Yurts & More

# *The Curator* CAFÉ & KITCHEN

**JUNCTION: BUCKFASTLEIGH; 14 MINUTES**

Laid out over two floors, adorned with vintage surfboards, custom cycles, prints and memorabilia for sale, The Curator is the perfect place to start a visit to the unique town of Totnes.

The café sits on the pavement level with outside seating and serves a range of woodroasted coffee beans, speciality teas and a selection of sandwiches and pastries. Focaccia, pizza and other Italian speciality breads and cakes are all prepared in an extension of The Curator just around the corner in Flour & Rice (12 Ticklemore Street).

Above the coffee shop is The Curator Kitchen, a lovely light modern Osteria with an open kitchen, serving locally sourced food with Italian flavours. Fresh pasta, small plates and brunch are served all day and evening meals are exceptional. Organic and bio-dynamic wines are imported directly from small vineyards in Italy, on the menu next to local craft beers.

Opening hours
Mon 7.30am-6pm
Tues-Fri 7.30am-9.15pm
Sat 9am-9.15pm (Sun 5pm)

The Curator Café & Kitchen, 2 The Plains, Totnes TQ9 5DR
**WWW.ITALIANFOODHEROES.COM  01803 865570**

ATTRACTION
# SALTRAM (NT)

JUNCTION: MARSH MILLS; 8 MINUTES

With glorious views over the Plym Estuary, this beautiful Georgian estate is a popular spot. During its rich history, it's been the choice of residence for both Plymouth's Mayor and the town's local MP. Arrive early and bag a seat by the pond to relax and watch the ducks with a cuppa whilst children revel in the play park.

The main café is elegant, bright and spacious; modern with a refined Georgian flavour. It's mostly light bites for lunch, seasonal and wholesome: perhaps a pea pesto and mozzarella panini or smoked mackerel and beetroot salad. The Chapel Tea-Room is hidden in the extensive gardens, a traditional tea room offering artisan loose leaf teas (served in dainty bone china), cakes and sandwiches. Try the cheese tea, a savoury twist on its cream cousin with cheese scone, cheese and chutney. Coffee and snacks can be taken away if you'd like to make the most of the estuary and woodlands, which lead down to the river. They play host to a vast array of wildlife to spy. Spotting a heron is a treat, and even better with an award-winning local ice cream in hand.

Opening hours
Mon-Sun 10am-5pm
Check website for seasonal variations

Saltram (NT), Plymouth PL7 1UH
**WWW.NATIONALTRUST.ORG.UK/SALTRAM  01752 333500**

# *Heskyn Mill* RESTAURANT

**JUNCTION: ST GERMANS; 1 MINUTE**

Atmospheric grade-II*-listed Heskyn Mill has to be a part of your trip to Cornwall, not just for the fabulous food on offer, but for the unique and fascinating gear workings of the original flour mill in the restaurant. These delightful relics last turned in the 1960s to grind corn for the Port Eliot Estate. Though just off the A38 it's hidden from view and so, undeservedly, is only frequented by those in the know or by those with eagle eyes to spot the tiny roadside sign.

Owners John and Ann (your maitre d' and chef) are ardent local food supporters. They are exacting about their ingredients, so most of them come from within the county – fish from West Country harbours, outdoor-reared meat and poultry from Cornish farms, vegetables from local gardens, herbs from hedgerows – to form a small menu of taste-focused dishes: perhaps foraged mushrooms on toast, Cornish sardine fillets, duck breast with red and blackcurrants, dressed crab or slow-cooked ox cheek. The zesty lemon posset is our tip for dessert.

Opening hours
Tues-Sat noon-2pm, 6pm-8.30pm
Sun noon-2pm

Heskyn Mill Restaurant, Tideford PL12 5BG
**WWW.HESKYN-MILL.CO.UK   01752 852127**

GARDEN CENTRE

# *Duchy of Cornwall* NURSERY

JUNCTION: TURFDOWN ROAD; 9 MINUTES

A plant lover's paradise. The Duchy of Cornwall Nursery has nested in a former slate quarry, a heavenly sanctum of tumbling flowers and sweeping views over the Fowey valley. Trail through the plants before heading to the café where you can slump into a sofa by the log burner and leaf through gardening books and newspapers at your leisure. Staff are attentive and friendly; breakfasts are made with the freshest ingredients – most from within the county limit – and washed down with free tea and coffee refills.

Enjoy the views to Restormel Castle from the terrace as you lunch on homemade bread, filled sandwiches, salads from the garden or heartier dishes – slow cooked pork belly, venison burgers, lemon sole. Cakes are expertly baked and afternoon teas are proper Cornish, piled with jam and daubed with clotted cream. There's a footpath linking the nursery to the castle if you fancy a leg stretch afterwards and if you can resist the lure of the fabulous garden and gift shop (Italian soaps, local ceramics, traditional toys), you're stronger than us.

Opening hours
Mon-Sat 9am-4.30pm
Suns & Bank Hols 10am-4.30pm

Duchy of Cornwall Nursery, Cott Rd, Lostwithiel PL22 0HW
**WWW.DUCHYOFCORNWALLNURSERY.CO.UK  01208 872668**

# LANHYDROCK (NT)

JUNCTION: BODMIN; 4 MINUTES

The grounds at Lanhydrock are looped with bike trails of varying degrees of difficulty, the immaculate lawns perfect for picnics, and the paused-in-time house packed with interesting artefacts and quirky collections. The late Victorian country estate that has been generously turned over to the public and being so wonderfully intact, it gives a vivid insight into the opulent, luxurious lives of a wealthy family. Today's atmosphere is probably not much changed: fun and adventure outside the house; formality and grandeur within.

There is a relaxed café in the former stable block that is buzzing and family-friendly, and a more formal tea room in the old servant's hall. The café menu is well-rounded, featuring local seasonal food and a balanced mix of 'wholesome' and 'treat' meals and snacks. Homemade burgers are a speciality and take-away lunch bags are available for kids.

Dogs are allowed in the grounds, but not the house.

---

Opening hours
Mon-Sun 10am-5pm
Check website for seasonal opening hours

Lanhydrock (NT), Bodmin PL30 5AD
**WWW.NATIONALTRUST.ORG.UK/LANHYDROCK   01208 265950**

CAFÉ

# *Woods* CAFÉ

**JUNCTION: BODMIN BYPASS: 4 MINUTES**

You'd be forgiven for looking for Hansel and Gretel as you arrive at this cottage café deep in 650 acres of Cardinham Woods. It's a cutesy stone cottage with open fire in winter and parasoled picnic benches in summer. Food and drinks are served on vintage crockery and floral curtains frame the windows.

It's a foodie's delight. Organic and locally sourced ingredients are rustled up into inventive dishes, such as homemade granola and compote, garlic mushroom and brie sandwiches, leek fritters with a herby yoghurt dip, sausage sandwiches with homemade onion marmalade and lip-smacking sausage rolls. Cakes and scones are baked every day by Lara (carrot with orange cream cheese icing and lemon berry drizzle are the most popular) are served with dollops of clotted cream and a steaming cup of locally roasted Origin coffee or Cornish Tregothnan tea. There are special carved posts for dog leads and the woodland trails are perfect for leg stretching once little people have exhausted the adventure play area.

Opening hours
Mon-Sun 10am-4.30pm

Woods Café, Cardinham Woods, Bodmin PL30 4AL
**WWW.WOODSCAFECORNWALL.CO.UK  01208 78111**

# *Miss Molly's* **TEA ROOMS**

JUNCTION: TOLVADON; 4 MINUTES

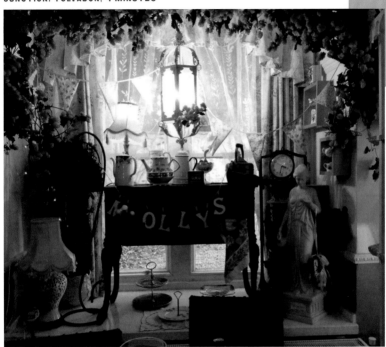

An unusual entrance leads through a courtyard full of bric-a-brac and junk shop treasures into a quaint, vintage tea room, where, tucked away in the mine counting house, Miss Molly's serves honest food made in the kitchen from scratch.

The cake is phenomenal, as are the freshly cooked bacon sarnies. Lunch on crusty sandwiches, cheese toasties, jacket potatoes and paninis. Indulge in a caramel flapjack or toasted teacake in the afternoon. Tea is served in delicate vintage cups with finger sandwiches, home-baked cakes, savouries and fruit, and scones with clotted cream – this, after all, is the scone's motherland.

Look out for seasonal, homemade additions (such as elderflower cordial in late spring )and the friendly in-house cat who is prone to commandeering laps. Dogs are welcome in the special dog area, which even has a special 'à la bark' menu of healthy canine treats. Browse the second-hand rooms before you leave to pick up your next upcycling project.

**Opening hours**
Mon-Sat 9am-5.30pm
Sun 10am-4.30pm

Miss Molly's Tea Rooms, The Old College, Dolcoath Rd, Camborne TR14 8RR
**WWW.MISSMOLLYSTEAROOM.CO.UK   01209 718196**

CAFÉ-DELI

# *Scarlet* WINES

**JUNCTION: ST ERTH ROUNDABOUT; 1 MINUTE**

An emporium of enticing food and wine, Scarlet Wines makes a fantastic pit stop when Cornwall's crowds get too much. Sitting above the Hayle Estuary (a haven for bird life and good for a stroll), this low stone barn is a popular destination for locals and tourists alike, drawn to the restaurant and amazing deli. You can find delicacies from Cornwall, Italy and Spain: smoked fish from Tregida Smokehouse, apple preserve from the Cornish Bee Farm, Tuscan olive oil, Spanish almond turron.

The cosy, stove-warmed restaurant is open for breakfast, lunch and dinner. Diners sit at sheepskin-covered benches inside or sunny tables outside and are plied with mouth-watering dishes – cinnamon toast or baked eggs with feta and chorizo for breakfast, warm beetroot salad or fresh seafood for lunch, baked cod with lentils and mezze platters for dinner. There are plenty of options for vegans and the coffee is excellent. Limited parking is available outside and dogs are welcome. Don't leave without browsing the wine shop for an arrival tipple.

Opening hours
Mon-Sun Breakfast 9am-11.30am
Lunch noon-3pm
Dinner 5.30pm-late

Scarlet Wines, The Old Forge, Griggs Quay, Hayle TR27 6JG
**WWW.SCARLET-WINES.CO.UK   01736 753696**

# *Lifton* FARM SHOP

**JUNCTION: LIFTON; 1 MINUTE**

A stop at Lifton Farm Shop makes any traffic jam on the way to Cornwall bearable. Swing in and let your nose lead you to the café, where the smell of freshly baked bread will draw you in.

The Mounce family started farming here more than 20 years ago with just a plot of strawberries: now their fields supply almost everything the kitchen needs for the farmhouse menu – meat, eggs, fruit and veg, often muddy from the field. It makes for excellent breakfasts and delicious cream teas, served with clotted cream and the farm's own strawberry jam. 'The scones would have made Mary Berry cry,' reported one customer.

Recreate it yourself at home by raiding the farm shop next door, which is stocked with irresistible goodies from home-reared beef and lamb to apple juice from the orchard, home-baked quiches, pies, hams and outrageously good ice cream made with the farm's soft fruit. Parking is plentiful and there are bowls of water for dogs on the patio by the lawn.

Opening hours
Mon-Sat 8am-6pm (5.30pm winter)
Sun 8am-5.30pm (5pm winter)
Restaurant closes half an hour earlier

Lifton Farm Shop, Lifton PL16 0DE
**WWW.LIFTONFARMSHOP.CO.UK   01566 784605**

One of the new wave of services, the Hog and Hedge is a breath of fresh air. Swing off the A30 on your way to or from Cornwall, and you'll be restored by freshly cooked food, organic teas and excellent coffee, with views over the Devonshire fields. Trestle tables stand in the middle of the dining room, heaving with help-yourself cakes and goodies. Red rugs are slung over polished concrete floors and scattered with stylishly mismatched tables; there are posh toiletries in the loos and charging points for mobiles and tablets.

Prices are reasonable and food includes full English breakfast, bacon rolls, porridge, soups, toasties and ploughman's made with the best West Country ingredients. Nothing is fried, so don't expect chips, but everything is delicious.

The kids will love the play area with Wendy house and toys, and there's a dedicated food station for little people, with plastic cups and plates, colouring sheets, a microwave and bottle warmer.

Opening hours
Mon-Sun 7am–7.30pm

Hog & Hedge, Whiddon Down Services EX20 2QT
**WWW.HOGANDHEDGE.CO.UK   01647 213588**

# QUICKE'S

JUNCTION: A377; 15 MINUTES

Listen out for skylarks when you visit, as Home Farm's sensitively tended 1,500 acres are a haven for wildlife, as well as home to Quicke'sartisan cheddar cheese. The team here subscribe to the old methods: grass-fed happy cows, heritage starters, cloth-binding and plenty of time to mature. Fourteen generations of the Quicke family have farmed this idyllic corner of Devon and Mary is the current guardian. Her passion for cheesemaking has seen her set up the Academy of Cheese and sometimes earnt her the nickname 'the Queen of Cheddar'. But the proof is in the eating, and this is tangy perfection.

Raid the farm shop shelves for fresh bread, milk, eggs, cider and superb cheeses, from here and across the West Country. The former café is not currently open, but the shop serves great coffee to take away. The website has terrific recipes (not all cheesy) if you're looking for inspiration for dinner at your destination, and there are wonderful trails around the farm if you're not in a hurry.

Opening hours
Mon-Sat 9am-5pm

Quicke's, Home Farm, Newton St Cyres EX5 5AY
WWW.QUICKES.CO.UK   01392 851222

The

# M5

Cotswolds, Quantocks
Malverns, Mendips & more

# M5 NORTH

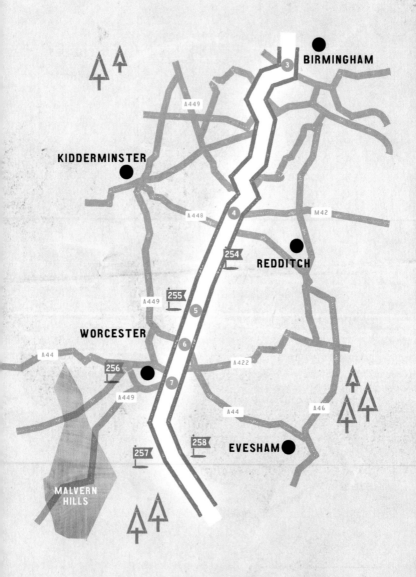

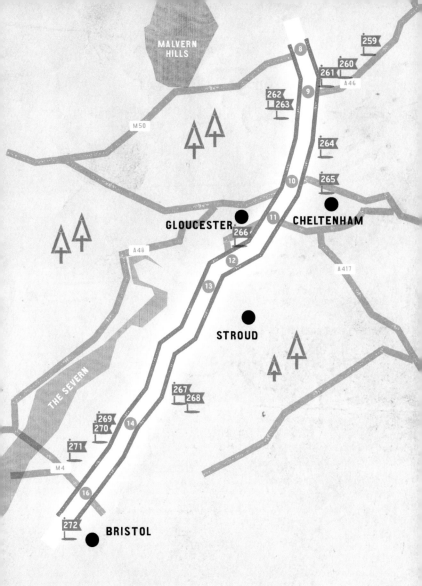

MALVERN HILLS

M50

GLOUCESTER

CHELTENHAM

A46

A48

A417

STROUD

THE SEVERN

M4

BRISTOL

8
9
10
11
12
13
14
16

259
260
261
262
263
264
265
266
267
268
269
270
271
272

254 The Restaurant at Webbs
255 Churchfields
256 The Fold
257 Clive's Fruit Farm
258 Revills Farm Shop
259 The Coffee Shop
260 Teddington Stores

261 Malt House Emporium
262 Café au Chocolat
263 Theoc House
264 Court Farm Shop
265 Central Cross Café
266 Gloucester Services
267 Wotton Farm Shop

268 The Edge
269 Hawkes House
270 Papilio at Heritage
271 Old Down Country Park
272 Morgans Coffee House

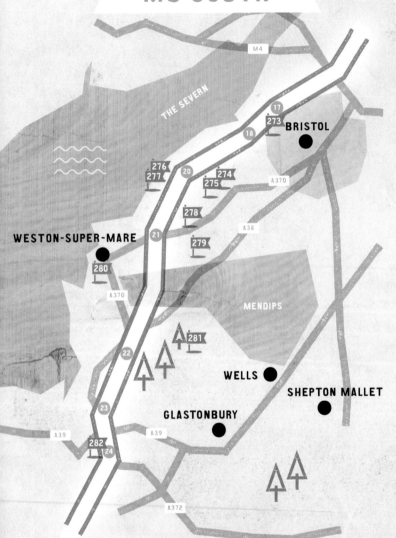

M4

THE SEVERN

17
273
18

**BRISTOL**

276
277

20

274
275

A370

278

A38

279

21

**WESTON-SUPER-MARE**

280

A370

MENDIPS

281

22

**WELLS**

**SHEPTON MALLET**

23

**GLASTONBURY**

A39

282
24

A39

A372

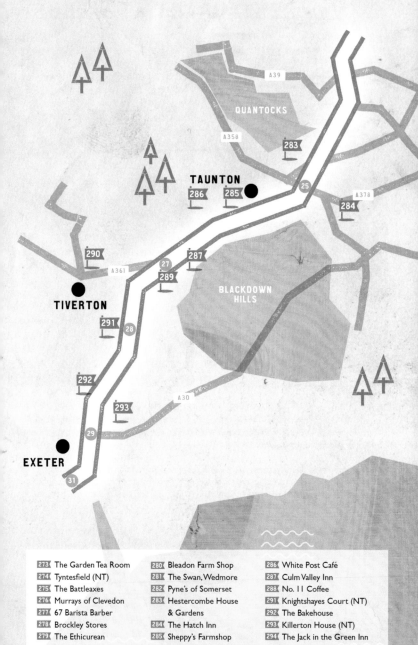

A39

QUANTOCKS

A358

283

TAUNTON

286  285 ●

25

A378

284

290

A361

287

27

289

TIVERTON ●

BLACKDOWN
HILLS

291

28

292

293

A30

29

EXETER ●

31

GARDEN CENTRE

# *The* RESTAURANT AT WEBBS

JUNCTION 5: 4 MINUTES

You'll feel your spirits immediately lift among the peaceful throng of flowers in Webbs' riverside gardens, which are free to visit. Amble through a wisteria walkway, marvel at the colour spectrum garden, let the kids delight in the Hobbit House and learn how vegetables can bring both form and function.

The renovated café seats 400 with more outdoors, plus a picnic area. The kitchen uses Worcestershire ingredients as far as possible – juices from Pershore, traditional farmhouse cheese from Ansteys and luxury ice cream from Bennetts – and serves tasty meals all day. There's a 'grab & go' counter for sandwiches, cakes and hot drinks if you're short of time.

The food hall sells deli delights, including honey and fig cheese, local beers, freshly baked bread, a chocolate library with more than 100 types of chocolate and a gelato bar. Stretch your legs with a riverside walk or, in winter, skate around the temporary ice rink and meet the reindeer.

Opening hours
Mon-Fri 9am-8pm
Sat 9am-6pm
Sun 10.30am-4.30pm

The Restaurant at Webbs, Worcester Rd, Droitwich WR9 0DG
**WWW.WEBBSOFWHYCHBOLD.CO.UK   01527 860000**

# CHURCHFIELDS

**JUNCTION 6: 8 MINUTES**

Hidden away among Worcestershire's small country lanes, Churchfields is a mecca for ice cream lovers, drawn to the lip-licking ice cream made from its pedigree herd of dairy shorthorns. Freezers are full of frequently changing flavours; stilton one of the most daring to date. People come to indulge in cones or sundaes, but the red-brick, wood-clad Barn Café also serves up a good selection of fresh sandwiches, pancakes, soups and salads. Seating is over two floors among wibbly oak beams, antler chandeliers and large windows. In summer you can tumble out onto the patio, looped with festoon lights, or slumber on the grassy terrace in the shade of a tree.

Kids can ride on tractors and enjoy the swings and slides in the playground, and an old milk float in the car park has been converted to dispense raw milk. Collect a reusable glass bottle and token from the café and take away a litre of creamy whole or semi-skimmed milk.

Opening hours
Mon-Sat 9am-6pm
Sun 10am-4.30pm

Churchfields, Salwarpe, Droitwich WR9 0AH
**WWW.CHURCHFIELDS-FARM.CO.UK   01905 451289**

ATTRACTION

# *The* FOLD

JUNCTION 7: 10 MINUTES

The eco-conscious will adore The Fold, a community enterprise on a rambling farm in the Worcestershire countryside with the gentle mission of encouraging sustainable living and escaping the commercial norm.

There's a farm shop selling seasonal, organic produce grown on site, an independent wine and spirits specialist, and artisan studios offering gifts, homewares and ethical haircuts. You can even find holistic treatments in the tranquil Therapy Centre. The café serves organic food in an arching 17th-century barn. Vegans and vegetarians are well catered for with soups, tarts, salads and freshly baked traybakes and scones. Sunday lunch is popular, with both traditional and modern twists always using good quality, local, organic meat plus something for the herbivores.

There's a fabulous wooden playground for the kids and a nature trail leading down to the river Teme where you can stretch your legs and meet the local wildlife.

Opening hours
Mon-Sat 9am-4.30pm
Sun 10am-4pm

The Fold, Bransford WR6 5JB
WWW.THEFOLD.ORG.UK   01886 833633

# *Clive's* FRUIT FARM

**JUNCTION 8; 12 MINUTES**

Hemmed in by the Malvern Hills on one side and the Severn on the other, this pocket of England is perfect for fruit growing. The Clive family have been tending the trees at their fruit farm since 1921, now under the watchful eyes of Jane and Charlie, and it's well worth swinging off the M5 to find. Once just a small shed and cash drawer, the farm shop and café now fill two long red-brick barns and are supplied by farmers from across the Vale of Evesham. Breakfasts are hearty, lunches liberal and the cakes worthy of a farmhouse kitchen. The shop provides everything you could need for a decent weekly shop or car picnic: the apple and pear juices, grown and pressed here on the farm, are unmissable.

The views over the countryside are sublime and kids will love the small play area and feeding the resident pigs, peacocks and hens, especially if you're passing in the morning when they can lend a hand with egg collecting.

Opening hours
Mon-Sat 9am-5pm
Sun 10am-4pm

Clive's Fruit Farm, Upper Hook Rd, Upton Upon Severn WR8 0SA
**CLIVESFRUITFARM.CO.UK   01684 592664**

FARM SHOP-CAFÉ

# *Revills* FARM SHOP

### JUNCTION 8: 12 MINUTES

Isabel Revill set up shop in the old stable 15 years ago with little more than a cash tin and a trestle table selling the farm's asparagus. From this rustic beginning has grown a thriving farm shop and tearoom, now run day to day by her son-in-law Darren and his team. You can still buy Revill's asparagus in season – and their carrots, beetroot, raspberries and baby courgettes – but the shop is also stocked with meat, game, vegetables, cheese and gifts sourced from fellow growers and producers across Worcestershire.

Once you've filled your basket, head to the tearoom to fill your belly. The breakfasts are excellent and the sandwiches, soups, towering cakes and cream teas served for the rest of the day are lovingly made to order. It's all served on charmingly mismatched crockery in a renovated timber-and-brick barn. Newspapers are sold in the shop, if you need any excuse to loiter longer. Or stretch your legs before resuming your journey with a stroll along the River Avon.

Opening hours
Mon-Sat 9am-5.30pm (café 5pm)
Sun & Bank Hols 10am-4pm (café 3.30pm)

Revills Farm Shop, Bourne Road, Defford WR8 9BS
WWW.REVILLSFARMSHOP.CO.UK  01386 750466

# *The* COFFEE SHOP

**JUNCTION 9; 11 MINUTES**

One of just a handful of independent silk mills still operating in the UK, Beckford Mill is a real treasure. A handsome redbrick building set in prettily landscaped gardens at the edge of the Cotswolds, it was set up in 1975 by James and Martha Gardner to revive the luxury silk industry.

Seamstress or not, it's wonderful to wander amongst the bolts of brightly coloured silk and velvet and to admire the hand-printed scarves. Enthusiasts can request a tour, the mildly curious can guide themselves to the newly renovated and extended tea room where Dani cooks up a storm. The coffee is flavourful and the cakes all homemade. Have a breakfast of yoghurt, honey and granola out in the sheltered courtyard, or lunch on a jacket potato stuffed with melted stilton, grilled pear and chunky walnuts.

The energetic may wish to yomp to the top of Bredon Hill just behind, which offers panoramic views over the Cotswolds, Malverns and Severn valley.

Opening hours
Mon-Sat 9am-4pm

GF V P

The Coffee Shop, Beckford Silk, Ashton Rd, Beckford GL20 8AU
**BECKFORDSILK.CO.UK   07568 170794**

FARM SHOP

# *Teddington* STORES

JUNCTION 9; 7 MINUTES

Former city worker Deborah has waved her magic wand over Teddington Stores, transforming it from a Little Chef into a delightful food hall to champion the good food of her Gloucestershire farming roots. The cut flowers greeting you in the foyer puts your average petrol station bunch firmly to shame. In the food hall beyond, broad oak tables sag under the weight of gargantuan stacks of freshly baked goodies, groceries and treats, including fruit from Hayles Farm, artisan bread, gorgeous local art, tasteful giftware, and a fantastic selection of wine and British chocolates. High-end frozen meals will dupe any in-law into thinking you've cooked it yourself.

The butchery counter is the piece de resistance, selling the finest cuts from local herds. It should be beef for dinner as the ribs and prime cuts here are dry aged in the store's own salt-lined ager and are melt-in-your-mouth delicious. The café at the entrance is where you can sup a Lavazza coffee and savour a light lunch or crumbly pastry at one of a handful of tables (with charging points). Everything is made in the kitchen and uses ingredients from the shelves.

Opening hours
Mon-Fri 8.30am-6.30pm
Sat 9am-6pm
Sun 10am-4pm

Teddington Stores, Teddington Hands, Evesham Rd, Teddington GL20 8NE
**WWW.TEDDINGTONSTORES.CO.UK   01386 725400**

# *Malt House* **EMPORIUM**

JUNCTION 9; 2 MINUTES

Lose yourself in the aisles of the gargantuan Malt House Emporium, a two-storey warehouse just off Junction 9 overflowing filled with tantalising homewares, antiques, clothes and gifts. It gathers together 70 traders whose alluring collections – old and new – range from farmhouse tables to upcycled chests of drawers, retro kitchenware, chandeliers and vintage clothes.

Browse the stalls then put your feet up in The Ferns Tea Room at the back. Its long run of floor-to-ceiling windows and the narrow terrace outside have lovely views over the Gloucestershire fields, though you'll have to ignore the fast road in the foreground. Devoted to tea, it has 15 types of loose leaf including the Flora Tea whose petals unfurl in the cup. Excellent barista coffee is also served alongside cakes, cheese scones, sandwiches and delicious homemade quiches. There's plenty of free parking outside and dogs are welcome inside on leads.

Opening hours
Mon-Sat 10am-5pm
Sun & Bank Hols 10am-4pm

Unit 2, Tewkesbury Retail Park, Northway Gate, Ashchurch GL20 8JP
WWW.MALTHOUSEEMPORIUM.COM   01684 423150

# *Café* AU CHOCOLAT

**JUNCTION 9; 6 MINUTES**

Francophiles will love this inviting café in the sleepy town of Tewkesbury. Café au Chocolat stands on the high street, distinguished by sage green paint, golden lettering on large windows and glowing filament lightbulbs. On sunny days, you can enjoy your coffee streetside at one of the pavement tables. Food is delicious and filling, perhaps a mozzarella and ham croissant, or a toasted bagel with smoked salmon, cream cheese and dill. For the sweeter tooth, try milkshakes, Salcombe dairy ice cream or homemade cakes – the flapjack with caramel, pumpkin seeds and cranberries is a staunch favourite.

Chocolate is definitely the main event; to titillate your tastebuds, try the chocolate indulgence challenge: a platter of cakes, chocolates, truffles and fudge designed for sharing. They have recently opened a chocolate shop next door which is definitely worth a browse – everything is hand-made on site using the finest Belgian chocolate. There's an hour's free parking on the street outside and dogs are welcome.

Opening hours
Mon-Thurs 9am-5pm
Fri-Sat 9am-5.30pm
Sun 9.30am-5pm

Café au Chocolat, 137 High Street, Tewkesbury GL20 5JR
**WWW.CAFE-AU-CHOCOLATE.CO.UK   01684 275 332**

# *Theoc* **HOUSE**

**JUNCTION 9; 6 MINUTES**

In a Tudor-style building amid the delightful architectural jumble that is Tewkesbury's high street, Theoc House is a relaxed café-bar to suit the most determined of lounge lizards. A community hub as much as an eatery, it has quizzes, live music, books and board games to encourage lingering on the squat chesterfields and mismatched wooden chairs and tables.

The coffee and on-trend breakfasts will set you up for the day: sourdough with local jam, eggs Benedict or a one-pan wonder incorporating bacon, onion, mushroom, potatoes, eggs and double Gloucester cheese. Lunch includes ciabatta with fries, super-food salads and burgers. Tasty tapas, beetroot and garlic pasta and balsamic rump of lamb star in the evening menu.

When you're fed and watered, wander around the pretty riverside town and glimpse its 1,000-year history in the abbey and half-timbered houses that bore witness to decisive battles in the War of the Roses. The abbey is exquisitely beautiful.

Opening hours
Mon-Sun 8.30am-11.30pm

Theoc House, 85 Barton Street, Tewkesbury GL20 5PY
**WWW.THEOCHOUSE.CO.UK   01842 296562**

FARM SHOP-CAFÉ
# *Court Farm* SHOP
### JUNCTION 10: 10 MINUTES

The long, dramatic ridge of Cleeve Hill runs like a spine behind Court Farm's fields. Starting life as a roadside egg shed, the farm shop now fills a purpose-built, red-roofed barn. Two-thirds of the produce on the shelves comes from within 30 miles: bread from Tewkesbury, cakes from down the road, honey from local hives. The hens roam free in acres of land resulting in beautifully fresh eggs with golden yolks.

Court Farm is primarily a livestock farm: cows, pigs and sheep are reared with love and butchered on-site for A-grade cuts, steaks, faggots, meatballs, burgers and a large variety of sausages including the award-winning Toulouse sausages. The butchery offers plenty of choice and has a fantastic BBQ selection. The deli is ripe for picnic plunder: homemade scotch eggs, lovely Court Farm cold ham and beef, Cotswold salami, cheeses, pork pies, sausage rolls, salad pots, local cider and filled baguettes. After you've met the pygmy goats and piglets, take your picnic and head up that hill for wonderful panoramic views.

Opening hours
Mon-Fri 8.30am-6pm
Sat 8.30am-5.30pm
Sun 10am-4pm

Court Farm Shop, Stoke Road, Stoke Orchard GL52 7RY
**WWW.COURTFARMSHOP.CO.UK   01242 678374**

# *Central Cross Café* (IN THE PARK)

**JUNCTION 10: 11 MINUTES**

Wide open spaces, lakes to walk around and an enormous adventure playground (complete with rabbits, guinea pigs, chipmunks, duck pond and an aviary); it's well worth zipping off at Cheltenham to drop into Pittville Park. Central Cross Café, an award-winning neighbourhood haunt from 'In the Park', has adopted an old Victorian park pavilion – green and white timbers, ornate fascia boards and blooming floral displays – and sells scrummy fair-trade coffee, hot chocolate, freshly baked cakes, breakfast rolls, pastries, salads and sandwiches.

Free blankets are slung over the outside chairs in winter and you can borrow a picnic blanket in summer. There are newspapers to read and pick-and-mix biscuits for dogs. A smaller Kiosk by the play area sells hot drinks, ice creams, cakes, and lunch boxes for kids; a third, The Boathouse, is nestled by the lower lake and has indoor seating – you can hire a boat out in the summer. The cafés are firmly linked to their green environment so packaging is 100% compostable and cardboard and plastic is recycled. Parking is free for up to four hours.

**Opening hours**
Mon-Fri 8.30am-4pm
Sat-Sun 9am-4pm

Central Cross Café (In the Park), Central Cross Drive, Cheltenham GL52 2DX
**WWW.INTHEPARK.CO.UK   01242 234907**

The latest in Westmorland's quiet motorway service revolution, this is a purpose-built Farmshop & Kitchen that blends in with its surroundings: natural stone walls, rugged landscaping and a grass roof over the timber-vaulted main building. A remarkable place.

Step inside the atrium to meet counters heaving with sandwiches, pies, stews, pastries, cakes and the reassuring burr of a barista coffee machine. All the produce is locally-sourced – they work with over 130 producers within 30 miles of the services. Enormous scrubbed tree trunks hanging overhead in a unique light underscore the Westmorland family's connection to the land. Seating overlooks a tranquil nature reserve and pond area, plus there's a rustic play area.

The Farmshop flanking the café on either side is impressive: from wild-boar pies on the deli counter to wooden spinning tops, heavenly macaroons and enamelware. Forget petrol station flowers: this is the place to get emergency gifts.

Opening hours
Mon-Sun 24 hours

Gloucester Services, Brookthorpe, Gloucester GL4 0DN
**WWW.GLOUCESTERSERVICES.COM  01452 813254**

# *Wotton* **FARM SHOP**

**JUNCTION 14; 10 MINUTES**

You won't regret breaking the journey for this prince among farm shops. Fuzzy-headed Bantam chickens scratch around in their pen, like little Cossacks. In spring you can buy an award-winning hanging basket; in summer, punnets of soft fruit from the pick-your-own fields.

The farm shop is a treasure trove: tayberry jam, Cotswold vegetables, local onion relish, a deli counter filled with pâtés, cooked meats, cheese, scrumptious frozen meals (no one need know) and posies of fresh flowers. The stack of ceramics, garden gifts and country homewares are expertly selected too; you will come away with a bag full of loot.

In the newly built café you can settle down to hillside views and food fresh from the farm kitchen: thick-cut bacon sandwiches, filled baguettes, jacket potatoes, quiches, sandwiches and cream teas. Mouthwatering cakes are carved in generous hunks; try the millionaire's shortbread or coffee and walnut. cake

Opening hours
Mon-Sat 9am-5.30pm
Sun 10am-4pm

Wotton Farm Shop, Bradley Rd, Wotton-under-edge GL12 7DT
**WWW.WOTTONFARMSHOP.CO.UK   01453 521546**

CAFÉ
## *The* EDGE

JUNCTION 14; 12 MINUTES

You'll find lusty, home-cooked food at the Edge, which stands in the centre of a photogenic high street in pretty Wotton-under-Edge. Huge windows painted spring green and hung with white curtains make for a bright café with plenty of opportunity for people-watching on the street outside. Floors are stripped and chairs painted various shades of green and cream. The brick-walled garden is a charming place to soak up the rays on fine days.

The café is run by father and daughter Chris and Beth, who stack the counter each day with oven-warm cakes and savouries. Churros, mocha loaf, and peanut butter brownies are among the sinful goodies.

Breakfasts and lunches are delicious, perhaps a butternut squash salad, spinach and sun-dried tomato flatbread or goat's cheese with red onion relish on homemade focaccia. Wotton is worth an afternoon, let alone a detour.

Opening hours
Mon-Sat 8.30am-4.30pm

The Edge, 44 Long Street, Wotton-under-Edge GL12 7BT
**WWW.EDGE-COFFEE-WOTTON.CO.UK   01453 844108**

# *Hawkes* **HOUSE**

JUNCTION 14: 10 MINUTES

An affable café-bar marooned in a 1960s shopping precinct in the thriving market town of Thornbury. Drop in here to enjoy the gentle murmur of gossip and live music, or kick back with the heaps of books and games.

The mottled stone building opened in 1859 as an off-licence and enjoyed a long spell as a pub before its reinvention as a community café. Owners James and Simon have played to its traditional roots, preserving the exposed stone walls, arching beamed ceilings and cosy nooks.

Food is fresh and delicious, the cake cabinet piled high. All-day brunch includes American pancake stacks, one-pan wonders and sourdough sausage sandwiches. The rest of the menu changes seasonally, but might include pork and apricot meatballs with tzatziki or a vegetable burger topped with avocado and baba ganoush. If you're here early, try the breakfast bowl, stuffed with fruit and homemade granola.

Opening hours
Mon-Sun 8.30am-11pm

Hawkes House, St Mary's Street, Thornbury BS35 2AB
**WWW.HAWKESHOUSE.CO.UK  01454 417621**

SHOP-CAFÉ

# *Papilio* **AT HERITAGE**

JUNCTION 15; 9 MINUTES

Spin across the Severn's flood plain to the traditional town of Thornbury with higgledy-piggledy roof lines, cascading floral displays and a castle where Henry VIII once stayed with his queen, Anne Boleyn.

Among the town's cafés and pubs, Papilio at Heritage is one of our favourites. The shop and café were badly damaged by fire in 2015, but have emerged like a phoenix from the flames under the guidance of owner, Tabi, whom you'll often find cheerily serving customers.

Wander through the beautifully stocked gift shop to a modern, light-drenched café with views onto a grassy garden where children can safely let off steam. Parents can delve into baskets of toys and books to keep little ones entertained, while grown-ups can pause over the newspapers and magazines with a light lunch or afternoon tea. Borrow a blanket to make the most of the fresh air, even on chillier days.

Opening hours
Mon-Sat 9am-5.30pm

Papilio at Heritage, 24 High Street, Thornbury BS35 2AH
**WWW.PAPILIOATHERITAGE.CO.UK   01454 415096**

# *Old Down* COUNTRY PARK

**JUNCTION 16; 8 MINUTES**

Swing off the motorway and wiggle down a few country lanes to find Old Down Country Park, a Victorian manor house and grounds perched on a hill overlooking the Bristol Channel. The licensed café stands in an old stone barn and serves tasty light meals (sandwiches, homemade soups with wedges of bread), and coffee. You're free to bring your own picnic if you prefer.

If you have time, it's worth paying to enjoy the full 66 acres of country park and visit the Victorian walled garden, small lake, play areas and oodles of wide open space. A pets' corner, zip wire and jumping pillow – a giant, multicoloured marshmallow – will keep little ones busy, while gardens and woodland with views of both bridges across the Severn will soothe frazzled grown-ups. The resident peacock, Kevin, is something of a local celebrity and roams freely.

Opening hours
Mon-Fri 10am-5pm
Sat-Sun 10am-5.30pm

Old Down Country Park, Foxholes Lane, Tockington BS32 4PG
**WWW.OLDDOWNESTATE.CO.UK   01454 414081**

CAFÉ

# *Morgans* COFFEE HOUSE

**JUNCTION 18; 5 MINUTES**

A cosy little hideaway in the arches, Morgans Coffee House is tucked away beneath Kings Weston House, a Grade I-listed mansion and little-known gem at the edge of Bristol. Completed in 1719 it was designed by Sir John Vanbrugh who also sketched Blenheim Palace.

Food is hearty – warming soups, delicious quiches, light bites and fantastic homemade cakes – and the atmosphere cosy. It's a haven for those travelling with dogs and kids. Original flagstones on the floor and colourfully tiled walls mean that dogs are welcome (on leads) to join their owners by the wood burners, and the house is ringed with acres of woodland and gardens, making for respectable leg stretches.

Don't miss the Compass Dial at Penpole Point (an ancient shipping marker used to navigate safely into the Avon) and Lodge gatehouse. A lawn overlooks the Severn and Avonmouth's port and is ideal for games and letting off steam. Parking is free and fairly abundant.

Opening hours
Mon-Fri 9am-4pm
Sat-Sun 9am-4.30pm

Morgans Coffee House, Kings Weston House, Kings Weston Lane BS11 0UR
**07954 324043**

# *The Garden Tea Room* **AT BRACKENWOOD**

**JUNCTION 19; 6 MINUTES**

It's six minutes from Junction 19 but a valuable time investment as the motorway services alternative is especially unattractive. Brackenwood Garden Centre is down a long driveway of the once private parkland of Leigh Court Estate. Its 12 acres of plants and ornamental trees are an oasis of calm, and back onto miles of woodland. The garden centre is family owned and it shows in the way the staff are exceptionally friendly and helpful.

In the midst of the plants you'll find the newly refurbished Garden Tea Room. It's in the capable hands of Mark and Dotti who load the counter with delicious cakes and ply tables with good honest food, including homemade quiches, parsnip soup and truffle oil and exciting seasonal specials. Further down the lane from the garden centre is a small parking bay where you can take a stroll to visit the grotto overlooking the River Avon, or explore the ponds and myriad footpaths lacing through the woods beyond.

Opening hours
Mon-Sun 10am-3.30pm (tea room)

Leigh Court Estate, Pill Road, Abbots Leigh, Bristol BS8 3RA
**WWW.BRACKENWOOD-PLANTANDGARDENCENTRE.COM 01275 374988**

## ATTRACTION
# TYNTESFIELD (NT)
### JUNCTION 19; 8 MINUTES

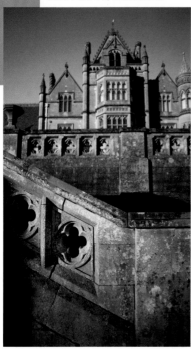

Tyntesfield House is a spectacular and gloriously preserved Victorian gothic pile built for the Gibbs family who made their fortune importing guano (bird poo) for fertiliser. Visit its graceful chapel, billiard room and staircase gallery, and then explore the grounds – with woodland paths, kitchen garden, lawns, rose garden and sculpture trail. There are three play areas for burning energy and dogs are welcome in signed areas.

You can eat in the self-service Cow Barn Kitchen with its high-beamed ceilings and stone floors. The seats are in old cattle stalls and the food is tasty – award-winning brownies, cream teas, substantial mains, bread-and-butter pudding and ice cream from the Marshfield dairy near Bath.

The smaller Pavilion café beyond the walled garden has beautiful views over the countryside and offers a bijou snack menu: hot cheese scones, sausage rolls, bacon butties and cakes.

Opening hours
Mon-Sun 10am-6pm

Tyntesfield (NT), Wraxall BS48 1NX
**WWW.NATIONALTRUST.ORG.UK/TYNTESFIELD   01275 461900**

# *The* **BATTLEAXES**

**JUNCTION 19; 9 MINUTES**

Cosy country pubs aren't hard to find in Somerset, but The Battleaxes is special for its mock Tudor gables and imposing roadside position. Just south of Bristol its soaring gothic roofline echoes that of its grander neighbour, Tyntesfield; indeed, it was originally the social club for the workers on that estate.

Still a very sociable spot, The Battleaxes' interior is now countryside chic – scrubbed wooden tables, slouchy leather chairs, patterned wallpaper and gilded portraits. It's cavernous too, with plenty of nooks to settle into. Striped deck chairs and white iron tables fill the lawn in summer.

Food is made from local produce: expect imaginative bistro and pub dishes such as ale battered cod and triple cooked chips, wild mushroom and baby spinach cobbler or slow cooked venison with suet pudding and pumpkin purée. Sunday lunches here have long been a neighbourhood mainstay.

**Opening hours**
Sun-Thurs 8am-9pm
Fri-Sat 8am-10pm

The Battleaxes, Bristol Road, Wraxall BS48 1LQ
**WWW.FLATCAPPERS.CO.UK/THE-BATTLEAXES/   01275 857473**

RESTAURANT-DELI

# *Murrays* OF CLEVEDON

**JUNCTION 20; 5 MINUTES**

Standing proudly on Hill Road and close to Clevedon's graceful Victorian pier (itself worth a visit especially for sunset), Murrays is a food emporium dedicated to the best produce that Britain and Italy can offer. Delicatessen, bakery, wine shop, café and restaurant rolled into one, it has become as much a community hub as a foodie destination, and John's Italian roots shine through in the cured meats, cheeses, anchovies, olive oil and Amalfi lemons as well as the friendly conversation.

The restaurant serves dishes lovingly made from fresh ingredients: chicken and artichoke rillette terrine, capellini with Cornish crab and fennel, slow braised beef neck. The hummus and freshly baked bread are famous, but whatever you do don't miss the Parma ham and cremini mushroom lasagne. Luckily for neighbouring Bristol, the Murray family continue to fly the flag over another outpost – a new café deli in Park Row.

Opening hours
Tues-Sat 9am-5pm (Deli)
9am-9.15pm last orders (Restaurant)

Murrays of Clevedon, 91 Hill Road, Clevedon BS21 7PN
**WWW.MURRAYSOFCLEVEDON.CO.UK   01275 341222**

# 67 *Barista* BARBER

**JUNCTION 20; 2 MINUTES**

It's an unique combination, a barber and a coffee shop, but owner Sue Cooper wanted to set up something a little different in her home town when she retired. As a result, 67 Barista Barber is overflowing with personality, from the retro furniture rescued from reclamation yards to the changing art exhibitions on the walls. Enormous windows framed by the darkest deep blue exterior are perfect for people watching as crowds mill in and out of Hill Road's trendy boutiques. It's a great refuelling stop after a walk along the seafront with its Victorian pier and bandstand.

The laid-back atmosphere means 'queuing was never this easy or enjoyable!' in the words of one customer, and we're inclined to agree. Whether or not you're in the market for a haircut, the coffee is excellent (fair-trade and sourced from Devon roastery, Voyager) and Sue's homemade cakes widely praised. It's dinky but delightful and one of the best spots in town.

**Opening hours**
Mon, Tues, Wed, Fri 8am-5pm
Thurs 8am-5pm
Sat 8am-4pm

67 Barista Barber, 67 Hill Road, Clevedon BS21 7RR
**01275 217740**

FARM SHOP

# *Brockley* STORES

### JUNCTION 21; 11 MINUTES

One of the best local food shops in Somerset, Brockley Stores started life 80 years ago as a roadside stall selling fruit and veg straight form the surrounding fields. Still very much wedded to the same ethos of fresh, local food – 'grown not flown', as they put it – the store is frequented as much by locals as tourists making the trip for the Brockley's delicious range.

Luxuriant bouquets from Kimberley's the Florist sit alongside crates of crisp fruit and vegetables, from peaty potatoes to rosy apples and crimson rhubarb harvested by candlelight, depending on the season. Fresh coffee from local roastery Extract is on sale at the door and the smell of baking wafts over the shop as the ovens are put hard to work creating Brockley Stores' praised goodies, with quiches and pies held in particularly high esteem.

There's a dedicated al fresco picnic area outside for lingering and plenty of gorgeous countryside on the doorstep for a leg-stretch.

Opening hours
Mon-Sat 8am-6pm
Sun 9am-5.30pm

Ⓥ Ⓟ

Brockley Stores, Main Road, Brockley BS48 3AT
WWW.BROCKLEYSTORES.CO.UK   01275 462 753

# *The* ETHICUREAN

**JUNCTION 22; 15 MINUTES**

15-minutes' drive from the motorway, the Ethicurean is one of our longest detours but trust us when we say it's worth it. The relaxed restaurant and café is set in the former kitchen garden and shabby chic glasshouse of grand Victorian residence Barley Wood – now separated by the road – with sweeping views towards the fern-mottled Mendip Hills.

Much of the food on offer is freshly plucked from the surrounding gardens – with a corresponding focus on vegetables – and transformed into an imaginative array of dishes. Drop in for coffee and cake and you'll be treated to delights such as parsnip, white chocolate and coconut cake from the daily changing menu. Linger for longer and you can lunch on super-food salads, soups and Welsh rarebit, or dine on more substantial feasts and renowned Sunday lunches (be sure to book in advance). Informal and friendly, there's parking on site and kids are safe to trundle around within the walled gardens. A touch pricey, but well worth it.

Opening hours
Tues-Thurs 11am-11pm
Fri-Sat 10am-11pm
Sun 10am-5pm

The Ethicurean, Long Lane, Wrington BS40 5SA
**WWW.THEETHICUREAN.COM   01934 863713**

FARM SHOP-CAFÉ

# *Bleadon* FARM SHOP

### JUNCTION 22; 10 MINUTES

A lovely farm shop and café in an old stone barn across the road from the village croquet green. Zoe is the energetic driving force behind the hub, priding herself on a cheerful atmosphere and hearty, satisfying food. Breakfasts are the toast of the town, sandwiches are freshly made, the coffee is smooth, tea is served in pots and cakes are baked in the kitchen, from classic Victoria sponge to fresh cream buns jewelled with strawberries.

Tables and chairs are set out at the front on sunny days (frequently occupied by cyclists, often a herald of good baking) and there is plenty of space inside when the weather is less kind.

The sandy beaches of Brean and Weston-super-Mare are within easy reach if children and pets need to run and play, and the blustery walk up to the headland at Brean Down is memorable. Pick up some tasty Somerset produce to take on your way from the pint-sized farm shop and post office next door.

Opening hours
Mon-Sat 9am-3pm

Bleadon Farm Shop, Purn Way, Bleadon BS24 0QE
**WWW.BLEADONCAFE.CO.UK   01934 814339**

# *The* SWAN, WEDMORE

JUNCTION 22; 15 MINUTES

An 18th-century beer house turned coaching inn, The Swan was refurbished by new owners in 2014 to become a much-loved village pub. Locals throng in the open-plan bar with its crackling fires, cosy corners and flagstone floors. In a sunny lounge with overstuffed chairs and a wood-burner you can kick back and tuck into the cake stand and all-day snack menu. Sundays are dedicated to lazy roasts, newspapers and Bloody Marys.

The menu changes regularly, inspired by chef Tom Blake's River Cottage training and fresh ingredients from the market – eggs from Burnham-on-Sea, fish from Bridport, meat from the local butcher's own herd. Loaves of bread are baked here, served with dinner and available to take away too. In summer, chefs make the most of a wood-burning oven and smoker in the lawned garden. Dogs are welcome in the bar area and there are some fabulous walks nearby on the Somerset Levels and around Cheddar Gorge.

Opening hours
Mon-Sun 9am-11pm

The Swan, Wedmore, Cheddar Road, Wedmore BS28 4EQ
WWW.THESWANWEDMORE.COM  01934 710337

FARM SHOP
# *Pyne's* OF SOMERSET
### JUNCTION 26; 4 MINUTES

Minutes from the motorway, Pyne's is a cracking farm shop and café serving exceptional food – fast. The steady stream of van drivers is testament to the melt-in-your-mouth breakfast rolls, proper pastries and unique roast-dinner-in-a-box. It's all available to take away, along with good coffee, or you can stop for a break at the farmhouse tables.

Sprightly Malcolm Pyne is in charge, together with his wife Julie. One in a long line of butchers, you can't miss him behind the counter sporting his trademark mutton chops whiskers and a bowler hat. There's nothing he doesn't know about the perfect cut and he is uncompromising when it comes to animal welfare, sourcing only from known local farmers. The in-house sausages change frequently and are deservedly described as legendary.

The farm shop showcases some of Somerset's best food, so you can fill your shopping bags from the cheese, fish and meat counters, or load up on locally-blended tea, veg and cider.

Opening hours
Mon-Wed & Fri 7.30am-5.30pm
Thurs 7.30am-6pm
Sat 7.30am-5pm

Market Way, Regional Rural Business Centre, North Petherton TA6 6DF
**WWW.PYNETHEBUTCHER.CO.UK   01278 663050**

# *Hestercombe* HOUSE & GARDENS

**JUNCTION 25: 14 MINUTES**

These magnificent 50 acres of garden, and the house, were a neglected secret for years after the last war. All is now in the benign hands of the Hestercombe Trust.

Stroll through three centuries of design: the Victorian Shrubbery, the Georgian Landscape Garden and the Edwardian Formal Gardens. The Great Cascade is a main feature and you feel your motorway strain subside as you gaze over one of the two great ponds. There is more: a Dutch Garden and Sir Edwin Lutyens' Daisy Steps and impressive Orangery. He also created the Rose Garden and collaborated with Gertrude Jekyll on some of the groundbreaking designs. This is as much a garden for gardeners as for those who just enjoy looking and strolling.

Dine in the refined Column Room, renowned for its traditional and champagne afternoon teas or eat more casually in the charming Stables Café. You can make use of the café without paying to enter the gardens.

**Opening hours**
Mon-Sun 10am-5pm

Hestercombe House & Gardens, Cheddon Fitzpaine, Taunton TA2 8LG
**WWW.HESTERCOMBE.COM  01823 413923**

PUB

# *The* HATCH INN

JUNCTION 25; 7 MINUTES

It is rare to find such a delightful family-owned pub so close to the motorway. You walk in to an immediate sense of welcome. On a cold day the open fire will warm your cockles; on a warm one you can sit outside and admire the scenery of the Blackdown Hills.

An old 18th-century coaching inn, The Hatch has had love and commitment poured into it, the rustic charm nurtured and improved. The welcome is real, the food traditional and delicious, the atmosphere cosy and friendly. If you are in luck there will be something special happening, for the pub is at the centre of things locally.

You may even want to plan your journey to spend the evening and night here. The rooms are perfect and for dinner you might have, for example, venison sausages or mussels or pork. Breakfast, with local meats and breads, is equally generous, and the Sunday roasts have the best cuts of meat and roast potatoes for miles around. The Hatch is a destination in itself.

Opening hours
Mon 5pm-11pm
Tues-Thurs noon-3pm, 5pm-11pm
Fri-Sat noon-11pm (Sun 5pm)

Ⓥ Ⓟ

The Hatch Inn, Hatch Beauchamp TA3 6SG
**WWW.THEHATCHINN.CO.UK   01823 480245**

# *Sheppy's* **FARMSHOP**

JUNCTION 26; 4 MINUTES

The Sheppy family have been pressing apples here for over two hundred years and the orchard is now under the care of David, a sixth generation 'Master of Cider'. Inside, the modern and rustic décor pays homage to the farm's long history of apple growing.

At The Apple Bay restaurant the menu is stacked with all things Somerset, such as in-house butchered sausages with caramelised onion gravy and cider battered fish and chips. If you fancy something lighter, the grilled goats cheese salad won't disappoint. This is artisan cooking at reasonable prices, and you can buy some of the ingredients in the farm shop, which may reel you in with its fresh greens, high quality meats and vast cheese counter.

If you can spare an hour, and have a (selfless) designated driver, hop on a tour of the orchard, see the apples go from branch to barrel and sample the excellent product en route. Take a quick look at the farm museum while the kids have fun in the play area and mini petting zoo.

Opening hours
Mon-Sat 9am-5.30pm
Sun 10am-4pm

Sheppy's Farmshop, Three Bridges, Bradford-on-Tone TA4 1ER
**WWW.SHEPPYSCIDER.COM  01823 461233**

CAFÉ

# *White Post* CAFÉ

**JUNCTION 26; 12 MINUTES**

Music hums gently but otherwise the only sounds here are the rush of wind through the corn and birds twittering in the trees. Masquerading as a potting shed, White Post Café stands quietly in the heart of a plant nursery with views over to the Blackdown Hills. If the M5 has your nerves jangling there are few better places to unwind.

The menu changes every fortnight or so, reflecting what's in season and includes in house pickles and ferments. You might breakfast on coconut french toast and granola with yoghurt and roasted fruit or lunch on dishes such as summer curry with griddled courgette, lime and fresh coconut chutney or a pea, ricotta and mint tart and salads. You can order small and sharing plates too. Cakes are made every morning and are complimented with locally roasted coffee or loose leaf teas. The café itself and its beautiful garden are designed for tarrying. Eclectic cooking books, design led magazines and inviting chairs near the stylish wood burning stove help you to while away time. Don't blame us if you're late home.

Opening hours
Tues-Sat 9.30am-5 pm

White Post Café, Langford Budville, Wellington TA21 0RW
**WWW.WHITEPOSTCAFE.CO.UK   01823 400322**

# *Culm Valley* INN

Standing alongside the river Culm, which is spanned by a low, multi-arched, stone bridge and fringed with grassy banks, the Culm Valley Inn feels quintessentially English. Yet the dodo logo and totem pole at the entrance to the car park tell another story.

The low-ceiling country pub combines old-world charm with trendy, left-field accessories. Walls painted a deep, cosy grey accommodate photo galleries, sculpture and taxidermy from antiques dealer and sister company, Stag and Squire. A sunny bay window has become a merry space for large parties; chairs are mismatched, fires open and tables decorated with fresh flowers.

Specials chalked on the board above the fireplace might include venison scotch eggs, spiced cauliflower soup, prawn and mussel curry, or an exotic avocado, peanut and coriander salad. It's still a village pub though, so dogs and kids are welcome and footpaths take you from the door for a turn in the countryside.

Opening hours
Mon-Thurs 12am-3pm, 5pm-11pm
Fri-Sun noon-11pm

Culm Valley Inn, The Riverside, Culmstock EX15 3JJ
**WWW.THECULMVALLEYINN.CO.UK   01884 840354**

# A LITTLE EXTRA

**SOME OF THE PLACES IN THE GUIDE** are kindly offering our readers (that's you!) a little extra: it may be a discount on your bill, a free coffee refill, a complimentary cup of tea when you buy a slice of cake… To redeem offers all you need to do is show your Extra Mile keyring fob at selected venues. The list is on our website and will be updated regularly so make sure you keep checking to snag the latest deals.

---

*Not got yours? Head to*

 **WWW.THEEXTRAMILE.GUIDE**

*and we'll pop one straight in the post.*

---

(While you're waiting for it to arrive you can still take advantage
of the offers by showing your copy of this book.)

CAFÉ

# *No.* 11 **COFFEE**

**JUNCTION 27; 4 MINUTES**

You'll see No.11's handsome shop front – large windows painted a soft shade of sage – standing at the centre of Uffculme. Inside, the décor is straightforward and minimalistic, with dark grey church chairs and wooden tables set against white walls. It's a friendly village coffee shop, where the service comes unfailingly with a smile and the coffee is both fair-trade and excellent. Owner Ian is uncompromising when it comes to food quality, serving delicious cooked breakfasts and then ciabatta (maybe brie and bacon) and fresh soup for lunch.
You can fill the gap with homemade cakes, savoury tarts served with crisp salads, filling soups and even an ice cream (the apricot is scrummy) for a sweet bite. Gluten-free diners are well looked after too.

Take time to explore riverside footpaths by the Culm before you head on your way; Coldharbour Mill on the riverbank is one of the UK's oldest woollen mills, part of the UK's industrial revolution in the 18th century.

Opening hours
Mon-Fri 9am-4.30pm
Sat 9am-2.30pm

No. 11 Coffee, The Square, Uffculme EX15 3AA
**WWW.NO11COFFEE.CO.UK   01884 842542**

ATTRACTION

# *Knightshayes* COURT (NT)

JUNCTION 27; 9 MINUTES

Follow a winding track through magnificent grounds to arrive at Knightshayes Court, where eccentricity and beauty combine in a Gothic revival mansion. The Victorian house was built on the back of a revolution in lace production by its owner, inventor (and local MP) John Heathcoat, who made sure his personality was stamped on the quirky architecture. The walled garden is wonderful: walls are reminiscent of a medieval castle and the gardeners have specifically chosen plants and growing methods that were popular in the Victorian era. Dogs on leads are welcome in the winter months.

Stop for a drink or a light snack in the luminous conservatory tea-room, surrounded by potted plants, or grab a taste of the West Country in the Stables Café. It serves homemade scones, cheesecake, filled sandwiches and hot meals, most made with ingredients from the kitchen garden and local farms. Drinks and snacks can also be taken away if yours is just a fleeting visit.

Opening hours
Mon-Sat 10am-5pm
check website for season variations

Knightshayes Court (NT), Bolham Tiverton EX16 7RQ
WWW.NATIONALTRUST.ORG.UK/KNIGHTSHAYES   01884 254665

CAFÉ
# *The* BAKEHOUSE

JUNCTION 28; 2 MINUTES

Once Cullompton's family grocer as the original signwork still proclaims, the Bakehouse is now a fabulous café and bistro just minutes from the motorway. Painted bright teal with bottle green tiles and a mosaic entrance, it's an eye-catching addition to the High Street. Inside, there's a homely collection of antique furniture with a large serving hub in the centre, buzzing with life and stacked with teetering cakes; the vegan sticky ginger cake is delicious. A corridor at the back opens up into another room where a wood burner crackles against the bare brick walls and broad windows in cooler months. It gives on to a narrow, flower-dressed courtyard for soaking up the sun over a latte.

Breakfast is served until 11.30am. Lunch is a simple and scrummy with soup and salads or homemade burgers or risotto for a bigger bite. In the evenings, the fairylights glimmer into life and the café becomes a bistro serving dishes such as duck confit, spicy meatballs, antipasti and meze platters; Wednesday is Italian night with pizza, pasta and weekly-changing specials.

Opening hours
Mon-Sat 9am-5pm (café)
Weds-Sat 6pm-10pm (bistro)

The Bakehouse, 3 High Street, Cullompton EX15 1AB
**WWW.THEBAKEHOUSECULLOMPTON.CO.UK   01884 35222**

ATTRACTION

# *Killerton* HOUSE (NT)

JUNCTION 29; 7 MINUTES

The South West's mild climate has allowed gardeners to create some spectacular creations including Killerton House's 18 acres of gently landscaped gardens, which were something of a testbed for exotic shrubs from around the world created by Scotsman, John Veitch. He is said to have walked from Edinburgh to London looking for work. However, the full estate extends for more than 4,000 acres so you can meander through the fabulous woodland and head up to the Iron Age hill fort – which local legend claims is protected by the Killerton Dragon – for views towards Dartmoor.

The house is a graceful Georgian villa, interesting for its costume collection and music room where you can try your hand on the pipe organ. As for food, you're spoilt for choice. The elegant Killerton Kitchen restaurant serves bistro-style lunches made with fresh ingredients from the estate, the Dairy café snacks and drinks in the heart of the garden, and the Stables café simple light bites overlooking a cobbled courtyard where plants and books are for sale.

Opening hours
Mon-Sun 10am-5.30pm
check website for season variations

Killerton House (NT), Killerton House, Exeter EX5 3LE
**WWW.NATIONALTRUST.ORG.UK/KILLERTON  01392 881345**

# *The* JACK IN THE GREEN

**JUNCTION 29; 5 MINUTES**

Leather sofas that could swallow you whole and roaring log-burners kicking out heat in the winter – a freshly ground coffee is your best defence against an unscheduled snooze. The bar area is warm and comfy, with old beams, low ceilings, and friendly staff.

There are three dining rooms – all charmingly rustic – named after nearby rivers, and an wide-ranging menu that isn't shy about listing suppliers. For a deep dive into local flavours, try the 'Totally Devon' menu which celebrates the county's produce with dishes such as bacon and crispy quail's egg, line-caught cod and rose crème brûlée with strawberry sorbet. Wash it down with apple juice pressed by Richard and Sue at Four Elms Farm down the road. This is on the finer side of pub dining but if it's a quick pit stop try a homemade Scotch egg.

Kids are very welcome with their own dedicated menu and space to play on the roomy, flower-fringed rear terrace.

Opening hours
Mon-Sat 10am-3pm, 5.30pm-11pm (6pm Sat)
Sun 10am-10.30pm

The Jack in the Green, Rockbeare, London Rd, Exeter EX5 2EE
**WWW.JACKINTHEGREEN.UK.COM   01404 822240**

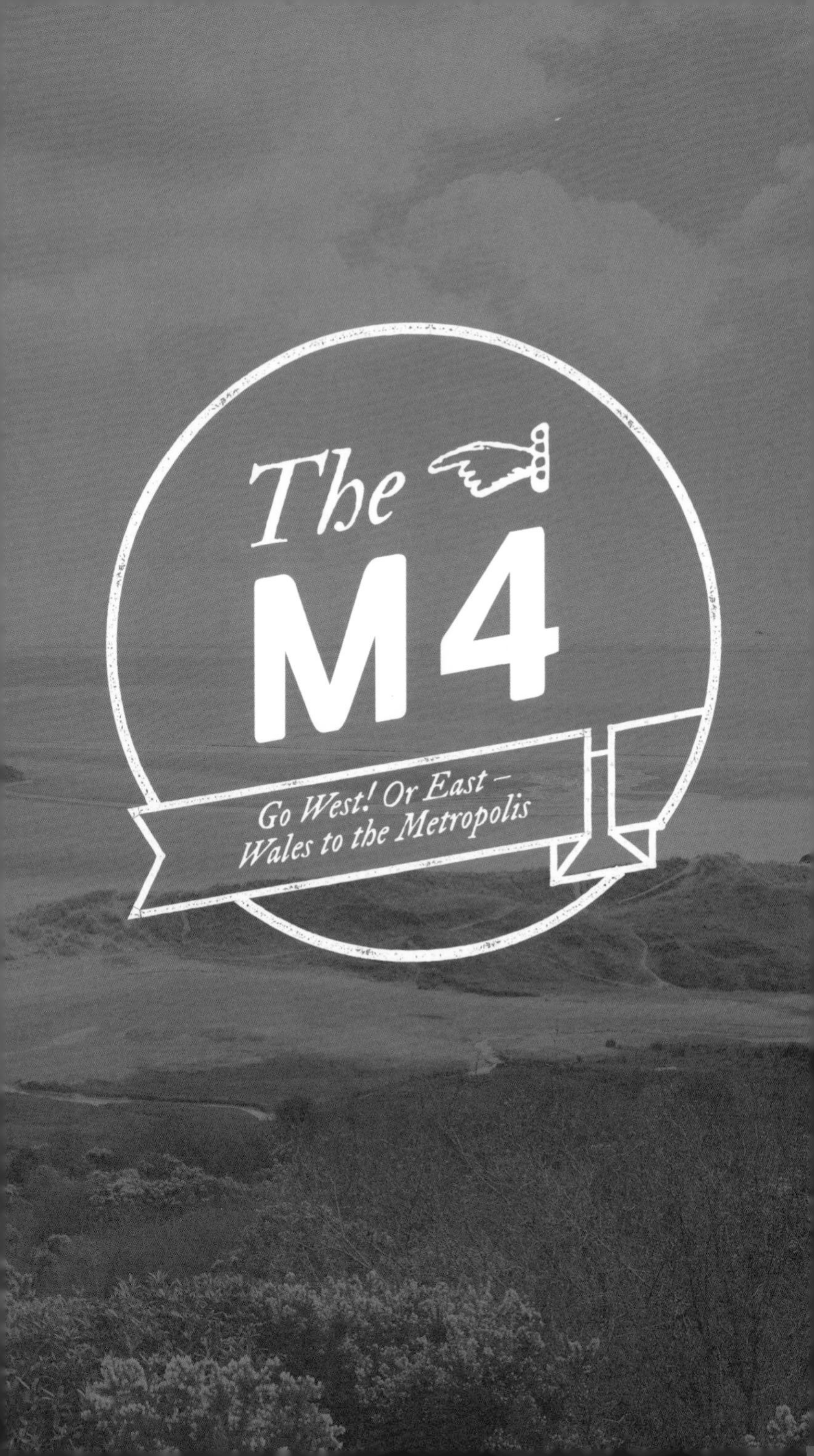

# The ☞

# M4

Go West! Or East —
Wales to the Metropolis

# M4 WEST

300
301
▲40
302
CARMARTHEN 303
304
▲48
▲40
43
305
NE
40
SWANSEA

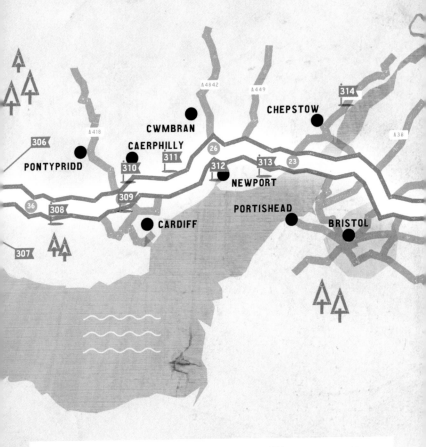

CHEPSTOW

CWMBRAN

CAERPHILLY

PONTYPRIDD

NEWPORT

PORTISHEAD

BRISTOL

CARDIFF

306

311

310

312

313

314

309

308

307

A418

A4842

A449

A38

26

23

36

# M4 EAST

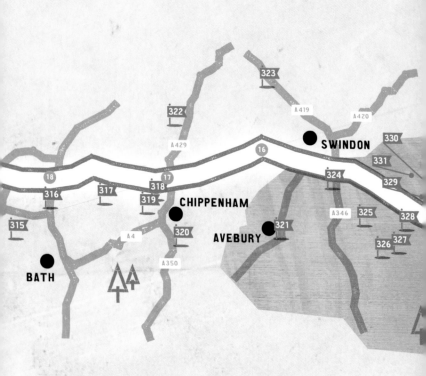

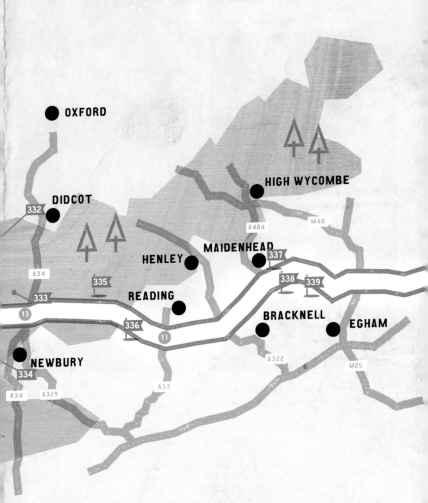

OXFORD

DIDCOT

332

HIGH WYCOMBE

A404

M40

MAIDENHEAD

HENLEY

A34

335

337

338    339

READING

333

13

BRACKNELL

EGHAM

336

11

A322

M25

NEWBURY

334

A34    A329

A33

# *Cwm Deri* VINEYARD & RESTAURANT

**JUNCTION CANASTON BRIDGE: 10 MINUTES**

Pembrokeshire's narrow country lanes will bring you, with a little perseverance, to the wine-making haven of Cwm Deri, where grapes thrive on low hills bathed in mild sunshine.

The restaurant is in a former bungalow, with a paved terrace and sunny conservatory overlooking the vines and curvaceous hills, and the room ringed with shelves of farm produce, including homemade liqueurs, cheese, chutney and biscuits. Eye which ones you'll be slipping into your shopping bag while you lunch on freshly baked bread, duck and cognac pâté, Pembrokeshire platters, and butternut squash risotto, followed up with a homely crumble. Fruit, veg and herbs are plucked from the kitchen garden.

Book ahead to enjoy a tasting of liqueurs and wines, or a tour of the vineyard and woodland, laced with footpaths to explore. Steer kids to the pets' corner where they can meet chickens, geese, rabbits, guinea pigs and Shetland ponies while grown-ups examine the vintage.

### Opening hours

Mon-Thurs 11am-5pm (4pm Nov-Feb)
Fri-Sat 11am-5pm, 7pm-11pm (4pm Nov-Feb)
Sun noon-5pm (4pm Nov-Feb)

Cwm Deri Vineyard & Restaurant, Martletwy, Narberth SA67 8AP
**WWW.CWM-DERI.CO.UK   01834 891274**

# *Café* MEDINA

**JUNCTION A478 ; 4 MINUTES**

Aromatic and welcoming, the earthy colours of Cafe Medina are inspired by Middle Eastern souks. Walls are painted a deep cinnamon red next to exposed stone and stained glass in the entryway. Wooden-topped tables with hairpin legs and sturdy farmhouse chairs pepper the room in front of a bay window streaming with exotic fabrics.

The scents of fresh herbs and spices greet you when you walk in; owner and head chef Helen insists on cooking everything from scratch, growing some ingredients herself in Narberth's community garden. There's a real community spirit here, thanks to chatty staff and a lovely programme of events, from open mic nights to TED talk screenings.

Food is wholesome and often inspired by Eastern flavours, from lentil and sweet potato soup to vegan mezze with homemade hummus. Teas are loose leaf and the coffee smooth. On fine days, you can take yours to tables in the courtyard garden which gives onto the town square.

Opening hours
Mon-Thurs 10am–5pm
Friday-Saturday 10am-5pm, 7pm-10pm

Café Medina, 5 Market Square, Narberth SA67 7AU
**07534 928102**

# *The Ferryman* DELICATESSEN

JUNCTION ST CLEAR'S; 6 MINUTES

A delicious little deli above the castle on Laugharne's main high street, the Ferryman is stuffed floor-to-ceiling with tantalising produce from Carmarthenshire and beyond: Perl Las blue cheese from Cardigan, môr seasoning and Welsh ales. Alongside local goodies, there's a strong Spanish theme, from the chorizo jam to alcaparras, treacly honey and el almendro nougat.

Step out the back and there's a dinky dining room where you can sit in and feast on those flavours. Lunch might be a bowl of lamb cawl, cauliflower and lentil pie, seafood chowder or a prawn open sandwich, open largely because it's too stuffed to close. The mixed meat and cheese platters are a smorgasbord of the most delicious charcuterie and pickles owner Tom can lay his hands on. Wrap up with a slice of apricot frangipane or salted caramel brownie.

The coffee is smooth and best paired with a Welsh cake – try the apricot and salted almond. It's a foodie's delight.

Opening hours
Tues-Sat 9am-5pm

The Ferryman Delicatessen, Exeter House, King St, Laugharne SA33 4SU
WWW.THEFERRYMANDELI.CO.UK   01994 427398

# *Blasus* DELICATESSEN

**JUNCTION CARMARTHEN: 1 MINUTE**

Foodies will love this family-run deli. Blasus means 'tasty' in Welsh, which is the founding philosophy of owners Paul and Delyth. The welcome is friendly – you may be handed a snifter of wine to taste or have a tempting plate of cheese wafted beneath your nose – and the staff are knowledgeable.

You'll find freshly made sandwiches on sourdough – perhaps goat's cheese and fig or sweet chilli crayfish – next to Spanish and Italian charcuterie and artisan cheeses. On the shelves are oils, vinegars and lip-smacking wines. In the main counter there are pastries (chorizo in puff pastry is a go-to favourite), savoury tarts and cauldrons of herby antipasti and fresh basil pesto. Baked goodies include frangipane tarts and pastries. The cheese counter is exceptional. Fill a hamper to the brim with focaccia, tapas and pâtés for the ultimate picnic. Carmarthen is a warren of narrow streets, but the town's huge St Peter's pay-and-display car park is a few minutes' walk away.

**Opening hours**
Mon-Sat 9am-5pm

Blasus Delicatessen, 58 King Street, Carmarthen SA31 1BD
**WWW.BLASUSDELI.CO.UK  01267 233811**

CAFÉ

# *Wright's* **FOOD EMPORIUM**

JUNCTION PORTHYRHYD: 7 MINUTES

Wright's Food Emporium sagely adopted the Golden Grove Arms, a former village pub, when it outgrew its previous home in a nearby farm shop. The network of rooms lend themselves perfectly to the holistic foodie concept, with a deli, café, weekend bistro and wine shop catering to almost every whim. Duck-egg blue panelling, mismatched chairs, repurposed bureaux, scrubbed wooden tables and vintage posters create a low-key, relaxed ambience. Munch generous antipasto platters (the charcuterie is second to none) and salads in the bright conservatory, and enjoy the much-celebrated pork belly Cubano in the dining room or in the courtyard garden.

Make the most of the refillable wine and cider (just buy a bottle and top it up from the barrel in the wine shop) or the pie of the day, which you can take away when you buy an enamel dish. Fill your tote bag with delicious homemade focaccia, lumps of Welsh cheese, Wright's signature chilli sauce and organic lavender hand creams.

Opening hours
Mon & Sun 11am-5pm
Wed & Thurs 11am-7pm
Fri & Sat 9am - late (last food orders 9pm)

(GF) (V) (P) (◊)

Wright's Food Emporium, Golden Grove Arms, Llanarthne SA32 8JU
**WWW.WRIGHTSFOOD.CO.UK   01558 668929**

# *The* **BRIT PUB**

**JUNCTION 41; 6 MINUTES**

Roaring fires, flagstone floors, a piano, friendly Welsh welcome and home-cooked food on the doorstep of Afan Forest Park, the Brit is a prince among pubs. Originally built in 1845, it has been eclectically made over with bare stone walls next to illustrated wallpapers, artful knick-knacks, a lamp made from a golden mannequin and Louis XV chairs upholstered in hot pink. Outside, there's a courtyard garden decorated just as quirkily with the River Afan running past.

Sitting a notch above pub grub, the award-winning food includes vegan pies, moules marinère and fresh mushrooms on brioche toast among the thoughtful lunch options, with heartier steaks and line-caught sea bass on the evening menu. Nearly all the food is homemade.

Walkers and cyclists are warmly welcomed and can stay in one of the four bunk rooms upstairs. The stunning Afan Forest, just up the hill, is a lovely spot to unfurl the legs and enjoy some beautiful scenery.

Opening hours
Mon 6pm-10pm
Tues-Wed, Sun 11.30am-10pm
Fri-Sat 11.30am-midnight (Thurs 11pm)

The Brit Pub, London Row, Cwmavon SA12 9AH
**WWW.THEBRIT.WALES  01639 680247**

# *Cedars* **TEAROOM**

JUNCTION 36; 6 MINUTES

There's nothing like a bit of greenery to soothe the mind after miles of motorway driving. Tucked behind Bridgend the stately Bryngarw Country Park has 113 acres of fabulous lawns, woodlands, wetlands, play areas and riverside paddling.

You'll find the lovely Cedars Tearoom here too, run by a formidable mother and daughter team who pride themselves on their fresh food and local ingredients, such as eggs, milk, butter and preserves. Cakes and pastries are baked here in the kitchen and the menu depends on what's available – maybe a butternut squash or a beetroot and goat cheese burger, chased down with a macaroon. Drink a speciality tea from vintage china or a strong coffee.

Download a free walking map from the park's website over a coffee or pre-order a picnic to take to the meadow – Jill and Hollie offer hampers with crockery and cutlery, fresh sandwiches, seasonal pies, fruit, scones with clotted cream, cakes and refreshing drinks.

Opening hours
Mon-Sun 10am-4.30pm  (April-October)
Mon-Sun 10.30am-3.30pm (November-March)

Cedars Tearoom, Bryngarw Country Park, Brynmenyn CF32 8UU
**WWW.CEDARSTEAROOM.CO.UK   01656 722288**

# Come and stay with us...

Visit the beautiful Easton Estate this year and stay in one of our luxury holiday cottages or new loft apartments.

Whether you choose to stay for one night or a fortnight, our dog-friendly accommodation includes exclusive access to Easton Walled Gardens for the duration of your stay.

*easton*
HOLIDAY COTTAGES

www.eastonholidaycottages.co.uk
01476 550227

# *Llanerch* VINEYARD

### JUNCTION 34: 3 MINUTES

Wales' oldest vineyard is a delight in 20-acres of woodland, landscaped gardens and, of course, vines, which run down to the Ely valley.

The bar and terrace offers a casual menu: grilled fish of the day, overstuffed ciabatta sandwiches, Middle Eastern mezze. Well-behaved dogs on leads are welcome and rewarded with a dog treat if they wear appropriate puppy eyes. Llanerch Restaurant housed in the old farmhouse with a sunny conservatory, offers more substantial meals, from pub classics like fish and chips and burgers as well as fine dining options, and the ever-popular afternoon tea.

A small admission fee lets you loose on the vineyard trail. Explore the beautiful grounds, lakes and precious woodland, rich with flowers and wildlife – eyes peeled for wild orchids, owls, dabchicks, Canada geese and kingfishers. Wine tasting is included in the fee and you can buy some at a small shop on the way out.

Opening hours
Mon-Sun 10am-9pm

Llanerch Vineyard, Hensol CF72 8GG
**WWW.LLANERCH-VINEYARD.CO.UK**  01443 222716

CAFÉ
# *The* ORCHARD CAFÉ

**JUNCTION 32: 5 MINUTES**

Across the road from a primary school in a quiet, residential neighbourhood on the Cardiff fringe, the Orchard is a relaxed café focused on excellent, freshly made food – right down to the bread and jars of confetti-like fruit tea. Owner Dawn is a welcoming and effervescent host, who will cheerfully sit down in her apron between serving for a chat.

Large floor-to-ceiling windows flood the simply decorated café with light and look onto a wide pavement where tables are set out on fine days. A little courtyard garden at the back not only provides a sunny sanctuary for visitors, it also provides herbs, leaves and produce for the daily changing and earthy menu. Alongside familiar café fare, you might find more substantial dishes, such as ham hock pie and quinoa salad with smoked salmon. Afternoon tea is a new and popular addition, with savouries such as garlic and mushroom bruschetta and roasted vegetables and capers next to the usual sandwich and scone suspects.

**Opening hours**
Tues-Sat 8.30am-5pm

The Orchard Café, 7 Park Road, Radyr CF15 8DF
**029 2084 2129**

CAFÉ
# PLAN2RIDE

JUNCTION 32; 2 MINUTES

Just off the motorway in the shadow of the fairytale Castell Coch, plan2ride is a pit-stop café on the edge of Fforest Fawr, which draws hikers, bikers and walkers to it like moths to a flame. Although born of cycling enthusiasts – they offer advice on local routes and a bike tune-up, and sell cycling-themed gifts and kit – the warm welcome is extended to all. You'd barely know it was once a garage. White walls, grey floors and open beams make it feel airy, and large patio doors from the small café give way to a sun-trap courtyard.

It's primarily a coffee and snack stop. Coffee is smooth, made with South American beans roasted in Caerphilly; teas are varied and smoothies freshly made. Locally baked cakes and pastries are enticing – from pear and chocolate to rhubarb and cinnamon, and rocky road. Gluten-free options are readily available. plan2ride is 100% powered by renewable energy and is committed to reusing or recycling every scrap of waste it produces.

Opening hours
Mon 8am-1pm
Wed-Fri 8am–6pm
Sat-Sun 9am-5pm (4pm Sun)

plan2ride, 51 Merthyr Road, Tongwynlais CF15 7LG
**WWW.PLAN2RIDE.CO.UK**  029 20 810868

Persevere down fiddly but well-signposted roads and you'll find the Moody Sow, a modern farm shop brimming with artisan food. It's housed in a well-lit, contemporary barn with a stream running by and pigs snuffling happily in the woods. Appealing counters are stacked with local cheese, homemade Danishes, Moody Sow jam, honey, fresh bread baked daily on-site, pink lemonade and craft beers ready to loot for finger-licking picnics. Scotch eggs are the speciality; enormous and award-winning. Try the sweet chilli chicken or black pudding.

The butchery is fabulous: pick up melt-in-your-mouth steaks, home-cured bacon, fresh sausages and juicy chops for the BBQ, then reward yourself with a coffee in the small café upstairs.

Animal lovers large and small will adore the farm park next door, part of the same complex, with a huge range of animals to meet and feed (ponies, sheep, goats, chickens, sheep and reindeer) as well as a soft play barn, go-karts and real diggers.

Opening hours
Mon-Sun 10am-5pm

Moody Sow, Cefn Mably Farm Park, Began Rd, Old St Mellons CF3 6XL
**WWW.MOODYSOW.COM  01633 680034**

ATTRACTION

# *Tredegar* HOUSE (NT)

JUNCTION 28; 5 MINUTES

© National Trust Images/John Millar

© National Trust Images/John Millar

© National Trust Images/John Millar

Lavish Tredegar House and the Morgan family have been an important part of the Newport community for over 500 years. Designed to impress, the house was once host to extravagant parties for the upper crust and comes alive through captivating tales of war heroism, inheritance disputes and Russian princesses.

These days, Tredegar is a destination in itself, with something for just about everyone: a stable block of craft shops, bags of green space, beautifully tended gardens, play areas, fitness stations, ducks to feed and an opulent historic house to explore. You're encouraged to unwind in the surroundings so you can loan a blanket from the Visitor Reception and lie out on the grass. The Brewhouse Tea-room is a perfect spot for refuelling on scrumptious, seasonal meals and snacks. Some ingredients are plundered from the kitchen garden to make soups, Welsh rarebit, quiches and carrot cake with profits going back into the conservation of the house. There's bags of parking (pay and display) and an electric car charging point..

Opening hours
Mon-Sun 10am-5pm

Tredegar House (NT), Pencarn Way, Newport NP10 8YW
WWW.NATIONALTRUST.ORG.UK/TREDEGAR-HOUSE 01633 815880

CAFÉ
# GRAZIA

**JUNCTION 23A: 3 MINUTES**

Swing off the motorway after crossing the Severn Bridge (and the border) to find sustenance in a stylish, white-hued café in the little Monmouthshire village of Magor.

Grazia is a family-run café and bar serving homemade meals and snacks with an Italian twist. It looks small from the outside, but it's like a tardis on the inside, with plenty of tables and sofas. Filament light bulbs give a warm glow to match the homely Mediterranean welcome. Abbie smiles broadly as she makes coffees behind the cake-studded, wood-clad serving counter, while husband Gianni – a classically trained chef and baker – cooks up a storm in the open-plan kitchen.

Nibble on a paninetti – their unique, miniature version of the panini – or chicchetti (Italian tapas) to stave off the hunger pangs; enjoy the signature antipasto misti platter or a hearty lasagne. Homemade ice creams are creative and tantalising flavours; cherry and custard is our tip.

**Opening hours**          GF  V
Mon 9am-4pm
Tues-Sat 9am-6pm
Sun 10am-1pm

Grazia, 1 Salisbury House, Magor Square, Magor NP26 3HY
**WWW.GRAZIAMAGOR.COM  01633 881817**

FARM SHOP-CAFÉ

# *Hanley* FARM SHOP

## JUNCTION 23: 15 MINUTES

Originally a disused 18th century barn and coach house, Hanley Farm Shop stands on the A48 between Chepstow and Lydney, overlooking the beautiful Severn Valley.

Now a farm shop with café, deli and butchery, it has become a culinary showcase for numerous local food and drink producers. Growers on a land share scheme in the field next door supply some of the seasonal vegetables, herbs and micro leaves to the shop. In the Butchery, organically reared beef comes direct from the farm and the lamb, pork and chicken sourced from other local farmers, and there's even an on-site florist and golf driving range.

With its exposed oak beams, comfortable sofas, armchairs and a wood burning stove the café is relaxed and homely; food is always freshly prepared. Pies, quiches, sausage rolls and fantastic cakes are all baked in the kitchen. If you're passing in spring, try to catch the Dancing Cow Day when the herd is gleefully released back into the field after a winter indoors.

Opening hours
Mon-Sat 9am-5pm (4.30pm café)
Sun 10am-4pm (3.30pm café)

Hanley Farm Shop, Tidenham, Chepstow NP16 7NA
**WWW.HANLEYFARMSHOP.CO.UK   01291 626642**

# *Manor* FARM SHOP

**JUNCTION 18: 15 MINUTES**

Birds chirrup, sheep bleat and the wind rustles the trees. Nuzzled in the hills between Bristol and Bath, Manor Farm is a working organic farm with traditional stone buildings, daisy-speckled fields and chickens roaming freely. The café is set in a stone courtyard, simply decorated with farmhouse tables, wooden chairs and chequered tablecloths. It serves unrivalled breakfasts made with meat reared entirely – they even grow the feed – on the farm, also available from the butcher next door. Lunches are filling and freshly made, perhaps a Ploughman's, poached eggs on toast or chunky soup; the organic ice creams are scrumptious.

A farm shop sells wholesome chutney, proper butter, homemade cakes and fresh chillis – this is one of only a handful of chilli farms in the UK (you can take a tour if you'd like). Ruby the sheepdog is popular with kids and will obligingly fetch sticks all day long, while piglets, lambs and cows can often be found in a paddock or sty nearby.

Opening hours
Fri-Sun 10am-5pm

Manor Farm Shop, Upton Cheyney, Bitton BS30 6NQ
**WWW.MANORFARM-SHOP.CO.UK  0117 932 88008**

CAFÉ

# *The* TOLLGATE

**JUNCTION 18; 3 MINUTES**

Uplifting views, honest cooking and alpacas, the Tollgate makes a refreshing pause from the motorway. The tea room is housed in a former turnpike, a sturdy building of stone, slate and arched windows, and looks to the sublime Welsh hills.

Settle in a corner next to the wood-burner or in the bright, Victorian conservatory for table service breakfasts of porridge, granola or eggs Benedict, and lunches of halloumi and avocado rarebit, cod and prawn fish cakes or falafel burger. Dainty afternoon teas are available to enjoy on the lawn – where you can also have a game of boules – and cakes are home baked, sticky and delicious. There's a 20% discount for 'cakeaway'. Tea is all loose leaf (speciality blends from Pukka) and coffee perfectly roasted.

Little people can canter around in the gardens, wolf down organic ice creams from Marshfield Ice Cream down the road, or feed carrots to Honey and Bumble, the resident Shetland ponies.

Opening hours
Mon-Fri 9.30am-5pm
Sat-Sun 9.30am-5pm

The Tollgate, Dyrham, Nr Bath SN14 8LF
**WWW.THETOLLGATE.CO   01225 891585**

# *Old Stables* **COFFEE SHOP**

**JUNCTION 17: 14 MINUTES**

Castle Combe is criminally pretty, which is why it's awash with tour groups and selfie sticks. Don't be deterred; the beautiful sandstone village with appealing gabled houses (notice that TV aerials are banned) and an arched bridge spanning a river is worth the hype.

Few places are more welcoming for a recharge than the Old Stables Coffee Shop, just off the main street. It's a relaxed home from home: stone walls painted cream are hung with bright local art. Loaf around by the log burner, relax on the sofa with a paper or play with Twiglet and Bumble, the often-resident dogs.

Owners Philippa and Yasmin are laid back and hospitable – muddy boots, mucky dogs, sweaty cyclists, even ponies are welcome. Food is flavourful and most of it comes from within a few miles of the door. Bacon rolls and excellent coffee for breakfast, paninis and sandwiches for lunch. Tempting cakes are baked each day – maybe a bakewell slice or a gingerbread muffin.

**Opening hours**
Tues-Sun 10am-5pm

Old Stables Coffee Shop, The Estate Yard, Castle Combe SN14 7HU
**WWW.OLDSTABLESDELI.CO.UK  01249 783872**

CAFÉ

# *Folly Row* CAFÉ

**JUNCTION 17; 4 MINUTES**

Dinky but delightful, Folly Row is cuddled into the high street of Kington St Michael. Panelled walls are painted cream and blue and host local artwork. Folly row is a little treasure where stacked crates display vintage teapots, china teacups and various leaf tea and yummy cakes baked on the premises. The gluten free brownies come highly recommended as does their coffee cake.

Their window displays are the talk of the village and their memorable toilet with a baking theme is well worth a visit.

Take advantage of the outside seating in the good weather or if sitting indoors, enjoy playing games or knitting while you wait for your food.

Dogs on leads are very welcome and can get a treat and a drink on the house!

Opening hours
Mon-Sat 10am-4pm
Closed Bank Holiday weekends.

Folly Row Café, 13 Kington St Michael, Kington St Michael SN14 6JB
**WWW.FOLLYROWCAFE.COM   01249 750887**

# *Allington* FARM SHOP & CAFÉ

JUNCTION 17: 7 MINUTES

The shop at Allington Bar Farm is cavernous. A wood-clad building at the roadside with sacks of potatoes piled outside the door, it hosts a butchery, delicatessen, locally produced store cupboard essentials and speciality grocery items and a considered range of tasteful cards, gifts including bespoke hampers and toys. The Reynolds family have worked the 700-acre farm for three generations, using low-intensity techniques to raise cereals, potatoes, cattle, pigs and sheep, much of which is available as produce to buy in the shop.

The conservatory café throngs with people enjoying wholesome farm food. Breakfast on sausages and bacon or almond and pumpkin seed granola with fruit and yoghurt; try the chicken chorizo burger, vintage mature Cheddar ploughman's or baked goat cheese, bacon and toasted walnut salad for lunch. Milkshakes are made with real strawberries and cakes and desserts all crafted by their in house pastry chef.. On sunny days, take advantage of the decked terrace or a picnic option in the glorious Wiltshire countryside.

Opening hours
Mon-Sat 9am-6pm (café 4.30pm, 5pm Sat)
Sun 9.30am-5pm (café 4pm)
Bank Hol 10am-4pm (café 3.30pm)

Allington Farm Shop & Café, Allington SN14 6LJ
WWW.ALLINGTONFARMSHOP.CO.UK   01249 658112

ATTRACTION

# *Lacock* ABBEY (NT)

### JUNCTION 17; 14 MINUTES

© *National Trust Images/John Miller*

© *National Trust Images/Alana Wright*

© *National Trust Images/James Dobson*

Harry Potter fans and culture vultures will love Lacock for its admirable version of an archetypal English village. It grew in the 13th century around the abbey, and its ancient graceful cloisters, higgledy-piggledy cottages and medieval tythe barn are much loved by film makers. In summer, villagers sell meringues, cakes and garden vegetables from their front gardens.

Lacock is the birthplace of British photography: William Henry Fox Talbot captured the world's first photographic negative at the abbey in 1835, a feat commemorated by a museum in the abbey grounds.

Replenish your energy in the Stables tea-room, a bustling café painted ochre and ivory, serving unpretentious lunches and snacks – jacket potatoes, seasonal salads, soups, cream teas and tempting cakes. Soak up any summer rays outside with views over the fields. Pooches are welcome on leads.

Opening hours
Mon-Sun 10am-5.30pm
Check website for winter opening times

Lacock Abbey (NT), Lacock, nr Chippenham SN15 2LG
**WWW.NATIONALTRUST.ORG.UK  01249 730459**

# AVEBURY (NT)

JUNCTION 16: 15 MINUTES

Stonehenge might have the limelight, but the Neolithic stone circle at Avebury is less crowded, just as bewildering and arguably as impressive. You can amble freely through Europe's largest henge and imagine Bronze Age rituals. Standing stones are clustered in circles and along the mysterious 'avenue'; barrow mounds pepper the landscape and man-made Silbury Hill was built from cattle bones. The pretty medieval village, curiously at the heart of the monument, is well worth a wander too.

Now under the watchful eye of the National Trust, Avebury has plentiful parking (free if you're a member) and lots of places to fuel up: you can enjoy grand afternoon teas in the blue-painted dining room at Avebury Manor, served on mismatched china, or more simple fare in the Circles and Coach House cafés – seasonal soups, sausage rolls, sandwiches, cakes and coffees. Eat in or make the most of the picnic area, where you'll also find ride-on tractors for the kids to enjoy.

Opening hours
Mon-Sun 11am-5pm
Check website for seasonal variations

Avebury (NT), High Street, Avebury SN8 1RF
**WWW.NATIONALTRUST.ORG.UK/AVEBURY   01672 539250**

A sunny welcome and homely cooking await you at the Summer Café on Malmesbury's chocolate-box high street. Space is tight so grab a table inside or wash out onto the pavement seats to watch the world go by with a cup of strong coffee or one of the many teas: Darjeeling, Assam, peppermint or rooibos.

Breakfasts are filling: scrambled eggs and smoked salmon, or poached eggs with hollandaise and bacon. Lunch includes fresh salads, sandwiches, beetroot, walnut and goat cheese tarts, Cornish pasties or flatbread wraps. Cakes are in a league of their own: chocolate and banana loaf, salted caramel brownies, lemon and blueberry polenta cake, all homemade – and the pancake stacks are a sure-fire hit with kids. Walk off any excess with a wander through the town, a visit to the museum to discover King Athelstan, the first king of all England, or a turn in the abbey gardens, which fizz with more than 2,000 roses and 100,000 tulips in spring.

Opening hours
Mon-Sat 7.30am-5.30pm
Sun 9am-5pm

The Summer Café, 4 High Street, Malmesbury SN16 9AU
**01666 822639**

# *The Cricklade* CLUB

**JUNCTION 15: 12 MINUTES**

Whip up the fast A419 towards the Cotswold Lakes (a popular spot for triathletes, stand-up paddler boarders, anglers, rowers and nature spotters) to find the Saxon town of Cricklade, where Alfred the Great once built a stronghold to defend Wessex from the invading Danes

Today, it is a quintessentially pretty town sitting at the top of the River Thames, with a traditional high street, ornate clock tower and frothy floral displays. Beautiful riverside and meadow footpaths radiate out from the centre, where you can catch some fresh air and work up an appetite before heading to the Cricklade Club.

The old Working Men's Club has been transformed into a quirky café-bar (Victorian bike, wind-up gramophone, scarlet phone box) with delicious, Ottolenghi-inspired menu to match. It's linked to the wonderful Purton organic farm down the road, which provides a rich gathering ground for the kitchen. Grab a menu and a pew on the patio for one of the best brunches around.

**Opening hours**
Mon-Thurs 8.30am-4pm
Fri-Sat 8.30am-11pm
Sunday 10am-3pm

The Cricklade Club, 38 High Street, Cricklade    SN6 6AY
**WWW.THECRICKLADECLUB.CO.UK    01793 299079**

# *Three Trees* FARM SHOP & CAFÉ

JUNCTION 15: 2 MINUTES

Three Trees is a family-run, mixed farm housed on what was once the Chiseldon army camp. Take a pew in the airy café and you can idly watch sheep and cows chew the cud against the backdrop of Liddington Castle.

The coffee is strong and can be boosted with farm-fresh cream. Cakes are varied and home-baked – the cheese scones have a devoted following. Tasty meals and snacks, such as Welsh rarebit, sandwiches, chilli con carne and jacket potatoes, are crafted from ingredients that you can buy in the well-stocked shop. Much of the meat comes from the fields (which makes for unbeatable breakfast sausages), the rest from a community of local Wiltshire producers.

Pick up a sirloin for dinner at the onsite butchery, a bag of fudge for the journey, some Cotswold Lavender hand cream or a cheeky tipple of Ramsbury vodka. Dogs can beg a bone from the butchery counter if they play their cards right.

Opening hours
Tues-Sat 9.30am-5.30pm (café 4.30pm)
Sun 10am-4pm
Please refer to website for opening times over Christmas

Three Trees Farm Shop & Café, The Ridgeway, Chiseldon SN4 0HT
**WWW.THREETREESFARM.CO.UK  01793 741436**

PUB

# *The Bell* AT RAMSBURY

**JUNCTION 14/15: 13 MINUTES**

The succour of this Georgian coaching inn, set at the edge of the Marlborough Downs, is not to be missed. The café, chic in shades of cream and sandstone, serves breakfast (organic sausages, free-range eggs, home-roasted coffee), lunch (toasties, home-cooked ham, egg and chips) and heavenly baking in the afternoon. Seasonal food in the tartan-upholstered restaurant will satisfy more substantial appetites: perhaps pea, lovage and courgette soup to start, mushrooms on toast to follow (don't underestimate these truffle-soaked lovelies) or pork loin with black kale and roast potatoes. Dessert might be a rhubarb and pear crumble with lavender ice cream.

Head chef Jonas notably uses ingredients from Ramsbury Estate, which is nearly all things to all men, with a brewery, distillery, oil press and smokehouse. Trout is cured in beetroot and the estate's vodka, partridge is smoked over beech. Much of the produce is grown in the kitchen garden at Priory Farm and tastes fantastic.

Opening hours
Mon-Sat noon-11pm
Sun noon-10pm

The Bell at Ramsbury, The Square, Ramsbury SN8 2PE
**WWW.THEBELLRAMSBURY.COM  01672 520230**

# *Cobbs* FARM SHOP & KITCHEN

**JUNCTION 14; 7 MINUTES**

A bone fide all-rounder, Cobbs Farm Shop has a butcher, fishmonger, delicatessen, florist, cheese counter – even a vineyard. The brightly lit shop has a country chic feel and scours the surrounds for the best local produce – cured meat, pork pies, salads, A-grade cuts of meat, all kinds of veg, and home-grown, Alder Ridge sparkling wine. You could do your weekly shop here and pick up gorgeous gifts at the same time, from handmade soap to ceramics and toys.

The chic café with leafy green plants, wooden tables and cream walls sells delicious breakfasts and lunches that vary from light bites to filling one-pot meals and caters for dietary needs with a seasonally changing menu showcasing homegrown produce.

Family fun is found in the pick-your-own fields, where you can pluck soft fruit in season, and kids will love the play barn, giant games and seasonal events such as pumpkin carving, open-air cinema and bird of prey displays.

**Opening hours**
Mon-Sat 9am–6pm
Sunday 10am-5pm

Cobbs Farm Shop & Kitchen, Bath Road, Hungerford RG17 0SP
**WWW.COBBSFARMSHOP.CO.UK   01488 686770**

# *The Garden Room* CAFÉ (LIBBY BLAKEY DESIGNS)

**JUNCTION 14: 6 MINUTES**

In a sunny conservatory behind the dove grey shop front and hushed calm of Libby Blakey's interiors shop, you'll find the Garden Room Café. It's is achingly refined, a vision of glass-topped tables, grey wicker chairs, quirky ornaments and hip design books. In the garden Parisienne wire chairs and tables are softened with cushions and tablecloths, the perfect invitation to a coffee and rustle of the newspaper.

This is a spot for elevenses or light bites, so a petit menu offers croissants stuffed with Parma ham and Gruyere, smoked salmon, avocado and mascarpone on rye bread, and a soup of the day. Cakes are impossibly perfect: plump sponges topped with nectarine and mascarpone, or a dense, multi-layered honey cake with salted caramel, walnuts and pecans. The counter is dominated by an enormous Italian coffee machine pumping out rich, dark blends; shelves behind are stacked with loose leaf teas.

Opening hours
Mon-Sat 10am-5.30pm

Libby Blakey Designs, 3 Bridge Street, Hungerford RG17 0EH
**WWW.LIBBYBLAKEYDESIGNS.CO.UK   01488 647440**

# *The* TALLY HO

JUNCTION 14: 1 MINUTE

A handsome, red-gabled pub on the road to Hungerford. Spirited too, as it was threatened with closure in 2012, forcing a community consortium to gallop to the rescue and reinstate it at the heart of the community. As a result, the atmosphere is now one of mellow conviviality. There's a toy box of books and jigsaws for kids, dog biscuits on the bar for four-legged companions and a couple of shelves in the corner put to use as a teeny shop selling, well whatever happens to need selling: eggs, marrows, honey and trinkets. There also comfortable bedrooms if you plan to break your journey overnight.

Food is classic pub fare, generously portioned and made with tasty local ingredients, including some veg from shareholders' allotments. Expect overfilled baguettes or fish and chips for lunch, which you can enjoy on the sunny terrace. Succulent steak, sweet potato curry and honeyed ham with free-range eggs and chips are on the dinner menu.

Opening hours
Mon-Sun noon–11pm

The Tally Ho, Hungerford Newton RG17 0PP
WWW.THETALLYHOHUNGERFORD.CO.UK    01488 682 312

# *The* PHEASANT

**JUNCTION 14; 1 MINUTE**

A country home tableau – wicker dog basket, newspapers, enormous exotic flower arrangement, milk pail lamp and taxidermy pheasant – greets you as you step through the doors of this countrified, clapboard pub which was once an old sheep drover's inn.

In the seagrass-painted bar you'll find open fires and bookshelves, busts, feathers and knick-knacks, and a cosy nook furnished with trunks and leather furniture – ideal for both a competitive game of Scrabble or kicking back with a newspaper. It's popular with the horse-racing crowd, which you'll notice in the racing TV coverage often buzzing in the background.

Food is excellent and flavoursome; the restaurant suave and animated. Cheese boards and duck spring rolls are offered as bar snacks; Bloody Mary gazpacho is on the menu for starters; Cornish cod with red pepper coulis and chorizo, and Wiltshire sirloin with garlic butter among the mains.

Opening hours
Mon-Sat 11am-11pm
Sun noon-10.30pm

The Pheasant, Ermin Street, Shefford Woodlands RG17 7AA
**WWW.THEPHEASANT-INN.CO.UK  01488 648284**

PUB

# The QUEENS ARMS

JUNCTION 14; 6 MINUTES

Just five minutes' drive from the roar of the M4, the Queens Arms is a peaceful country pub in the heart of the Wessex Downs and an ideal stop between London and the West Country. It's a centrepiece for the pretty village of Garston, which has the River Lambourne running through it and Winterbourne Bottom Down rising above.

Work up an appetite following the footpaths out of the village and up past the gallops – this is horse-racing country – before taking a table in the wood-panelled dining room. Candles and a log burner add to the 18th century atmosphere.

Food is led by the seasons and the plates are generous: Cornish mussels, local pork tenderloin, falafel burger and wild mushroom risotto have all featured on the menu. Bellies filled, head to the bar to rub shoulders with the regulars or spill out onto the sunny lawn where kids can run about while parents enjoy the impressive views over this area of outstanding natural beauty.

Opening hours
Mon-Sun 11am-11pm

The Queens Arms, East Garston, Hungerford RG17 7ET
QUEENSARMSEASTGARSTON.CO.UK   01488 648757

# *The* **EASTBURY PLOUGH**

**JUNCTION 14: 7 MINUTES**

Slate-roofed and washed in cream paint, this lovely beamed pub stands in the heart of the countryside. The kitchen, ably headed by Graham, sends out wave after wave of delicious plates to the dining room. He's an ardent local food supporter and it shines through in the flavours. Starters of king scallops and black pudding, honey and sesame sausages and Goan fishcakes flow into mains of slow-cooked oxtail, local pheasant, Berkshire mushroom and parmesan tart. Desserts (Bakewell tart with homemade marmalade ice cream or sticky bourbon pudding) do not disappoint. Fat, gourmet sandwiches and bowls of soup will fill you up at lunchtime.

In summertime, dine al fresco in the verdant garden (say hello to Arthur the rooster and Billy the goat) and stretch your legs with a stride across the fields to the neighbouring villages of Woodland St Mary and East Garston.

Opening hours
Tues-Sat noon-3.30pm, 6pm-11.30pm
Sun noon-10.30pm

The Eastbury Plough, Newbury Road, Eastbury RG17 7JN
**WWW.EASTBURYPLOUGH.COM 01488 71312**

# *Saddleback* FARM SHOP

JUNCTION 14: 12 MINUTES

You'll find Saddleback at the edge of the North Wessex Downs, housed in a converted piggery. Farmers Clare and David are enthusiasts of the field-to-fork philosophy and supply the farm shop with as much locally sourced produce as possible.

The café is snug and welcoming and the menu, like the shop, proudly local. Bunting hangs over scrubbed wooden tables and pew benches and from the sunny patio terrace you can enjoy the Berkshire hills rising to a copse on the brow, or watch the combine harvester at work in the fields. Kids can bowl about on the large lawn, visit the chickens and tire themselves out in the play house.

The countryside around is ripe for exploring so if you've got time before heading on, ask staff for a map and explore the nearby footpaths. If you call ahead, the kitchen will prepare you a picnic.

Opening hours
Mon-Sat 8.30am-5.30pm
Sun & Bank Hol 10am-4pm
Café closed 30 mins before shop

Saddleback Farm Shop, California Farm, Brightwalton RG20 7HR
**WWW.SADDLEBACKFARMSHOP.CO.UK  01488 638806**

# *Crab &* **BOAR**

**JUNCTION 13: 7 MINUTES**

The entrance to this classic, thatched pub in the Berkshire countryside is round the back, flanked by gravelled seating areas and a large canopy covering a fountain-adorned patio.

Inside, the bar is dressed in copper and topped with a grand silver tureen of fruit. Scarlet rugs cosy up the stone floors and battered leather chairs beg to be claimed for a mellow game of chess. The comfortable candlelit dining room, in what was the original bar, has low beams, earthy tones and tartan upholstery.

Bar snacks are a cut above the norm: rollmop herring, boquerones, wild boar salami and Porthilly Rock oysters. The food is outstanding. Lunch on smoked salmon and crème fraîche sandwiches, pea risotto or beetroot and chick pea burgers. The dinner menu combines surf and turf, featuring mackerel, pheasant breast, venison and pork belly, as well as a number of flavourful vegetarian options. Save space for the strawberry roulade afterwards.

**Opening hours**
Mon-Sun noon-11pm

Crab & Boar, Wantage Road, Chieveley RG20 8UE
**WWW.CRABANDBOAR.COM   01635 247550**

PUB

# *The* FIVE BELLS

**JUNCTION 14; 3 MINUTES**

Pies are the speciality at The Five Bells – all handmade, encased in shortcrust pastry and served with mash or triple-cooked chips and gravy (of course). But you'll also find crisp, wood-fired pizzas, gourmet sandwiches and fresh fish dishes from the day's catch at Brixham.

The 400-year-old thatched pub stands in the rolling Berkshire countryside and makes a cracking stop on the way to or from London, not just for the pies. Staff are cheerful and familiar, joking with the natives at the bar and making a fuss of visiting dogs. A ceiling covered in beer mats is a conversation starter and you can sit in the grassy beer garden on blue-sky days.

There are some fantastic country walks nearby if you fancy wearing off the pie before you depart. Start from the lovely old church of St Swithun, not far from the pub, with its original Saxon tower, and you can head off through woodlands and meadows towards the River Lambourne at Boxford.

**Opening hours**
Mon-Sat 11am-11pm
Sun 11am-10.30pm

The Five Bells, Baydon Road, Wickham RG20 8HH
**WWW.FIVEBELLSWICKHAM.CO.UK  01488 657300**

# *The* ROYAL OAK

**JUNCTION 13; 11 MINUTES**

This red-brick, 17th-century village inn effortlessly combines old-world charm with modern comfort; smooth leather sofas sitting above chequered tiles in the lobby, chunky wood furniture over a rugged parquet floor in the dining room.

Food is unfussy but delicious, as evidenced by the Michelin rating, and flavour is king. Beef and game are reared on the Yattendon estate and eggs come from a local farm. Dishes take inspiration from around the globe: katsu curry with panko aubergine and pak choi, risotto primavera with dukkah roasted vine tomatoes or the classic slow roasted lamb shoulder.

The candle-lit dining room is cosy, with open fires in winter, and come summer the walled garden throngs with people enjoying the borders and a game of petanque. It's dog-friendly, so much so that they'll get roast beef if they're lucky, and the countryside nearby is blissful and laced with footpaths.

Opening hours
Mon-Sat 11am-11pm
Sun noon-10.30pm

The Royal Oak, The Square, Yattendon RG18 0UF
**WWW.ROYALOAKYATTENDON.CO.UK  01635 201325**

# *Cobbs* AT ENGLEFIELD

**JUNCTION 12; 2 MINUTES**

Formally known as Fielders Farm Shop, Cobbs at Englefield is a popular farm shop and delicatessen at the edge of Englefield Estate, between Theale and Pangbourne.

This cheerful establishment offers a fantastic array of local and British food. It sells everything from fresh fruit and vegetables, eggs, honey and bread to cakes, local beers, cider and wine. Visit the delicatessen for a wide range of quality British cheese, free-range pies and Scotch eggs. Always well stocked with British meat; you'll find pork, beef and lamb from across the south of England, free-range chicken, sausages, dry-cured bacon and locally shot game (when in season).

To top it all off, homemade soup, sandwiches and delicious coffee are all available to take away for lunch on the go. Keep an eye out in 2019 as their new build is planned to open early in the year and will include a new delicatessen, butchery, café and florist.

Opening hours
Mon-Sat 9am–6pm
Sun 10am–4pm

Cobbs at Englefield, Wickcroft Farm, Pangbourne Rd, Theale RG7 5EA
**WWW.FIELDERSFARMSHOP.CO.UK   0118 9304064**

# *The Crown* **AT BRAY**

**JUNCTION A308M; 4 MINUTES**

Heston Blumenthal's foray into pubs has been a riotous success, combining atmospheric, chic country surroundings with Heston's much-celebrated flair for food. The Crown has an old world feel to it – dark wood bar, brass ornaments, low timbered ceilings and the scent of open fires: rumour has it that Charles II would call in for a drink here while visiting his mistress – but has been flawlessly updated. In summer, you can spill out into the newly landscaped garden, sheltered from any breezes by high brick walls.

Food is excellent – pub food done well. Options might include pastrami and smoked cheese burger, steak with marrowbone sauce, crispy cauliflower cheese or beer-battered fish and chips (sometimes available to take away). Save space for the signature spit roasted pineapple sundae with salted caramel when the BBQ is fired up, or sticky toffee pudding in winter. It's mid-way between Reading and London so a perfect pit stop if you're meeting relatives in the middle, or if you're running early for Heathrow.

Opening hours
Mon-Sat 11.30am-11pm
Sun 11.30am-10.30pm

The Crown at Bray, High Street, Bray SL6 2AH
**WWW.THECROWNATBRAY.COM  01628 621936**

# *Crocus at* DORNEY COURT

**JUNCTION 7: 5 MINUTES**

This gorgeous walled garden near Eton plays host to a garden centre that transforms the idea of a local garden centre into a celebration of plants and nature, often featuring difficult-to-find plants. As the name suggests, this was once the kitchen garden that supplied the manor house at Dorney with fresh fruit, vegetables and flowers and is even rumoured to be the place where England's first pineapple was grown. For eco-friendly growing supplies, covetable home and garden décor and gifts from around the world, you need look no further than the well-stocked shop.

Basket filled, head for the newly revamped café. It's filled with restful greenery and serves wholesome seasonal produce, delicious cakes and afternoon teas, all made in the kitchen. There's plenty of seating in the modern, oak-beamed café but when the sun shines, make the most of the shady garden with its large play area, featuring a Wendy house, ride-on tractors and a fort for lively little warriors.

**Opening hours**
Mon-Sun 9am-5.30pm

Crocus at Dorney Court, Windsor SL4 6QP
**WWW.DORNEYCOURT.CO.UK  01628 604638**

RESTAURANT-BAR

# *Eton* MESS

**JUNCTION 6; 10 MINUTES**

Eton is precisely the sort of place you see on postcards: a sea of appealing shop fronts decorated with fluttering Union Jacks and hanging baskets frothing with petunias. Ensconced in the high street is the Eton Mess, a relaxed kitchen and bar. The main bar has a stylish mismatch of chairs, filament lights and walls strewn with old photographs. Sash windows give onto the street and peep onto the antiques bookshop across the way. The dining room feels like home, lit with table lamps perched on old suitcases

The menu changes throughout the day, starting with tasty breakfasts and strong coffee. From lunch onwards there's a varied menu: stuffed red peppers, lobster roll, courgette and toasted quinoa salad, poached River Dart trout and celeriac spaghetti with braised lentil Bolognese.

There are lovely walks along the Thames and in the Brocas meadow; Windsor Castle, just across the bridge, is well worth a stroll.

## Opening hours

Mon-Thurs 8am-3pm, 6pm-9.30pm
Fri 8am-3pm, 6pm-10pm
Sat 9am-10pm (Sun 6pm)

Eton Mess, 55 High Street, Eton SL4 6BL
**WWW.THEETONMESS.CO.UK  01753 865516**

Go the Extra Mile
**RHUG ESTATE ORGANIC
FARM SHOP #355**

# WALES & THE BORDERS

*From the Servern estuary to Snowdonian Mountains*

LLAND[

352
353
A470
354

BANGOR

BETWS-Y-COED

# WALES & THE BORDERS

SNOWDONIA
PARK

TEA ROOM

# *Davenports* TEA ROOM

JUNCTION WILLOW GREEN: 1 MINUTE

A vintage van parked outside signposts this quintessential English tea room. It sits at the side of the canal in the idyllic Weaver Valley and is adorned with antique furniture, William Morris wallpaper and murals of Alice in Wonderland, making it look like the Mad Hatter's Tea Party.

It's open for breakfast, snacks and light lunches (think sandwiches and ploughman's), but the afternoon teas are the real speciality, and need to be pre-booked. Cakes are homebaked by ladies in nearby villages; china cups will be pre-warmed and the array of teas available is bewildering, from English Breakfast imported from Kwazulu Natal Tea Plantation in South Africa to mint choc Rooibos. Owner Belinda will happily advise on the perfect blend for you.

Roll out onto the gravelled terrace on fine days to listen to the birds singing and admire the donkeys and alpacas. The tea room is popular and can get very busy, so if you're set on the Davenports experience it's a good idea to call ahead and book

.Opening hours
Wed-Sat 10am-5pm
Sun-Mon 10am-4pm
Last orders for light lunches/afternoon tea 3pm

Bridge Farm, Warrington Rd Bartington, Nr Northwich CW8 4QU
WWW.DAVENPORTSTEAROOM.CO.UK   01606 853241

# *The Devonshire* **BAKERY**

**JUNCTION 12: 6 MINUTES**

Nestled on Frodsham's pretty high street the Devonshire Bakery is a welcome break from the M56. Follow your nose to find its vast array of artisan breads (sourdough, rye, ciabatta, spelt, baguette) made on site from recipes honed over five generations.

Pull up a chair at a window table to enjoy a smooth coffee and made-to-order sandwich as you watch the world go by. There's a cosiness to the interior which is hung with bold artwork and in summer tables are set on the pavement. The beef and pork pies are famously good and it's worth picking up a golden-crusted pie or spiced chutney sausage roll for later – we're loved the steak and blue cheese. Don't miss the handmade chocolates at Christmas and Easter too.

There's a pay-and-display car park just round the corner. Make time to browse the Lady Heyes Craft and Antiques centre nearby before you go. The old farm buildings are now host to a run of alluring vintage shops.

Opening hours
Monday, Weds 8.30am-4.30pm
Tuesday, Thurs, Fri 8.30am-5pm
Satu 8.30am-4pm

The Devonshire Bakery, I High Street, Frodsham WA6 7AH
**WWW.DEVONSHIRE-BAKERY.CO.UK  01928 731234**

# *JTO Vintage &* *The Old Bank* **TEA ROOMS**

Filled with a steady stream of visitors, it's hard to believe that the Old Bank Tea Rooms came about by happy accident. Owner Diane Ormrod planned to relocate her furniture restoration business from Frodsham to a larger space in Helsby's old bank building, including a small space where customers could enjoy tea and cake. But such was its popularity that the furniture was quickly replaced by a full tea room serving crumpets, homemade soup, panini and generous slices of cake baked by women in the village. 'It was bonkers from day one,' says Diane.

Vintage light fittings hang over the counter and tables are dressed with country-chic table cloths; the room rings with chatter. You can find a range of heritage items and gifts for sale on the shelves and dressers. Out back there's a large covered garden decorated with the same thoughtful panache. If you're feeling energetic, earn some extra space for cake with a hike up the iron age hill fort just over the road at Helsby Hill.

Opening hours
Tues-Sat 10am-5pm

JTO Vintage & The Old Bank Tea Rooms, Helsby WA6 0DA
**01928 724846**

# *Lynda's* CAKES

**JUNCTION A540; 3 MINUTES**

Cake lovers on the move should look no further than Lynda's Tea Room for their sugar fix. Her home baking keeps the counter of her new café well supplied, as well as half of Cheshire in birthday cakes. From coconut and pineapple, to rhubarb and almond, the flavour combinations are fantastic. But it's not just her cakes that are fêted: the light lunches and afternoon teas are every bit as good. The clotted cream for the beautifully light scones comes from the family dairy farm and the sumptuous sausage rolls are made down the road.

Lynda's sits behind the town hall (easily spotted thanks to its clock tower) in a retro wooden hut that has seen countless previous lives, including one as an operating theatre during the war. Inside is whitewashed and trimmed with bunting; embroidered cloths dress the tables and tea is served in proper china. The tea room has a firm community vibe as host to a small library and craft cupboard stocked with gifts, as well as locals stopping for a natter.

Opening hours
Tues-Sun 9am-4.30pm

Lynda's Cakes, Vernon Institute, Church Rd, Saughall CH1 6EN
**07817 082339**

FARM SHOP-CAFÉ

# *Hawarden* FARM SHOP

JUNCTION SAINT DAVIDS PARK INTERCHANGE; 6 MINUTES

The enthusiasm this Flintshire farm shop has for sustainable local produce is catching. Provenance is key: kindly reared meat is sourced from the estate and neighbouring farms, milk is produced over the road and fruit and veg are grown just outside the shop. Local game is stocked in the freezer, and sausages and pies are made on site with meat raised at Hawarden. The Christmas turkeys are particularly sought after – lovingly tended, they have music piped into their barn to keep them calm.

Fill your shopping basket with all manner of countryside treats, from artisan bath oils to indy beer and cast-iron camping pans. Then step through to the airy café to taste the difference that good provenance makes to flavours. Try a black pudding and pork burger for a late breakfast or a farmland platter of local meats and cheeses for lunch. Outside, a huge play fort and a mile-long nature trail will keep kids entertained, and there's PYO fruit in summer and a weekend marketplace twice a month.

Opening hours
Mon-Fri 9am-6pm
Sat 8.30am-5.30pm
Sun 9.30am-4.30pm

Hawarden Farm Shop, Chester Road, Hawarden CH5 3FB
WWW.HAWARDENESTATE.CO.UK   01244 533442

CAFÉ
# Jacob's LADDER

JUNCTION 27A; 1 MINUTE

There's a Wild West feel to the balconied veranda of Jacob's ladder as it faces out towards the town's main crossroads. But if outside reminds you of outlaws, inside couldn't be more different: the tribe of regulars is testament to the convivial, community atmosphere that owner Lowri has created. The welcome from behind the counter, heaped with her home baking, is unfailingly friendly.

Once the town's Postal Sorting Office, the two rooms of the café have been given a modern makeover: grey walls and wooden cladding stand above the original terracotta floor tiles. Throw yourself into a cosy sofa at the fireside in the back room and indulge in the simple, hearty fare, which includes bacon and brie sandwiches, leek and potato soup, jacket potatoes. The coffee is excellent and tea loose leaf. Parking is available on the street or in the pay-and-display car park near the cathedral opposite (famous for being the smallest in Britain). A lovely stop when travelling to or from North Wales.

Opening hours
Mon-Sat 10am-4pm

Jacob's Ladder, Mount Street, St Asaph LL17 0DB
01745 582577

# CAFÉ
# PROVIDERO

**JUNCTION 19; 3 MINUTES**

Beginning life in an achingly cool Citroën van, Providero's bricks-and-mortar café sits at the top of a steep hill just off the North Wales Expressway in Llandudno Junction. Blow the cobwebs away with a walk along the prom (take a peek at the Chapel of St Trillo, reputedly the smallest church in the UK) before heading to Providero to reward yourself with some of the best tea and coffee in Wales.

Smartly dressed on the outside with its grey-painted render and wood cladding, inside you'll find the exposed brick walls and stripped wood floors of a very hip coffee house. Flat whites are exceptional, matched by the Turkish apple tea. The menu is predominantly vegetarian – think falafel, hummus, artisan breads with homemade jams or roasted root vegetable salad with lemon tahini. If you can resist the cakes and traybakes, you're stronger willed than us. Grab a stool at the breakfast bar in the window, sunnily decorated with jam jars of fresh flowers, or find a sofa in the roomy lounge upstairs.

Opening hours
Mon-Fri 8am-5pm
Sat 9am-5pm
Sun 10am-4pm

Providero, 148 Conway Road, Llandudno Junction LL31 9DU
**PROVIDERO.CO.UK   01492 338220**

# *Bodnant* WELSH FOOD CENTRE

JUNCTION 19; 7 MINUTES

Foodies will love the Bodnant Welsh Food Centre, a wholehearted celebration of Welsh artisan produce. It's the latest addition to the sprawling, beautiful Bodnant Estate, which stretches across a wooded hillside above the River Conwy, overlooking the mountains of Snowdonia.

Prince Charles cut the ribbon here in 2013, and the converted 18th-century farm buildings are now home to a cookery school, beekeeping centre, enticing café and fantastic farm shop. You can pick up almost everything you need for your destination at the butchery, delicatessen and bakery, as well as Welsh-made gifts.

Food in the café – slate-floored, whitewashed and long – is simple and made with ingredients from the shop. Eat inside on chillier days, but if the sun shines, take your lunch out to the lovely sheltered courtyard to eat by the water fountain. Visit the estate's gardens, now under the capable stewardship of the National Trust, if you have time before heading on.

Opening hours
Mon-Sat 9am-5.30pm (Tea room 4.30pm)
Sun 10am-4.30pm

Bodnant Welsh Food Centre, Furnace Farm, Tal-y-cafn LL28 5RP
WWW.BODNANT-WELSHFOOD.CO.UK   01492-651100

# *Ffin y Parc* COUNTRY HOUSE & GALLERY

### JUNCTION A470; 5 MINUTES

The luminous café alone at Ffin y Parc is worth a detour from the A5. The stately manor house sits splendidly in 14 acres of gardens overlooking Snowdonia National Park. Previously used by the council it has been rescued and restored to its former glory by owners Ralph and Roland, who have a passion for 20th-century contemporary art. The gallery has changing exhibitions, including works by the finest Welsh artists, but there's art in every room here.

Mind suitably nourished, head to the café for sustenance. The menu is simple – sandwiches, quiches, salads and daily specials – the coffee great and homemade cakes widely lauded. There are slouchy leather chairs in the adjoining room, warmed by a log burner with the refined feel of a gentlemen's club, where you are invited to sit and ruminate on the paintings over your coffee. In the halcyon days of summer you can settle at one of the tables on the lawn to make the most of those glorious views; if the weather is inclement enjoy the Conwy valley panorama from the large airy conservatory.

Opening hours
Wed-Sat 10am-5pm
Sun 11am-5pm

Ffin y Parc Country House & Gallery, Betws Rd, Llanrwst LL26 0PT
**WWW.WELSHART.NET** 01492 642 070

# *Rhug Estate* ORGANIC FARM SHOP

JUNCTION TYN-Y-CEFN; 0 MINUTES

The sprawling Rhug Estate covers a remarkable 12,500 acres in the rugged Dee Valley. For 20 years it has been a bastion of organic farming and animal welfare, with Lord Newborough at the helm. You might well see his Labrador 'Truffles' roaming around on the scent of a sausage. The dedication to planet and people can be tasted in every bite of the beef, lamb, chicken and game.

If you're on your way to Snowdonia, stop off to enjoy the estate's walks (pick up a map from the shop), play area and treat-yourself, award-winning Bison Grill. Browse the farm shop's local products, from Snowdonia cheeses and Penderyn whisky to Rhug Estate wool duvets.

If you're in a rush, On The Hoof serves fast food a class apart from other takeaways (try the bison burger), while the drive-thru coffee shop is an inspired idea and blows your average café chain out of the water. Drive up to the hatch for farm-grade drinks, sausage rolls, paninis and cakes cheerily served in compostable packaging.

Opening hours
Mon-Thurs 8am-5pm
Fri-Sat 8am-5.30pm
Sun 8.30am-5pm

Rhug Estate Organic Farm Shop, Corwen LL21 0EH
**RHUG.CO.UK   01490 413000**

# *Arthur's Farm Kitchen* AT FORDHALL FARM

JUNCTION B5065; 15 MINUTES

Camped in the Tern Valley, Fordhall Farm is a beacon of organic farming, taking the bold step of eschewing chemicals more than 65 years ago. These days the community-owned farm showcases its light environmental touch in its strikingly renovated Old Dairy building, which houses its shop and dog-friendly organic café.

The slate floors, log burner and sturdy wooden tables give the café a farmhouse kitchen warmth. Fill your bellies with sumptuous plates of grass-fed beef, lamb and Gloucester Old Spot pork – the farm's pigs feast on the by-products of Joules' brewery down the road – all served with locally sourced and organic, where possible, vegetables. Or buy a feast in the farm shop and take it out front to enjoy in the picnic area.

Before you go, take the kids off to make dens in the woodland and climb on the rope trails, or give the kids and dogs some exercise on one of three farm trails (you may need wellies!).

Opening hours
Tues-Fri 9.30am-4.30pm (5pm April-Oct)
Sat 9.30am-5pm
Sun & Bank Hols 10am-4pm

Fordhall Organic Farm, Market Drayton TF9 3PS
WWW.FORDHALLFARM.COM   01630 638696

# BATTLEFIELD 1403

JUNCTION BATTLEFIELD; 1 MINUTE

Named rather gruesomely after a bloody battle here more than 600 years ago, Battlefield 1403 stands in an idyllic corner of Shropshire, just north of Shrewsbury. It's part of the Albrighton Estate, which has been farmed sympathetically by the same family for six generations. You can learn about the site's historic significance in the on-site exhibition (keep kids quiet with a game of knights and princesses), but today the only bloodshed is in the outstanding butchery.

The farm shop gathers the estate's harvest and that of neighbouring farmers in a superior celebration of local food – cheese, charcuterie, fresh vegetables and free-range meat alongside proper ready meals cooked up in the kitchen.

Across the courtyard, the Sparrow cafe buzzes with life, and it's a fantastic lunch stop. Chefs plunder the shelves of the farm shop and local suppliers to conjure tasty cafe fayre, hot and cold: the award-winning Battlefield beef and Shropshire ale pie will melt in your mouth.

Opening hours
Mon-Sat 9.30am-5.30pm
Sun 10am-4pm

Battlefield1403, Upper Battlefield, Shrewsbury SY4 3DB
**WWW.BATTLEFIELD1403.COM 01939 210905**

RESTAURANT

# CSONS

JUNCTION EMSTREY ISLAND; 6 MINUTES

CSONS roosts in the heart of historic Shrewsbury in a 16th-century building that combines Tudor panelling with zingy yellow banquette seating. It's a labour of love for the four brothers behind it, and their excellent food is inspired by their ex-pat experiences. Crafted from local ingredients, the menu changes almost daily depending on the produce available that day.

The English breakfast is served with chorizo and chipotle sauce, granola with house lemon curd. Lunch might be labneh and caponata with flatbread, salted beef or hummus and red pepper sandwiches. Try the cinnamon buns or gluten-free chocolate and quinoa cake with a coffee. Dinner is served from Wednesday to Saturday and is a real flavour adventure (think sesame salmon with kimchi teriyaki) particularly Friday's Mystery Menu.

There's a lovely courtyard garden for soaking up the sun on fine days, and high chairs and colouring pages for little people.

Opening hours
Mon, Tues 9am–3.30pm
Weds-Sat 9am-4pm, 6pm-10pm
Sun 10am-3pm

CSONS, 8 Milk Street, Shrewsbury SY1 1SZ
WWW.CSONS-SHREWSBURY.CO.UK   01743 272709

The heady, scented gardens set The Hundred House apart, encircling the eclectic Shropshire hotel with raised flower beds, running streams and more than 100 varieties of herb. If you've had enough of the M54, you'll be revived the moment you step out of the car here.

The building's name reveals its rich history, Hundred House being the term for an ancient administrative centre and court of law. The hotel and restaurant are an unusual warren of buildings, from 14th century to Georgian, red brick to thatched. They are quirkily decorated and show their age in parts. In the cosy farmhouse kitchen restaurant – hexagonal floor tiles, dried herbs hanging from the rafters – flavour is king: chef Stuart prioritises home-grown produce and herbs, which are plucked liberally from the garden.

It's on the pricier side, so it's worth factoring in a longer stop to savour your meal and explore the Severn Valley, rose centre and famous Ironbridge Gorge nearby.

Opening hours
Mon-Sat 11am-11pm
Sun 11am-10.30pm

Hundred House, Norton Telford TF11 9EE
WWW.HUNDREDHOUSE.CO.UK   01952 580240

FARM SHOP-CAFÉ

# *Apley* FARM SHOP

JUNCTION 4; 12 MINUTES

Shropshire's rippling hills pass through the beautiful Apley Estate – 8,500 acres of gorgeous countryside bisected by the upper reaches of the Severn. It's not far from the M54 at Telford so a perfect border stop-off on your journey between England and Wales. At the pint-sized Apley Shopping Village old farm buildings arranged around a square courtyard have been returned to use for the farm shop, deli and café, alongside a handful of local businesses. They hum with life from passing visitors dropping in to pick up groceries or have a quick bite. Trestle tables in the shop sag beneath the weight of tasty produce from nearby farms.

The café is housed in the old creamery, where the award-winning Apley cheese was once made. Chefs draw many of the ingredients from the walled garden (returned to service in 2013) and the wider estate. Tasty tarts, freshly baked cakes, unsparing sandwiches, delicious afternoon teas and seasonal soups are served; the roasts on Sunday come highly recommended. and the children can let off steam in the soft play area, Pigg's Playbarn.

Opening hours
Fri-Sat 9.30am-5.30pm
Café closes 30 mins before the shop

Apley Farm Shop, Norton TF11 9EF
**APLEYFARMSHOP.CO.UK   01952 581 002**

# *The* GREEN DRAGON

**JUNCTION LITTLE STRETTON; 1 MINUTE**

The Green Dragon bustles with customers day round, a sure sign that Jay brothers Adam and Jonathan at the helm are getting it right.

It stands at the roadside in the border town of Little Stretton. Whitewashed and climbing with ivy on the outside, inside it's smart and well-kept without losing the village pub vibe: terracotta floor tiles, horse brass by the fire and dried hops above the bar. Polite, smiling staff deliver a regular stream of excellent plates to tables. Mushroom and paprika stroganoff, duck breast with black pudding, and steak and blue cheese melt are just some of the flavourful dishes you can expect, and there's a dedicated menu for vegans.

In good weather, you can sit in the shade of a parasol in the garden, where kids can keep themselves out of mischief on the sturdy climbing frame. If you've time before you head on your way, hike up to the top of Long Mynd for uplifting views over Shropshire. Breathtaking.

**Opening hours**
Mon-Sun 11.30am-11.30pm

The Green Dragon, SY6 6RE
**WWW.GREENDRAGONLITTLESTRETTON.CO.UK  01694 722925**

RESTAURANT

# *The French Pantry* BAR & BISTRO

JUNCTION SHEET ROAD; 5 MINUTES

Ludlow is a heaven for foodies – a castle-topped town with a passion for brilliant and flavourful food. The French Pantry in the town centre is a shining example of this trend. Just like chefs across 'La Manche', the team here encourage slow dining on simple but extremely flavoursome dishes. The garlic mushrooms on toast and dressed crab with salad are mouthwatering and the wine list is exceptional (sorry drivers).

Food is the star of the show, but there's a wonderful shabby Parisien chic to the dining room itself: an inky blue wall, battered wingback chairs and antique maps. On summer evenings it would be hard to find a more romantic place to dine than in the red-brick courtyard, strung with festoon lights. The nearest, easiest parking is at Smithfield, a four minute stroll away. Do pay a visit to the the 11th-century castle if you have time: its history is varied and intriguing and the views over Shropshire and the Welsh Marches are spectacular.

Opening hours
Mon, Wed, Thurs 9am-10pm
Fri-Sat 8.30am-10pm
Closed Tues & Sun

The French Pantry bar & bistro, 15 Tower St, Ludlow SY8 1RL
WWW.THEFRENCHPANTRY.CO.UK   01584 879133

# FROGGATTS

**JUNCTION ASHFORD BOWDLER; 1 MINUTE**

It's hard not to love Froggatts Tea Rooms and Vintage Shop, and those who follow the sign from the road on a whim are invariably delighted. Standing at the side of the farm track, overlooking fields of sunflowers, this former farm shop is now an adorable café packed with upcycled furniture – either to buy or to sit at while you have a bite to eat. Sally Froggatt and Helen Cooper love all things vintage and have painted, embellished, reupholstered and restored a wonderful range of items. They too are responsible for many of the home-made cakes, scones, jams and pickles on sale alongside appealing retro homewares, tins of chalk paint and home-reared rare breed pork.

It's an eclectic mix, just like the family's Featherknowle Farm, which has added fishing ponds and a caravan park to its portfolio after centuries of rearing livestock. A light lunch on the tea room's covered terrace watching bees drift among blooming pots of flowers is pure bliss.

Opening hours
Weds-Sat 9am-4pm

Froggatts, Meadowside, Ashford Bowdler SY8 4AQ
**WWW.FROGGATTS.ORG.UK   07837 644896**

SHOP-DELI
# *Carrot &* WINE

**JUNCTION MUCH BIRCH; 2 MINUTES**

For a small shop Carrot&Wine packs one hell of a punch. One of a group of three stores across Hereford, it's a tremendous reimagination of the traditional village shop and supplies everything you could need from a local store, emphasising low food miles and nearby producers. This is the food revolution in full swing.

The shelves provide everything you need for the store cupboard, with decent organic, vegan and gluten-free ranges. Bottles can be refilled with wine shipped directly from France, vegetables are loose in crates and the deli counter stocks delicious olives, scotch eggs and cheeses. Croissants are delivered daily, the coffee is rich and bars of Hereford chocolate are a tempting pick-me-up. Staff are friendly and can be relied on to tip you off on the best products.

It's near the upper part of the gorgeous Wye valley (looped walks start from Hoarwithy, about 9 minutes' drive away), so consider a restorative riverside walk while you're out of the car.

Opening hours
Mon-Sun 7am-9pm

(GF) (V) (P) (↻)

Carrot & Wine, Wormelow HR2 8FD
**01981 540126**

# *The* MALTHOUSE

**JUNCTION 2; 9 MINUTES**

Swathed in Virginia creeper, you'll find the Malthouse tucked away off the lane up to the church in the heart of handsome Ledbury. Its cobbled courtyard is brimming with flowers and perfect for a chilled lemonade on a hot day. Inside is beamed and cosy.

Customers are struck by the friendliness of the self-effacing owners. Food is reliably tasty: the American pancakes with bacon and berries are hard to resist for breakfast; salmon, leek and tarragon tart or tomato and basil soup are perfect for lunch. The coffee is excellent and the dresser is crowded with scones, cakes and bakes under various glass domes to tempt even the most steadfast dieter. We loved the lemon meringue pie and fig frangipani. Even those on a gluten- or dairy-free diet have a choice of treats to indulge in here.

Take a look at the gallery displaying local art upstairs and make time to stroll through the centre of Ledbury to see its famous 'black-framed' Tudor buildings.

| | |
|---|---|
| **Opening hours** | GF V |
| Sun-Mon 10am-4pm | |
| Tues-Sat 9am-5pm | |

**The Malthouse, Church Lane, Ledbury HR8 1DW**
**01531 634443**

ATTRACTION

# *Three Choirs* VINEYARD

JUNCTION 3; 10 MINUTES

It's all about the views at Three Choirs Vineyard, which is frequently likened to the Napa Valley. From the brasserie terrace you're bathed in bird song and transported to the vineyards of hotter climes. Vines spool down the hillside, bordered in the distance by the Malvern Hills, Cotswolds and Black Mountains, which give the vineyard its unique microclimate.

Homely and informal, the brasserie is relaxed and welcoming with beamed ceiling, and colourful chandeliers made of recycled glasses and decanters. As stops go, it's tremendous: different to a pub, more than a café but not as formal as a restaurant. Ease yourself onto a fireside sofa and revive yourself with a rich coffee, or park yourself at a table for food. The charcuterie, featuring wild boar salami from neighbouring Forest of Dean and pressing of duck, fig and quince is sensational as is the local cheese platter; burgers and hearty soups are always on the menu. Take time to walk the footpaths that lace the vineyard before you go, or take a tour and pick up a bottle in the shop to uncork at your destination.

Opening hours
Tues-Sun noon-2pm, 6.30pm-9pm

Three Choirs Vineyard, Newent GL18 1LS
**WWW.THREE-CHOIRS-VINEYARDS.CO.UK  01531 890223**

# *Ross* GARDEN STORE

**JUNCTION WILTON ROUNDABOUT: 5 MINUTES**

Isambard Brunel could scarcely have imagined that his Engine Shed at the edge of Ross on Wye would one day become a flower-filled garden centre. Tucked away on a small industrial estate, the enormous doors at one end stand as a reminder of its former life. Have a look at the walls inside for the black and white photos of how it once looked.

A sea of flowers and plants fans out to the boundary of the garden centre, while inside the Shed is a cavern of considered gifts and homewares arranged on trestle tables against the stone walls. A clapboard entrance signals the way into the homely café and gives the air of a station waiting room. Old-fashioned home-cooked values reign in the kitchen where everything is made from scratch – the cheese scones and cream teas are held in particularly high regard.

There's an overflow car park over the road if spaces inside the gates are all taken. A wonderful place to pause on the way to or from Wales.

Opening hours
Mon-Sat 9am-5pm
Sun 10am-4.30pm

The Engine Shed, Station Approach, Ashburton Ind Estate, Ross-on-Wye HR9 7BW
**WWW.ROSSGARDENSTORE.COM   01989 568999**

# The 👉

# M6

*Natural Lakeland glory*
*& industrial landmarks*

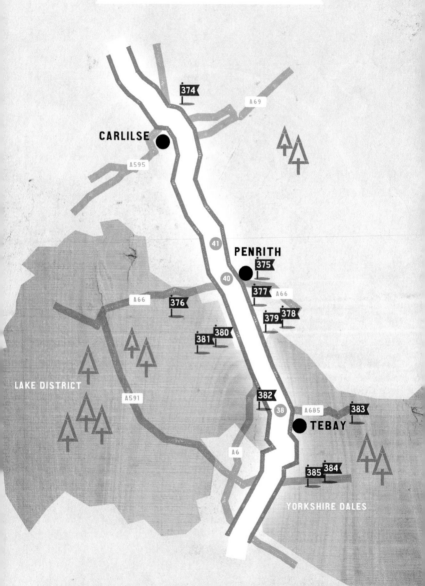

# M6 NORTH

374

A69

**CARLILSE**

A595

41

40

**PENRITH**

375

377

A66

376

379 378

381 380

382

38

A685

383

**TEBAY**

A591

A66

A6

385 384

**LAKE DISTRICT**

**YORKSHIRE DALES**

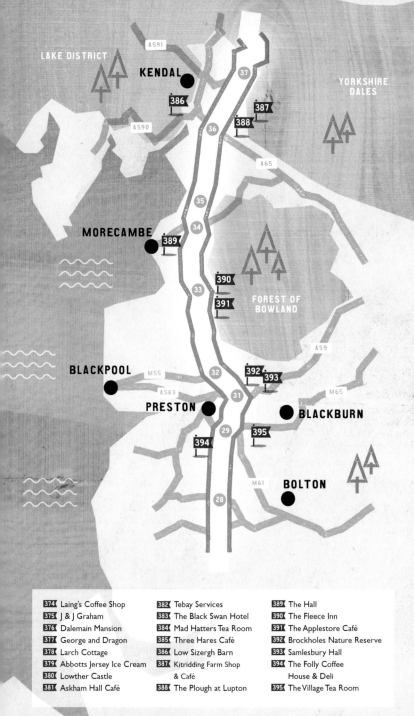

LAKE DISTRICT

A591

KENDAL

386

387

388

A590

YORKSHIRE DALES

37

36

A65

35

34

MORECAMBE

389

33

390

391

FOREST OF BOWLAND

A59

BLACKPOOL

M55

A583

32

392

393

M65

31

BLACKBURN

PRESTON

29

395

394

M61

BOLTON

28

374 Laing's Coffee Shop
375 J & J Graham
376 Dalemain Mansion
377 George and Dragon
378 Larch Cottage
379 Abbotts Jersey Ice Cream
380 Lowther Castle
381 Askham Hall Café

382 Tebay Services
383 The Black Swan Hotel
384 Mad Hatters Tea Room
385 Three Hares Café
386 Low Sizergh Barn
387 Kitridding Farm Shop & Café
388 The Plough at Lupton

389 The Hall
390 The Fleece Inn
391 The Applestore Café
392 Brockholes Nature Reserve
393 Samlesbury Hall
394 The Folly Coffee House & Deli
395 The Village Tea Room

# M6 SOUTH

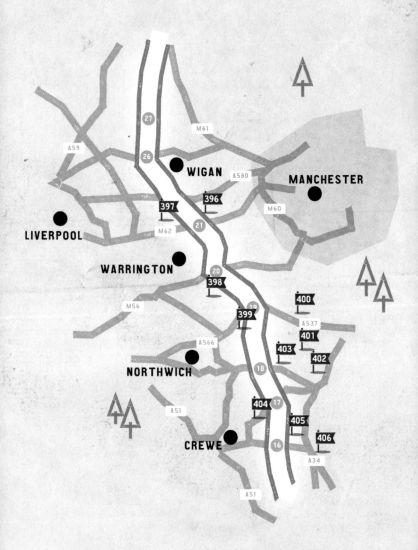

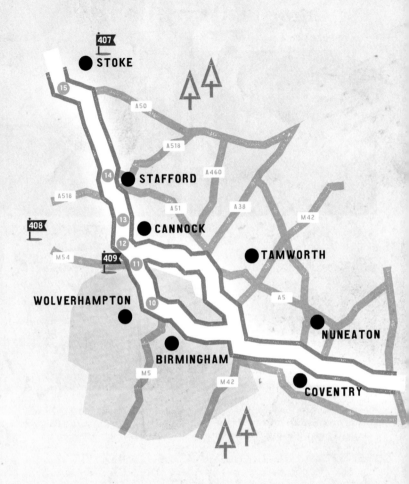

STOKE

STAFFORD

CANNOCK

TAMWORTH

WOLVERHAMPTON

BIRMINGHAM

NUNEATON

COVENTRY

395 The Village Tea Room
396 Kenyon Hall Farm
397 Red Bank Farm
398 Arley Hall
399 Tabley Tea Rooms
400 The Lambing Shed

401 Jodrell Bank
Discovery Centre
402 Chapeau! Café
403 The Vicarage
404 The Wheatsheaf
405 Hall Farm Shop & Café

406 Middleport Pottery
407 Emma Bridgewater
Café & Garden
408 The Granary Grill & Deli
409 Essington Farm

FARM SHOP-CAFÉ

# *Laing's* COFFEE SHOP

JUNCTION 44; 1 MINUTE

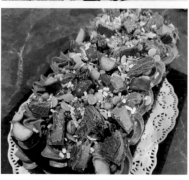

If you love glamping, you'll love ogling Laing's gorgeous, hand-crafted shepherd's huts and camping pods. Farmers-turned-timber-artisans, George and Judith Laing started manufacturing wooden buildings in 2001 after a devastating bout of foot-and-mouth hit their farm.

Today their family-run business has flourished. A modern farm shop filled with gifts and produce from the surrounding area stands alongside a roomy coffee shop. The welcome is warm and friendly, the breakfasts hearty, and Judith's cooking comfortingly home-made. Don't miss out on their in-house jam and biscuits.

In winter months you can snuggle up around the warming wood burner; in summer, spill out onto the sunny terrace. You'll find it hard to crowbar your kids away from the play area: swings, a playhouse and mini tractors provide welcome respite from in-car squabbles. Children's hats, bibs, wipes and sun cream are kindly provided if your bag is buried in the boot.

Opening hours
Mon-Sat 10am-5pm
Sun 10am-4pm

Laing's Coffee Shop, Reiver House, Harker CA6 4DS
**01228 672269**

DELI

# 𝒥 & 𝒥 GRAHAM

**JUNCTION 40; 5 MINUTES**

M6

Penrith stands on a route to Scotland that's been strategically important since Roman times and its historic standing shows in the hodge-podge of cobbled lanes, castle ruins, arcades and red stone buildings arranged around a lively square. In the heart stands J&J Graham, an old-fashioned grocers with traditional signage and ornate shop windows still intact.

Established in 1793, these days it's more an artisan deli and perfect for picnics and holiday hampers. The shop is dominated by an enormous counter, a treasure chest of Cumbrian delicacies, and ringed with shelves of groceries. Resist, if you can, the local gingerbread, chutneys, sticky toffee puddings, own-blend teas and chilli sauces, all sourced from the Eden Valley. An in-house bakery provides daily bread, scones, pies, quiches, soup and freshly cooked ham.

If you're here in October, look out for the Winter Droving, an annual festival with a torch-lit procession and rural games.

Opening hours
Mon-Sat 8.30am-5.30pm

J & J Graham, 6-7 Market Square, Penrith CA11 7BS
**WWW.JJGRAHAM.CO.UK   01768 862281**

ATTRACTION

# *Dalemain* MANSION

JUNCTION 40; 5 MINUTES

Just like Paddington Bear, it's marmalade that Dalemain is known for. Each spring the centuries-old manor house plays host to a marmalade celebration, featuring demonstrations, talks and shows that celebrate the not-so-humble preserve. The hotly contested awards are a big draw, often attracting more than 3,000 entries from all over the globe.

The winning marmalades are available to buy in the shop if you miss the show. The house – still home to the Hasell-McCosh family – is worth the ticket price for the fabulous jumble of passages, graceful rooms and décor, from hand-painted wallpaper in the Chinese Room to staggering panelling in the Fretwork Room.

If you don't have time for the tour, the medieval tea room is free to access, an atmospheric stone room filled with dark wood antiques and open log fires, serving piping hot tea, Kendal-roasted coffee, hot meals and the famous chocolate cake from a well-worn, old oak table.

Opening hours
Sun-Thurs 10am-4.30pm (from April–October)
Sun-Thurs 11am-3pm (from October–December)

Dalemain Mansion, Dalemain, Penrith CA11 0HB
**WWW.DALEMAIN.COM  017684 86450**

# *George and* DRAGON

JUNCTION 40; 5 MINUTES

Sister to the glamorous Askham Hall down the road, the George and Dragon is a classy country inn with gourmet food to match. Long, low and whitewashed, it's been lovingly restored, decorated in period colours and reinstated as a community hub. The run of interconnecting rooms feel intimate with flagstone floors, sanded floorboards, scrubbed tables and walls hung with period photographs. There's a sunny courtyard with chunky benches out front and an enclosed garden beyond where kids and dogs can cheerfully run free – ask behind the bar for suggested walking routes if you're after a longer hike.

Food is foraged, organically home-grown and home-reared, and prepared with finesse. The menu is changed seasonally and may include potted crab, beef and ale cottage pie, venison haunch with bitter chocolate, Askham Hall cured meats with pickles, Lowther honey parfait and cherries, or dark chocolate tart with pistachios. Once you're fed and watered, mingle with the locals in the cosy bar or slump into a sofa next to the smouldering fire.

Opening hours
Mon-Sun noon-2.30pm, 6pm-9pm

George and Dragon, Clifton, Penrith CA10 2ER
WWW.GEORGEANDDRAGONCLIFTON.CO.UK  01768 865381

GARDEN CENTRE

# *Larch* COTTAGE

JUNCTION 40: 10 MINUTES

A labour of love for owner Peter Stott, Larch Cottage Nursery is a rambling, theatrical beauty, a maze of Romanesque ruins, sculptures and individual, carefully designed gardens. Pass through a modest entrance at the side of a country lane and it's like stepping onto a stage. An elaborate clock tower stands sentry over a wonderland of winding paths and distinctive gardens.

The restaurant, La Casa Verde, is just as magical, a little chink of Italy with tiled floors, wooden beams and a vine-strung veranda overlooking the pond and gardens. Fresh food is hand-picked from the organic kitchen garden or sourced locally and slanted towards Italian cuisine – marinated olives, panzanella (a Tuscan salad with chunks of bread and fresh vegetables), smoked salmon crostini, thin-crust pizzas and wild mushroom risotto. Soup is served all day and cakes are freshly baked daily. Visit Red Barn Art Gallery before you leave to discover a hoard of paintings, sculptures, ceramics and handmade jewellery, together with the unique and unusual gifts.

Opening hours
Mon–Sun 9am-5pm

Larch Cottage Nurseries, Melkinthorpe, Penrith CA10 2DR
**WWW.LARCHCOTTAGE.CO.UK   01931 712404**

# *Abbott Lodge* JERSEY ICE CREAM

**JUNCTION 40; 9 MINUTES**

A family-run dairy farm at the edge of the Eden Valley and Lake District, people flock here for the ice cream – all 40 fabulous flavours of it. Choose from Just Jersey classic, mint choc chip, tiramisu, passion fruit, trifle, raspberry pavlova and a host of other delicious concoctions.

The charming, circular café is housed in a former gin case (horse-powered engine house: ask farmers Steve and Claire how it used to help thresh the harvest) and serves good tea and coffee along with traybakes and freshly made waffles; you can watch the milking on cow cam which shows the three robots that work 24-hours a day milking the free-range cows. Kids can burn off the ice cream in the playground at the front, which has a large, wooden play frame, ride on a tractor circuit for under-eights and charge about in oodles of space.

Be sure to visit the adorable calves in the barn alongside the café to meet the next generation of ice cream makers.

**Opening hours**
Mon-Sun 11am-5pm

Abbott Lodge, Clifton CA10 2HD
**WWW.ABBOTTLODGEJERSEYICECREAM.CO.UK   01931 712720**

ATTRACTION

# *Lowther* CASTLE

### JUNCTION 40; 12 MINUTES

For history lovers and energetic kids, Lowther Castle is unmissable. It's a gloriously wrecked relic surrounded by acres of grass and woodland; a rescued fragment of a grand old castle that once claimed to have a room for every day of the year. After much was mystifyingly demolished in the 1950s, a multi-million pound scheme restored the building in 2012.

The café is modern with an enormous Flemish painting on the wall, and large arched windows give way onto the sunny courtyard. Food is freshly made and filling – wraps, fishcakes, falafel pitta bread with hummus, butternut squash and sun-dried tomato linguine. A Hansel-and-Gretel-style hut deep in the forest sells simple refreshments.

Wander through the 130 acres for glorious views of the fells and wonderful gardens. Don't miss the Lost Castle adventure playground, the structure an echo of Lowther itself; whole families enjoy the tunnel slides, zipwires, fireman's poles and swings. Unbeatable fun.

Opening hours
Mon-Sun 10am-5pm (Apr-Sept)
Mon-Sun 10am-4pm (Oct-Mar)

Lowther Castle, Lowther Castle, Penrith CA10 2HH
**WWW.LOWTHERCASTLE.ORG   01931 712192**

# *Askham Hall* CAFÉ

**JUNCTION 40; 10 MINUTES**

Once the Lonsdale family pile, this former manor house at the edge of the Lake District has been turned into an informally elegant hotel by Charlie Lowther, who grew up here.

Tucked away in a Grade II-listed barn in the beautiful gardens, the Kitchen Garden Café has low-beamed ceilings, cobbled floors and white-washed walls – and a counter filled with home-baked cakes and sausage rolls. The food is unmatched (stews, soups, fell lamb with wild garlic risotto) and the kitchen gardens provide much for the table. The oven outside is fired up on busy days for crispy pizzas, which can be enjoyed on benches in the scented orchard if the sun is shining.

Families will love exploring the animal trails, which take in the hall menagerie – shorthorn cattle, boer goats, ducks, chickens and rare-breed piggies. Signs point the way from the village road to the rear car park dedicated to café customers.

**Opening hours**
Sun-Fri 10am-5pm (Easter-Oct)
Reduced hours and days in winter.

Askham Hall Café, Askham Hall Askham Penrith CA10 2PF
**WWW.ASKHAMHALL.CO.UK   01931 712350**

# *Tebay* SERVICES

JUNCTION 38-39; 0 MINUTES

The mothership of good motorway services, Tebay sits amid the pitching, fern-dabbled Cumbrian hills, a paragon of pit stops. In the Kitchen, delicious home-cooked food is heaped upon counters: sausage rolls, shortbreads, sausage and mash, frittata, sweet potato chilli and wedges of cake. Sup your coffee or freshly-squeezed juice by the picture windows and watch the famous Tebay ducks dabbling in the pond, while the kids frolic in the play area in the corner. On sunny days a BBQ is fired up on the terrace.

Before you leave, stock up at the Farmshop a wonderland of Cumbrian produce and covetable gifts: jams made from forest fruit, homemade pies, toffees from Penrith and artisan focaccias; the butchery counter stocks beef and lamb from the family farm. They are supplied by over 70 local producers within 30 miles of the services, many exclusive to Tebay. Order ahead and a cool bag will await you on arrival. At the back, you'll find a hotel where ski-lodge chic intermingles with excellent food, smiley service and more of those wonderful views.

Opening hours
Mon-Sun 24 hours

Tebay Services, Orton, Penrith CA10 3SB
**WWW.WESTMORELAND.COM  01539 624511**

# *The Black Swan* HOTEL

**JUNCTION 38; 12 MINUTES**

An idyllic country pub, with stately proportions and Victorian roots, the Black Swan roosts in fabulous, sheep-speckled hills. The bar is a warm affair of tartan carpets, dried garlands and interesting curios, where staff are jolly and locals play darts. The heart of the inn, it connects to a fire-warmed sitting room and an airy, panelled dining room.

Head chef Scott Fairweather creates a tremendous Cumbrian menu, which changes with the seasons and uses ingredients from local farms and fields. Expect goat's cheese with gingerbread and balsamic vinegar, rump of lamb with pomegranate and chickpea dahl, bouillabaisse with samphire and pistachio soufflé. The bar serves coffee and snacks all day maybe duck nuggets with hoisin, steak and blue cheese sandwiches and Judith's meringues.

A stream runs past the garden and a glade-like beer terrace with free-range chickens, firepit, rope swings and three enviable glamping tents. Keep an eye out for red squirrels.

Opening hours
Mon-Sun 8am-11pm

The Black Swan Hotel, Ravenstonedale, Kirkby Stephen CA17 4NG
WWW.BLACKSWANHOTEL.COM   015396 23204

SHOP-CAFÉ

# *Mad Hatters* TEA ROOM

**JUNCTION 37; 10 MINUTES**

Little flags in the Alice in Wonderland-themed tea room at No.6 Finkle Street instruct you to eat and drink. As if you need encouragement. Gold-dusted Ferrero Rocher cupcakes, millionaire's shortbread oozing with caramel, and hot crumpets dripping with butter practically leap onto your plate.

Coffee is freshly ground and loose teas are presented in little glass bottles to sniff before deciding on your blend. It's a good place to pull in for lunch, but afternoon tea is the real pièce de résistance: sandwiches, cakes, shortbread, heart-shaped pavlova served on vintage cake stands with proper teacups.

You'll find the Mad Hatter's Tea Room above a wonderful gift and homewares shop (it's a temptress), up a steep and narrow flight of stairs. Tables are dressed with crisp tablecloths, sugar bowls and posies of flowers, and surrounded by dressers of covetable trinkets.

Opening hours
Mon-Fri 9am-4.30pm
Sat 10am-4.30pm
Closed Sun & Bank Hols

Mad Hatters Tea Room, 6 Finkle Street, Sedbergh LA10 5BZ
**WWW.NO6FINKLESTREET.CO.UK   015396 20298**

# *Three Hares* CAFÉ

**JUNCTION 37; 10 MINUTES**

For delicious, freshly baked goodies, look no further than the Three Hares, run with love by couple James and Nina. Nina is chief baker and her imaginative recipes are influenced by her upbringing in Dusseldorf (expect a range of ryes and sourdoughs), Japanese parents and her time with bakers of the north. Sweet treats might feature red wine and chocolate cake, banana and maple syrup loaf, and overfilled doughnuts.

The tiny shop in charming Sedburgh's old lanes is also a bustling café and bistro, often crowded with people savouring coffee and a book, and a large bay at the back looks out onto the garden.

Nearly all bakeries can be relied on for a good breakfast but here you can lunch too on smoked mackerel, blue cheese and walnut risotto, or Japanese-style rabbit with curd cheese salad. Game often features alongside standard meats, perhaps hare, saffron and caper stews, or pork chops marinated in Zhoug. Ingredients are sourced or foraged locally.

**Opening hours**
Tues-Sat 8.30am-5pm
Fri-Sat 6.30pm-11pm
Sun 10.30am-4pm

Three Hares Café, 57 Main Street, Sedbergh LA10 5AB
**WWW.THREEHARESCAFE.CO.UK  01539621058**

FARM SHOP-CAFÉ
# *Low Sizergh* BARN
JUNCTION 36; 7 MINUTES

Low Sizergh is a paragon of happy animals, community growing schemes, environmental stewardship and delectable local food. If only all farms were like this. A cafe, farm and gift shop are housed in a 17th-century barn cuddled around a grassy courtyard where tables are set out in summer and chickens scratch around your feet. A trail loops around the pond, woodland and fields, so don your wellies and work up an appetite.

Food is inspired by the farm kitchen: thickly sliced bacon, vegetable soups, hunks of quiche and farmer's salads on chunky crockery. Thick milkshakes are a sure-fire hit with children. Gallery windows in the café look down into the milking parlour - where else can you watch cows being milked while enjoying a cream tea? The farm shop is stacked with groceries and delicacies – game salami, organic vegetables, salad dressings, the farm's eggs, damsons from the orchard, Morecambe Bay shrimp, as well as freshly baked cakes and shortbread. Do try the raw milk from the dispenser – it's unpasteurised and tastes fantastically fresh and creamy.

Opening hours
Mon-Sun 9am-5.30pm (5pm café)

Low Sizergh Farm Sizergh, Kendal LA8 8AE
**WWW.LOWSIZERGHBARN.CO.UK   01539 560426**

# *Kitridding* FARM SHOP & CAFÉ

**JUNCTION 36: 13 MINUTES**

Not the easiest place to find, but worth the exertion; Kitridding Farm has previously worn the Cumbrian Farm Shop of the Year crown, in a county that really knows a thing or two about farm shops. It's burrowed into the scenery: big skies and low, rounded hills scattered with sheep and livestock. Pull off the road and skirt past the man-made lake (there are paths and benches for peaceful, digestive strolls) to find the compact farm shop and café on one side of the yard.

A triumph of the field-to-fork philosophy, the café uses produce from the farm as far as possible. Lunch on sausage and mushroom quiche, minted lamb crumble or strapping ploughman's. Don't miss the caramel shortbread if you're just stopping for a bite.

The farm shop sells flavourful meat from the farm (an on-site butchery makes sausages and burgers), Kitridding's speciality pies, local produce, cheeses and preserves, as well as lovely gifts – chinaware, local artwork and unusual finds.

Opening hours
Weds 11am-3pm
Thurs-Sun 9.30am-5pm

Kitridding Farm Shop & Café, Old Town, Nr Kirkby Lonsdale LA6 2QA
**WWW.KITRIDDINGFARMSHOP.CO.UK   01539 567484**

PUB

# *The Plough* AT LUPTON

JUNCTION 36; 3 MINUTES

The modern incarnation of a classic coaching inn, The Plough is a popular stop on the way to or from Scotland. It's set in the picturesque hamlet of Lupton, sandwiched between the Yorkshire Dales and Lake District, and draws travellers in with its welcoming log fires, sumptuous rooms and delicious menu.

In the stylish restaurant you can dine on dishes such as chargrilled octopus with padron peppers and chorizo, roasted squash flatbread or beef, onion and stout pie. You can enjoy the same menu in the bar, where dogs are very welcome too. Then melt into one of the leather sofas by the hearth with your coffee, or in summer take it out to the garden to drink in the fell views. If you arrive mid-afternoon treat yourself to an unforgettable Plough High Tea.

If you have time to spare before heading on, take a look at the unique, almost lunar landscape of Hutton Roofs Nature Reserve: it boasts some of the best limestone pavement in Britain.

Opening hours
Mon-Sun 8am-11pm

The Plough at Lupton, Cow Brow, Lupton LA6 1PJ
**WWW.THEPLOUGHATLUPTON.CO.UK   01539 67700**

CAFÉ
# *The* HALL

JUNCTION 34: 10 MINUTES

The flat whites at The Hall, an inauspicious looking 1930's Art Deco parish hall, have been voted the best in the UK. The secret to their success lies next door in the coffee roasters and tea merchants, known as Atkinsons, who have been trading here since 1837. It is steeped in tea and coffee history, with many artefacts, like canisters and scales, still in daily use. The old roaster in the window still puffs out its white smoke heralding every batch of freshly-roasted coffee; on entering the shop the smell alone is worth a visit. Behind the scenes the operation is a hotbed of innovation.

That same blend of heritage and innovation is evident in the café, where the materials palette is all stripped back maple and furniture constructed of upcycled coffee paraphernalia. This is a café run by coffee roasters who really know what they're doing and love to share their passion with their customers. Enjoy cake made daily in-house by The Bakery, sourdough sandwiches and live music on Saturdays. Worth going the extra mile for...

Opening hours
Mon-Fri 8am-6pm
Sat 8.30am-6pm
Sun 10am-5pm

The Hall, 10 China Street, Lancaster LA1 1EX
**THECOFFEEHOPPER.COM   01524 65470**

PUB

# *The Fleece* INN

## JUNCTION 33; 3 MINUTES

Walking and cycling routes abound in the Trough of Bowland, a wonderfully named Area of Outstanding Natural Beauty in Lancashire, and where good tramping lies, good pubs normally follow. Enter the Fleece, built in the 1600s as a farm and now transformed into a lovely local. It has the original exposed beams, stone fireplaces and flagstone floors that you'd expect from a character pub, updated with tartan upholstery, woollen rugs, Laura-Ashley-style blinds and cosy banquette booths. The menu has the same updated-traditional vibe: sausage and mash or vegetable cheese roulade for lunch; and then for dinner, crispy whitebait, seared scallops with crispy pork belly, steak and ale pie and rack of Pilling Marsh lamb with black cherry and rosemary jus.

A pleasant terrace garden features a log cabin for kids. Cementing its place in village life, a small shop to one side of the front door sells groceries (Atkinsons' coffee, Dolphinholme honey, Pennine Way preserves), local artwork and hand-whittled walking sticks.

Opening hours
Mon 4pm-10pm (drinks only)
Tues-Sat noon-11pm
Sun noon-10pm

The Fleece Inn, Dolphinholme, Lancaster LA2 9AQ
**WWW.FLEECEINN.CO.UK  01524 791233**

# *The Applestore* CAFÉ

**JUNCTION 33; 11 MINUTES**

Greenhouses, it seems, make wonderful cafés. The Applestore fills a beautifully rustic glasshouse – an old vinery. Scarlet rugs thrown over the stone floor, comfortably mismatched tables and turquoise pendant lights have turned it into a gastronomic den with a beautifully landscaped, sunny walled garden. Walk further to a fantastic adventure play area fashioned from fallen trees, stately redwoods and views over to the fells. For a longer leg stretch, the route to Nicky Nook viewpoint is close by; Tipsy the house dog has been known to tag along.

Specials include jacket potatoes with mushrooms in blue cheese, bean and chorizo soup, or a goat's cheese salad with fig chutney. You can normally expect overfilled barmcakes (rolls) served with coleslaw, salad and crisps, cured meat platters or sausage and mash.

Baking is an art form here and there's always a healthy selection to choose from: blackbean chocolate brownies, sultana and blueberry scones, strawberry gateaux. Fabulous.

Opening hours
Weds-Sun 9.30am-4pm

The Applestore Café, Wyresdale Park, Snowhill Lane, Preston PR3 1BA
**WWW.WYRESDALEPARK.CO.UK   01524 791011**

ATTRACTION

# *Brockholes* NATURE RESERVE

JUNCTION 31; 2 MINUTES

© Bentham Imagery

© David Gaskell

Brockholes is a nature lover's paradise on the site of a (huge) former quarry. The visitor village is one-of-a-kind: strikingly modern and floating on the water. Here you'll find an informative visitor centre, activity room and good value café where you can fill up on simple, home-cooked dishes – full breakfasts, boiled eggs, jacket potatoes with homemade coleslaw, fresh soups and minced beef cobbler – while enjoying panoramic lake views. Pop in to the ice cream parlour for scoops of Lancashire ice cream before exploring the network of well-signposted paths around the expansive 250-acre site and the large adventure playground.

Shop at The Nest where you'll find a good range of gifts and local crafts and you'll be supporting the work of the Lancashire Wildlife Trust too.

The parking charge applies to everyone, regardless of how swift the visit, so it's worth making it a longer break.

Opening hours
Mon-Sun 10am-5pm (Apr-Oct)
Weds-Sun 10am-4pm (Nov-Mar)

Brockholes Nature Reserve, Preston New Rd, Samlesbury PR5 0AG
**WWW.BROCKHOLES.ORG   01772 872000**

# *Samlesbury* HALL

JUNCTION 31; 3 MINUTES

The folks at Samlesbury Hall have made a tremendous job of its rescue after the grand house was almost scrapped for timber in the 1920s, restoring the historic home and its impressively ornate, black-and-white exterior to glory. Witch hunts, priest holes, ghost stories – there's plenty of history to explore as well as the blooming gardens. Tours of the house are free and on Sundays are led by gruesome Janey the witch or portly Henry VIII.

Kids will love the fantastic, galleon-themed adventure playground as well as the host of animals – hens, rabbits, goats, sheep and Elvis and Ozzie, the Kunekune pigs. A fabulous restaurant serves simple dishes (the onion soup is highly recommended), afternoon teas and roasts on a Sunday, all made with ingredients from the estate. At Dottie's, claimed to be England's first wafflery, you can feast on sweet and savoury waffles (obviously), Lancashire ice cream and milkshakes. You could make your stop off a longer one and spend the night glamping in one of their fantastic Shepherd's huts (you can even bring the dog!).

Opening hours
Sun-Fri 10am-4pm.
Occasionally closed for weddings – call ahead to check.

Samlesbury Hall, Preston New Road, Samlesbury PR5 0UP
**WWW.SAMLESBURYHALL.CO.UK  01254 812010**

CAFÉ

# *The Folly* COFFEE HOUSE & DELI

JUNCTION 28; 9 MINUTES

Leyland's Worden Park is a haven of mature woodlands, meadows and playgrounds. The 18th-century outbuildings and parkland of what was once Worden Hall (destroyed by fire in 1941) have been rescued and the old stables colonised by the wonderful Folly Coffee House and Deli.

It's a family affair: sisters Lisa and Paula at the helm, Grandad (a farmer) supplies the veg and Mum and Nan bake magazine-worthy cakes. You can take away a picnic basket to enjoy in the glorious grounds, though many prefer the cosy, almost Victorian-style tea room, where breakfasts of avocado and feta on toast or lunches of black pudding ploughman's are cheerily served.

Dogs are as welcome as people: there's a dedicated shower in the car park for sluicing off furry friends after muddy walks and the Folly has a doggy deli selling canine treats. The large public car park is a five-minute stroll and staff can provide a permit for the small, adjacent car park in inclement weather.

Opening hours
Mon-Sat 9am-4pm
Sun 10am-4pm

Wordern Arts & Crafts Centre, The Avenue, Leyland PR25 1DJ
01772 622707

# *The Village Tea Room* AT WHEELTON

**JUNCTION 28; 13 MINUTES**

The Leeds and Liverpool Canal washes through the former weaving village, bringing with it crowds of narrow boats in the summer, and from the top of nearby Heapey's Hill you can see stunning views towards the West Pennine Moors and, on a good day, Blackpool Tower. It's worth stretching your legs and exploring Wheelton's Hovis-style sloping streets to make room for the much-fêted afternoon tea at the Village Tea Room. It's served in an individual picnic basket and includes finger sandwiches, fruit scones with cream and paper-wrapped slices of cake. Lighter lunches, such as Welsh rarebit and homemade soup, are also served. Eyes bigger than your belly? They'll pop it in a take-away bag for your onward journey.

The relaxed welcome encourages you to linger. Tables are arranged cosily over three levels, though the best seats in the house are undoubtedly those outside – weather permitting – overlooking the beautiful memorial clock tower. Revel in the tranquility - it's hard to believe you're so close to the M6 and only a couple of miles from the M61.

Opening hours
Tues-Sat 9am-4.30pm
Sun 10am-4.30pm

The Village Tea Room at Wheelton, 202 Blackburn Road Wheelton PR6 8EY
**WWW.THEVILLAGETEAROOMATWHEELTON.CO.UK  01254 830160**

FARM SHOP-CAFÉ

# Kenyon Hall FARM

**JUNCTION 22; 1 MINUTE**

A working farm on the Cheshire and Lancashire countryside, Kenyon Hall Farm has been tended by the Bulmer family for generations, and the personal touch shows. In the shop you'll find fresh seasonal fruit and veg, home-cooked jams, chutneys and cakes, speciality cheeses and meats, honey from the hives and oven-warm bread – perfect for a gold-standard picnic.

Everything served in the café – soups, stews, sandwiches, salads and cakes – are made fresh in the kitchen using local ingredients. Breakfast is a vision of proper farmhouse cooking – hearty fry ups with potato cakes, sausage and bacon, organic porridge with cream – served with rich Italian coffee and pots of tea.

In spring, the Plant Centre is in full bloom and a delight to browse. Come summer, the pick-your-own fields open for harvesting strawberries, raspberries, currants and more. Kids will love the outdoor play area, autumn maize maze and pumpkin-picking festival.

Opening hours
Mon-Sun 9.30am–5.30pm

Kenyon Hall Farm, Winwick Lane, Croft WA3 7ED
**WWW.KENYONHALL.CO.UK   01925 765531**

# *Red Bank* **FARM**

**JUNCTION 22: 5 MINUTES**

A pen of goats bleat for their breakfast outside Red Bank Farm Shop, while Limousin and Angus cows graze in the fields behind. The meat is as fresh as it comes, with much of the produce reared here, and convenient BBQ or breakfast boxes make picking the best cuts easy.

Step through the racing-green doors and you'll find shelves loaded with free-range eggs, flours, preserves, Cheshire honey, dipping crackers and fresh pies to take away. A small but stylish café – painted a charcoal grey with dark wood cladding and cheery festoon lights, and decorated with vintage posters and hessian coffee sacks – serves excellent breakfasts, lunches and coffees.

Breakfast might be bacon on barm cake (bread roll) or smoked salmon and cream cheese on toast; lunch a hot roast beef baguette with caramelised onion gravy or meatball sub, slathered with cheese. In the afternoon, snack on pork pies, sinful gluten-free brownies or chocolate and peanut butter flapjacks.

Opening hours
Weds-Fri 10am-6pm
Sat 10am-5pm
Sun 10am-3pm

Red Bank Farm, Winwick Rd, Newton Le Willows WA12 8DU
**WWW.FARMSHOPNORTHWEST.CO.UK   01925 292 470**

# *Arley* HALL

You'll find this characterful Jacobean-style gem down Cheshire's leafy lanes, in a sea of magnificently tended gardens. The fine stately home (still home to Lord and Lady Ashbrook) and its grand clock tower, intricate carvings, Elizabethan cruck barn and grand state rooms are well worth the entrance fee. Horticulturists will love moseying around the vast, effervescent gardens, celebrated borders and hothouse, while you can tire out the kids and dogs on the woodland walk.

The Gardener's Kitchen is open to all, even those not visiting the house; just get a free sticker from the kindly volunteers at the entrance. Cross the cobbled courtyard and you'll find a vaulted barn strung with lights and proudly decorated with the family heraldry. Specials are chalked up behind the modern counter, which is filled with salads, sandwiches and cakes, many prepared to the 18th-century recipes of Elizabeth Raffald, the Delia of her day who learned her craft here.

## Opening hours
Mon-Sun 10am-5pm (11am winter)

Arley Hall, Arley Hall & Gardens, Northwich CW9 6NA
**WWW.ARLEYHALLANDGARDENS.COM   01565 777353**

# *Tabley* TEA ROOMS

**JUNCTION 19; 3 MINUTES**

Tabley Tea Room is an infinitely superior stop to the mediocre services at nearby Knutsford. Tucked away beneath Tabley House – a grand Palladian pile built using red Runcorn sandstone – there's a quaintness to the atmospheric cafe, with its lace tablecloths, mismatched china and ornately carved fireplace.

You'll get a friendly reception and efficient service from Deb and Mark and their team, who took over the café here after the success of their Victoriana Tea Room in town. Kids will love the milkshakes and grown-ups can feast on excellent breakfasts (try the eggs Benedict), light lunches and home-baked cakes. Run off any excess energy in the wonderful grounds.

You can use the tearoom without paying to visit the house, but do make time to see it if you can: it's stuffed with fine art and antique furniture and features a 17th-century chapel, which was moved here, brick-by-brick, from Tabley Old Hall in 1927.

Opening hours
Thurs-Sun noon-5pm

Tabley Tea Rooms, Northwich Road, Tabley WA16 0AR
**01565 625745**

FARM SHOP-CAFÉ

# *The Lambing* SHED

JUNCTION 19; 10 MINUTES

Lambs once took their first tentative steps in this wooden barn. Today, the sheep have gone and the Lambing Shed has become a modern farm shop stocking Cheshire's finest produce. A bank of floor to ceiling windows make the former barn sunny and light and the shop is stocked to the brim with delicious products sourced to the philosophy of 'fresh, local and simple'. Head to the deli for hamper-worthy cheese, charcuterie and homemade pies and coleslaw.

From an elegant patio studded with neatly trimmed box hedges and shady tables you can glimpse the 400 acres of Cheshire fields from which the Mitchell family have been producing award-winning meats for decades. The meat is available to buy in the butchery (ask Master Butcher Stewart for advice) or to eat in the deli and café, where you'll find burgers, house-cured bacon and freshly baked sausage rolls; all the lamb and beef comes straight from the farm. For lighter bites, there's Tatton rarebit, quiche of the day or a slab of home-baked cake.

Opening hours
Mon-Sat 9am-5.30pm
Sun 10am-4pm

The Lambing Shed, Moseley Hall Farm, Chelford Rd, Knutsford WA16 8RB
**WWW.THELAMBINGSHED.COM  01565 631027**

# *Jodrell Bank* DISCOVERY CENTRE

JUNCTION 18; 14 MINUTES

© Mike Peel, Jodrell Bank Centre for Astrophysics

Earthlings and would-be astronauts pull in here to be wowed by the enormous, 90m-high Lovell Telescope. Built in 1957 and the world's first steerable radio telescope, the Cheshire landmark is still a working part of Manchester University where scientists probe the cosmos to reveal its secrets. You'll need to buzz to enter and turn your phone off to avoid interference with the radio signals. Educational and interactive displays in the space, star and planet pavilions are fascinating for children and adults alike, teaching the curious about the Big Bang, how the telescope works and mysteries of the observable universe.

Mind filled, turn your attention to tummies in the Planet Pavilion Café, which serves hearty breakfasts and appetising lunches. Cakes, salads, pasties and sandwiches are made on-site every day and can be enjoyed in the airy café or on the terrace. There are 35 acres of tended grounds where you're welcome to stroll and picnic.

Opening hours
Mon-Sun 10am-5pm

Jodrell Bank Discovery Centre, Macclesfield SK11 9DL
WWW.JODRELLBANK.NET  01477 571766

CAFÉ

# *Chapeau!* CAFÉ

JUNCTION 17/18; 15 MINUTES

A dash through leafy Cheshire towards Macclesfield leads to pretty countryside and breakfast or lunch at Chapeau!. Housed in a red-brick stable block, the cycle-friendly café is bright and unfussy with oak beams. Parasolled tables are hemmed in by troughs of lavender and greenery.

The menu is simple but tasty, making good use of the farm produce: cooked breakfasts, sandwiches and deep-filled pies, as well as quiche, pie and soup of the day – perhaps carrot and red lentil soup, or stilton, bacon and mushroom quiche. The counter is loaded with cakes beneath shiny glass domes, with flavours from Ferrero Rocher (sublime) to cherry frangipane. You can pick up groceries from the shelves in the café – milk, bread, meat, eggs, and some of those delicious pastries – so you won't have to go without a cuppa on arrival at your destination.

 Next door, the old farm shop has been converted into a game café, so if you've had enough of I Spy, select a board game and pull up a chair!

Opening hours
Wed-Sat & Bank Hol Mon 9.30am-4pm

Chapeau! Café, Manchester Road, Marton SK11 9HF
WWW.FACEBOOK.COM/CHAPEAUCAFESHOP   01260 224344

# *The* VICARAGE

**JUNCTION 18; 3 MINUTES**

It's hard to believe but this 17th-century coaching inn was a crumbling relic as little as four years ago. Seeing its potential, owner Dominic Heywood has created a wonderfully period hotel-restaurant enlivened with a mane of wisteria and junkyard finds. Panelled walls, beamed ceilings and flagstone floors rub shoulders with a bar made from a French altar, polo mallets and gilt mirrors; perfect for this well-heeled corner of Cheshire. Sofas are arranged invitingly around fires and corners, while the spacious dining room is decorated in dark tones and dimmed lights, balanced by a luminous conservatory beyond.

Full breakfasts are available from 7.30am, as well as lighter bites, including toasted crumpets and porridge. Nibble on glazed chipolatas and homemade dips between meals or tuck into a locally sourced lunch, perhaps Shropshire blue salad, club sandwich or braised beef pie. Dinner is a variation on the same theme, followed by sweet treats, such as pear and almond tatin.

**Opening hours**
Mon–Sun 7am–midnight

The Vicarage, Knutsford Road, Cranage Holmes Chapel  CW4 8EF
**WWW.THEVICARAGECHESHIRE.COM  01477 533393**

# *The* WHEATSHEAF

### JUNCTION 17; 3 MINUTES

The ever-hospitable Pear family, who are also behind the popular (and posh) Pecks restaurant down the road in Congleton, continue to improve the Wheatsheaf. Since taking over the down-at-the-heel hostelry just a few years ago, they have restored its coaching inn gl ory. Behind heavy front doors, the large Victorian pub – red brick with castellated bays and gables peeping out of the attic – has been turned into a gleaming gastropub with nine chic bedrooms above.

The dining room has had an art deco facelift: shimmering velvet banquettes, golden pineapples and dusky lighting. Blankets hang considerately on the back of chairs on the terrace, which twinkles with fairy lights. It's opulent but comfortable; you could just as easily drop in for a coffee or a three-course meal. Start the day right with a Wheatsheaf breakfast or fill up properly at lunch and dinner with a well-rounded menu, including dishes such as beef and mushroom pie or pan-fried hake and baby octopus. Round off with a passion fruit and white chocolate cheesecake or an old English trifle.

Opening hours
Sun-Thurs noon-midnight
Fri-Sat noon-1am

The Wheatsheaf, I Hightown, Sandbach CW11 1AG
**WWW.WHEATSHEAFSANDBACH.CO.UK   01270 762013**

# *Hall* FARM SHOP & CAFÉ

**JUNCTION 16; 5 MINUTES**

Skirt Alsager's mill pond and countryside pub to find the Hall Farm Shop, a friendly family business housed in an old stone milking parlour at the edge of the farmyard. The shop is known for its butchery, stocking meat from neighbouring farms. It has a good range of homemade sausages, burgers, cuts and ready-to-cook options for cheats (meatballs, chicken carveries in the fresh counter, plenty more in the freezer). The deli is perfect for picnics and pantries. Stock up on cooked meats, a delicious range of cheeses (Caerphilly and leek our favourite), olives, jams, chutneys, fresh bread and sausage rolls. There's also a range of gifts, greeting cards and books.

The café has a warm feel, with tiled floor, chunky wooden furniture and copper pendulum lights hanging over the sage-green counter. Dishes are made to order by the cook, who has a talent for soups, quiches, sandwiches and cakes; cooked breakfasts are a real crowd-pleaser and are served till 2pm.

Opening hours
Tues-Sat 9am-4pm
Sun 10am-3pm

Alsager Hall Farm, Alsager, Stoke-on-Trent ST7 2UB
**WWW.HALLFARMSHOPALSAGER.CO.UK  01270 876449**

ATTRACTION

# *Middleport* **POTTERY**

### JUNCTION 16; 11 MINUTES

A canalside café true to its industrial roots, Middleport Pottery's Tea room is a gem. Obsolete machine bases have been turned into tables, lightshades fashioned from teapots and a delicate blue mural reflects the Burleigh pottery made here. Only a few years ago the factory was facing closure but it was rescued by the Prince's Regeneration Trust and turned into a wonderful heritage centre that gives a real glimpse of industrial, Victorian England.

Unpretentious homemade food is served on blue and white china, naturally. Rich coffee and various teas are on offer. The Staffordshire oatcakes with bacon and cheese are a firm favourite; cooked breakfasts are generous and lunches simple but filling – toasties, jacket potatoes and paninis. Sit on the outdoor patio and watch the narrowboats glide past.

The museum is well worth a visit and there's a year-round programme of events to entertain kids, from clay craft to a Mad Hatter's Tea Party.

Opening hours
Mon-Sun 10am-4pm

Middleport Pottery, Port Street, Stoke-on-Trent ST6 3PE
**WWW.MIDDLEPORTPOTTERY.ORG   01782 499766**

# *Emma Bridgewater* CAFÉ & GARDEN

**JUNCTION 15; 10 MINUTES**

Cosy and inviting with iron windows, bare brick walls and wooden panelling, the café at the Emma Bridgewater factory is a diamond of a staging post. Colourful walls, industrial accents, steel girders and low hanging lights remind you that this is a working factory. There's even a cream Aga decorated in the same coloured dots that have made Emma Bridgewater a household name.

The coffee is smooth and the tea delicate, and the tasty food is often inspired by Emma's recipes. The menu includes seasonal specials, such as homemade marmalade on toast, quiches, sandwiches, daily soups, yummy cakes and children's lunchboxes. The secret walled garden is a thoughtful, environmentally considerate haven overflowing with colourful blooms.

If you've got time to spare, the experience day is worthwhile: a factory tour, afternoon tea, lunch and a session in the decorating studio.

**Opening hours**
Mon-Sat 9.30am-5.30pm
Sun 10am-4pm

Emma Bridgewater Café & Garden, Lichfield St, Hanley ST1 3EJ
**WWW.EMMABRIDGEWATERFACTORY.CO.UK   01782 201 328**

CAFÉ-RESTAURANT

# *The Granary* GRILL & DELI

**JUNCTION 12; 11 MINUTES**

The Granary Grill & Deli stands in the Weston Park estate, a grand pocket of Shropshire that harks back to Georgian days of fine buildings and elegant landscapes. The granary, built in 1767, is now a contemporary space shared by the café and an art gallery; the grill is large, open and relaxed, with warm spotlights illuminating bare brick walls and wooden floors.

Sophisticated lunches might start with wild mushrooms and truffle cream on toasted brioche, followed by whole roasted trout and samphire, and finish with peanut butter parfait. The more informal deli serves lighter options: mezze platters, breakfasts, filled bagels, flavourful salads, savoury tarts, tea, barista coffee and homemade cakes. Raid the shop for cured meats, bakery goods, cheese and nibbles.

For furry friends, there's a jar of treats and miles of woodland paths to explore. For kids, there are giant games in the courtyard and an adventure playground.

Opening hours
Tues-Sun 9.30am-5pm

The Granary Grill & Deli, Weston Park, Weston-under-Lizard TF11 8LE
**WWW.GRANARYGRILL.COM   01952 852107**

# *Essington* FARM

JUNCTION 11: 7 MINUTES

The sprawling Essington Farm has been run by the Simkin family since 1892, selling field-fresh produce year-round (sometimes only hours out of the ground) as well as hosting a pick-your-own field and plant nursery.

Newly renovated, the farm shop and deli is large and stacked with islands of fresh and store-cupboard produce to plunder for a very respectable picnic – award-winning pork pies, fresh juices, slabs of pâté and local honey. The butcher's counter sells free-range pork and Hereford beef reared in the fields outside the window, priding itself on traditional service with a smile. Pick up some speciality sausages made in-house for a delicious BBQ treat.

Head chef Amanda Kellar also raids those shelves for the delicious restaurant food, whether fresh pies, salads, traybakes, soups or roasts with all the trimmings: straight to the fork without even leaving the farm.

Opening hours
Mon-Sun 9am-5pm (4.30pm for restaurant).

Essington Farm, Bognop Road, Essington WV11 2AZ
**WWW.ESSINGTONFARM.CO.UK  01902 735724**

# A LITTLE EXTRA

**SOME OF THE PLACES IN THE GUIDE** are kindly offering our readers (that's you!) a little extra: it may be a discount on your bill, a free coffee refill, a complimentary cup of tea when you buy a slice of cake… To redeem offers all you need to do is show your Extra Mile keyring fob at selected venues. The list is on our website and will be updated regularly so make sure you keep checking to snag the latest deals.

---

*Not got yours? Head to*
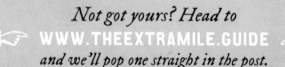
**WWW.THEEXTRAMILE.GUIDE**
*and we'll pop one straight in the post.*

---

(While you're waiting for it to arrive you can still take advantage of the offers by showing your copy of this book.)

# ☞ *The* INDEX ☜

# *The* INDEX

# 👉 *The* INDEX 👈

# *The* INDEX

# 👉 *The* INDEX 👈

# HOW TO USE THIS GUIDE

**MAPS** Maps are, as you can see, not to scale. They're intended as a guide to show you the approximate location of each place (shown on the map by a flag with the relevant page number), but you'll need a sat nav or smart phone to guide you in; or a detailed road map if you're feeling adventurous.

**OPENING TIMES** We generally list the times a place is open but, this doesn't always mean the kitchen is open. Do check ahead (we've listed websites and phone numbers) to make sure you won't go hungry.

**SYMBOLS** Below each entry you'll see a run of symbols indicating what you can expect. They're based on information given to us by owners but things do change, so treat them as a guide rather than gospel.

 **Dog friendly:** places that accept dogs in some or all inside areas. Be aware that sometimes these areas are restricted and dogs must be on leads. Some have seasonal variations so it's worth checking ahead.

 **Kid friendly:** Specific attractions for kids of places with good play areas.

 **Disabled access:** People with limited mobility can access the main venue. Some of our venues are old and listed, so won't always be fully accessible.

 **WiFi:** Free WiFi for visitors.

 **Vegetarian or vegan options:** A good range of vegetarian options for our meat-free friends, vegan if possible.

 **Gluten-free:** One of the most common dietary restrictions these days, so we've highlighted places which can accommodate gluten-free diets and have alternative options on their menus.

 **Organic:** Food produced with a lighter environmental touch, or with a good number of options made from organic ingredients.

 **Parking:** Parking available onsite.

 **Electric car-charging:** Though this is a book centred on the car, it is also devoted to doing things better, so, being firm advocates of the electric car, we've noted any places where you can charge your electro-steed.

 **Recycling/sustainability practices:** Solar panels, bio fuels, recycled water and sustainable materials; we've marked out the venues going the extra mile towards minimising their impact on the planet.